AF653967

HIGH RELIGION

A Cultural and Political History of Sherpa Buddhism

HIGH RELIGION

A Cultural and Political History of Sherpa Buddhism

SHERRY B. ORTNER

MOTILAL BANARSIDASS PUBLISHERS
PRIVATE LIMITED • DELHI

*Reprint : Delhi, **2012***
First Indian Edition : 1992
By arrangement with Princeton University Press

© 1989 BY PRINCETON UNIVERSITY PRESS
All Rights Reserved

ISBN : 978-81-208-0949-9 (Cloth)
ISBN : 978-81-208-3553-5 (Paper)

MOTILAL BANARSIDASS
41 U.A. Bungalow Road, Jawahar Nagar, Delhi 110 007
8 Mahalaxmi Chamber, 22 Bhulabhai Desai Road, Mumbai 400 026
203 Royapettah High Road, Mylapore, Chennai 600 004
236, 9th Main III Block, Jayanagar, Bengaluru 560 011
Sanas Plaza, 1302 Baji Rao Road, Pune 411 002
8 Camac Street, Kolkata 700 017
Ashok Rajpath, Patna 800 004
Chowk, Varanasi 221 001

FOR SALE IN INDIA ONLY

Printed in India
By Jainendra Prakash Jain at Shri Jainendra Press,
A-45, Naraina, Phase-I, New Delhi 110 028
and published by Narendra Prakash Jain for
Motilal Banarsidass Publishers Private Limited,
Bungalow Road, Delhi 110 007

In memory of Nyima Chotar
(1927–1982)

Nyima Chotar is getting competitive about this project. [He asked rhetorically] Did [a certain anthropologist] photograph a particular set of documents as we did? No. Did [another anthropologist] interview [a certain very knowledgeable informant] at length as we did? No. He is now referring to "our book" and saying it's going to be good.

—from the field notes, 1979

Contents

Illustrations

MAPS

Acknowledgments

LET me first explain the dedication. Nyima Chotar, of Khumjung, was my field assistant for this project from January to June of 1979. I cannot imagine a more perfect assistant. He was intelligent, responsible, knowledgeable, well-connected, sensitive to the problems of a well-meaning but clumsy anthropologist, and more. He helped me in innumerable ways, including—as indicated in the quote from my field notes on the dedication page—identifying with the project and making it as much his own as mine.

What was particularly fine about Nyima Chotar, over and above his rock-solid and dignified character, was the fact that although he had worked much of his life for Westerners—on mountaineering and scientific expeditions—he was nonetheless utterly at home in his own village context, in which he was an active and highly respected citizen. He managed to use the resources of the world system to the fullest, without any hint of being corrupted by it.

While I was writing the first draft of this book in 1982–83, I got word that Nyima Chotar and his wife, Sumjok, had been killed along with twenty-six other Sherpas in a bus accident, on the way back from a pilgrimage to see the Dalai Lama in Dharamsala. I am sorry for many, many things about his death, and all the other deaths in that terrible accident, but one thing I particularly regret at this moment is that I cannot send him "our book." I dedicate it to him.

Many others in Nepal helped facilitate this project in one way or another. I mention them here in no particular order.

Harka Gurung set up some critical interviews for me in Kathmandu, and also shared with me some good conversations over Star Beer in the rooftop garden of the Crystal Hotel.

Mahesh Chandra Regmi was kind enough to make himself available to me for several useful conversations on Solu-Khumbu taxation, and to provide me with several valuable research leads.

Mingma Tenzing Sherpa and his family provided me with hospitality and friendship in Kathmandu, and worked with me in Khumbu for part of the fieldwork.

Dawa Namgyal, a Tengboche monk and a relative of Nyima Chotar's, was my host at Tengboche monastery for several weeks. He also became my good friend. He is a devoted monk, as well as a person of great warmth and wry humor. He teased me and my anthropologist ways all the time, and I loved it. He also knew many good stories. I

Dawa Namgyal, my host at Tengboche monastery, 1979.

especially wish to thank him here for his hospitality and his friendship.

My domestic staff included Nyima Chotar's daughter, Ang Teshi, as kitchen girl. Ang Teshi was beautiful and cheerful, a delight to have around. She held my hand in an hour of particular tribulation. The staff also included Mingma Tenzing's brother-in-law, Ang Pasang, as cook. Ang Pasang, whom we all called Tsak (Brother-in-law) Pasang, was a wonderful human being, whose special culinary talent was making delicious mo-mo dumplings. His place was taken on the last leg of the trip by Serki, who showed what a professional expedition cook could do.

The Center for Nepal and Asian Studies approved my research project, despite all the rumors I had heard that projects on impractical subjects like religion were having trouble receiving approval. I am acutely aware that I still owe them a final field report, and I hope this book will serve the purpose.

Mike Cheney and the people at Sherpa Cooperative Trekking Ltd. did an excellent job as my agents in Kathmandu, handling much of the dreadful paperwork before I got there, and keeping me well supplied when I was up in the mountains.

The National Science Foundation (Grant No. BNS-7824925) paid for the entire field research, and I am happy to acknowledge their support here. John Yellen, then director of the Anthropology Program at NSF, was particularly helpful and considerate when the grant ran into certain problems later.

For various reasons (including the completion of Ortner and Whitehead [1981]), I was forced to postpone the writing on this project for several years after the fieldwork. It was not until the academic year 1982–83 that I was finally able to take the field notes out of the closet and begin a first draft of this book, with the support of a Solomon R. Guggenheim Memorial Fellowship and of the Center for Advanced Study in the Behavioral Sciences (National Science Foundation Grant No. BNS-8206304). I am extraordinarily grateful to both the Guggenheim Foundation and the Center for that productive year. I have also subsequently received funding from the University of Michigan Faculty Fund toward the completion of this book.

The manuscript has had many readers. It is impossible to describe the various ways in which each made useful comments. I will simply say that I am blessed with an exceptionally smart and perceptive group of friends and colleagues, who have individually and collectively tried to save me from everything from deep conceptual murkiness to irritating stylistic tics. If they have not succeeded, the fault is entirely my own. Thomas Fricke, Raymond C. Kelly, Joyce Marcus, Harriet Whitehead, and one extremely well informed but anonymous press reader read the entire manuscript thoroughly from beginning to end, and gave detailed, page-by-page criticisms, for which I am deeply grateful. Nicholas Dirks, James Fernandez, Clifford Geertz, David Kertzer, Gananath Obeyesekere, and William H. Sewell, Jr., as well as one other anonymous press reader, plus the students in my Himalayan seminar and the students in Sewell's and my seminar on "Culture, Practice, and Social Change," all read the manuscript and gave me valuable reactions and insights. There is no doubt whatsoever in my mind that this book would be infinitely poorer without all these contributions.

Others provided special bits and pieces that went into making the whole. Håkan Wahlquist has extensive bibliographic knowledge and files on Nepal, and gave me several crucial references that I would never otherwise have found. Ang Gyelzen Sherpa went far out of his way to do some interviewing for me after I left the field, and to retake some pictures for me after mine did not come out. Kathryn March very kindly sent me copies of chunks of her field notes on Sherpa rituals; I have not used them in this book but plan to do so in the next one. Tom Fricke was extraordinarily helpful in several ways, beyond his careful reading of the entire manuscript. He gave me many useful references (usually taking the time to copy whole articles rather than just sending me the titles), and he answered all of my naive demographic questions with carefully worked out responses that were virtual minipapers in themselves. He also went over the Nepali words in the Glossary with me. I particularly want to thank him here. Ray Kelly and Bruce Knauft provided some critical buoying up as the book and I went into our final agonies. My heartfelt thanks to all.

On the technical front, John Klausmeyer was both expert at his mapmaking and marvelously patient with me in the process. Alisa Harrigan cheerfully ran back and forth to the map library some large number of times. She was aided in her task of map retrieval for me by the great helpfulness of the map librarians at the University of Michigan map library. Carol Goldberg tracked down many Tibetan spellings of Sherpa words, and helped to finalize the Glossary. She in turn consulted with Geleg Rinpoche, who was kind enough to assist. Mary Steedly did an excellent job of typing the first draft of the manuscript, and Rachael Cohen did her usual brilliant job on the final version, managing somehow to make it all look easy.

Note on Orthography

As IN *Sherpas through Their Rituals,* I have adopted the strategy of spelling Sherpa words the way I, as an English speaker, heard them, and the way in which they would be spelled if they were English words. There seemed no sense in spelling them in the text in their Tibetan spellings, since the uninitiated reader would produce from those spellings pronunciations that bore little or no relation to spoken Sherpa. I have, however, included a Glossary of all non-English words at the end of the text, and where a Sherpa word had an ascertainable Tibetan counterpart, I have included the Tibetan spelling in the Glossary entry.

Readers of Chinese may be interested in consulting an article by the Chinese linguist-ethnologist Qu Ai-tang (n.d.) comparing the spoken language of a Sherpa group in Tibet with several other spoken Tibetan dialects. Professor Qu was kind enough to spend time with me in Lhasa (where he was attending a Tibetology conference, and where I was engaged in discussions with Tibet University about an exchange program), going over some of the main points of the article in English.

Dramatis Personae

I HAVE generally included here only individuals who play an active role in the events (or in the recounting of the events) that follow. I have excluded individuals whose names appear merely in lists of names—for example, all the members of the founding cohort of a particular monastic institution.

Ani Tarchin *Karma's daughter, one of the founding nuns of Devuche nunnery*

Chak Pön Dudjom Dorje *leader of first group of Sherpas to move to Solu*

Chopal of Gole (see Gembu Tsepal)

Dawa Tenzing *youngest son of Sangye, former Tashilhunpo monk; assisted in the founding of Chiwong monastery*

Donka Ringmo *ancestor of one of the original Sherpa clans*

Dorje Zangbu *founder of Gompa Zhung, rival of Lama Gombu (see also Ngagchang Dorje Zangpo)*

Gaga Mangden *younger brother of the Kusho Tulku, assisted in the founding of Chiwong monastery*

Gelungma Palma *female monastic, heroine of the charter myth for the observance of Nyungne*

Gembu Tsepal *head tax collector (*gembu*) of Solu-Khumbu, sponsor of Tengboche monastery*

Guru Rinpoche *(Skt., Padma Sambhava) founder of Buddhism in Tibet in the eighth century*

Karma *senior sponsor of Tengboche monastery*

Karma Chotar *married lama and tax collector, father of monastery founders Karma and Sangye*

Kemba Dorje *youngest brother of Ralwa Dorje and Lama Sangwa Dorje; founder of Rimijung temple*

Kusang *youngest sponsor of Tengboche monastery, son-in-law of senior sponsor Karma*

Kusho Dongumba *a lama of the Sakya region of Tibet who authorized the founding of Khumjung temple*

Kusho Mangden *(see Gaga Mangden)*

Kusho Tulku *son of the last married head lama of Thami temple, reincarnation of the Chalsa lama of Solu, first head lama of Chiwong monastery*

Lama Budi Tsenjen *father of Lama Sangwa Dorje, reincarnated in Lama Gulu*

Lama Gombu *the* pembu (*tax collector, "big man"*) *of the Zhung area in the early eighteenth century, rival of Dorje Zangbu*

Lama Gulu *first head lama of Tengboche monastery*

Lama Pakdze *Solu lama, father of Dorje Zangbu*

Lama Rena Lingba (Ratna gling-pa) *one of the ancestral Sherpa lamas, teacher of Lama Sangwa Dorje*

Lama Sangwa Dorje *founder of the first Sherpa temple, at Pangboche*

Lama Tenzing *the head lama of Kyerok gompa*

Lama Tundup *married head lama of Thami temple, 1923–58*

Ngagchang Dorje Zangpo *ordained name of Dorje Zangbu*

Ngawang Norbu Sangbu *religious name of Lama Gulu*

Ngawang Samden (a) *one of the senior monks of Thami monastery, regent during the current head lama's childhood and permanent assistant to the head lama*

Ngawang Samden (b) *one of the leaders of the founding cohort of Devuche nuns*

Ngawang Tenzing Norbu Sangbu *religious name of the Zatul Rinpoche*

Phule *an affine of Karma, one of the sponsors of Devuche nunnery and of the rebuilding of Tengboche after the earthquake of 1933*

Ralwa Dorje (a) *member of the Lama clan, leader of a move from Solu to Deorali Bhandar between 1725 and 1750*

Ralwa Dorje (b) *younger brother of Lama Sangwa Dorje, legendary founder of Thami temple*

Sangye *sponsor of Chiwong monastery, younger brother of Karma*

Sangye Tenzing *head lama of Sehlo monastery, author of a history of Sherpa religion*

Sehlo lama *(see Sangye Tenzing)*

Sherap Tsepal *(see Gembu Tsepal)*

Tengboche Reincarnate Lama *the reincarnation of Lama Gulu, current head of Tengboche monastery*

Thami Rinpoche (Thami reincarnate lama) *current head lama of Thami monastery, reincarnation of Lama Tundup*

Tushi Rinpoche *reincarnation of the Zatul Rinpoche's teacher in a former existence, leader of the Rumbu monks who went into exile from the Chinese and settled in Solu-Khumbu*

Zamte Lama (a) *figure in the Lama Sangwa Dorje cycle of tales, killed by Zongnamba; his followers in turn killed Zongnamba*

Zamte Lama (b) *son of a tax collector, first fully ordained monk of Sherpa birth to be active in Solu-Khumbu, founder of Nauje temple ca. 1905*

Zatul Rinpoche (Ngawang Tenzing Norbu Sangbu) *founder of Rumbu monastery, instigator of the founding of Tengboche, reincarnation of Lama Sangwa Dorje*

Zongnamba *legendary* pembu *and political rival of Lama Sangwa Dorje*

Chronology of Sherpa History

(Most dates are only approximate.)

1480	Sherpas leave Kham and settle in south-central Tibet.
1533	Sherpas cross into Nepal and settle in Khumbu.
1553	Settlement of Solu
1667	Founding of Pangboche temple
1667–77	Founding of temples at Thami and Rimijung
1717	Submission of Sherpas to the Sen king
1720	Founding of Zhung temple
1769	Gorkha conquest of Kathmandu
1772	Gorkha conquest of eastern Nepal and apparently peaceful acquisition of Solu-Khumbu by the Gorkha from the Sen
1786, 1791, 1805, 1810, 1828, 1829	Gorkha state documents establishing state policies vis-à-vis the Sherpas
1831	Founding of Khumjung temple
1846	Beginning of Rana regime
1850	Birth of Karma, the senior founder of Tengboche monastery
1856	Birth of Sangye, Karma's younger brother and the sole founder of Chiwong monastery
1865	Final establishment of the borders surrounding the Darjeeling-Kalimpong area
1866	Completion of road between Darjeeling and the Indian plains
1885	Birth of Kusang, a Tengboche sponsor
1902	Founding of Rumbu (celibate) monastery in the D'ingri region of Tibet, over the Himalayas from Khumbu
1905	Founding of Nauje temple
1916	Founding of Tengboche monastery
1923	Founding of Chiwong monastery
1925	Founding of Devuche nunnery, near Tengboche
1952	Transformation of Thami noncelibate temple into a celibate monastery

HIGH RELIGION

CHAPTER I

Introduction: The Project, the People, and the Problem

THIS is the story of the establishment of the first celibate Buddhist monasteries among the Sherpas of Nepal—of how the monasteries were founded, and by whom, and especially why. It is also an essay on the relationship between worldly dominance and spiritual striving, between power and merit, politics and religion. And at the broadest level, it is an essay in thinking about human action in the world, about how people can be both created and creators, products and producers, symbols and agents, of that world.

Early in the twentieth century, the Sherpas began to build Buddhist monasteries. They had always practiced a "folk" form of Tibetan Buddhism, in which local married priests (*lama*) conducted rituals in village temples and in households for the benefit of the general populace. But the Sherpas had never before had the more "orthodox" monastic institutions, in which celibate individuals live and practice religion on a full-time basis. Unlike the married lamas, the monks and nuns withdraw from social life, do no (materially) productive labor, and devote their whole lives to the practice of religion.

The founding of the celibate monasteries thus represents, in about as visible a form as this sort of thing ever takes, the birth of a new (for Sherpa society) institution—an institution with its own rules, its own forms of social organization, its own values and ideals, its own raison d'être. Once the Sherpa monasteries were built, a whole new process was set in motion: the monks launched a campaign to upgrade popular religion and to bring it into line with monastic views and values. The monasteries were thus to have a far-reaching impact on Sherpa society over the course of the twentieth century.

The effects of the newly established monasteries on Sherpa popular religion, culture, and society are the subject of a separate work (Ortner n.d.b). In the present work I will be concerned to illuminate the forces and processes that led up to the foundings in the first place. Who built the monasteries, and why? Who filled the monasteries, and why? What were the constraints—social, economic, political, cultural—on the people involved, and what were the provocations? In order to answer these questions, I have had to write a history of Sherpa society—of the society's internal dynamics, and of the external forces that interacted with those dynamics, from the time of the Sherpa settlement in Nepal in the early sixteenth century to the time of the monastery foundings in the early twentieth.

Who Are the Sherpas?

It is relatively standard practice to start a work in anthropology with a brief sketch identifying and situating the people to be discussed. This is problematic in the present case for two reasons: first, because who the Sherpas are (in terms of institutional configuration) depends on what historical period one is talking about, and second, because who the Sherpas are (in terms of cultural configuration, or ethos) is a matter of quite divergent assessments on the part of their main ethnographers. I will be brief on both points, and provide more ethnographic detail as the need arises throughout the text.

Institutionally, the modern Sherpas are an ethnically Tibetan group living at high altitudes (between about 8,500 and 14,500 feet) in the Himalayan mountains of northeast Nepal. (Nepal is a Hindu kingdom of about 15.6 million people [Nepal 1984]; the Sherpas constitute one of many ethnic minorities within it.) They are thought to have migrated from Kham, in northeast Tibet, in the late fifteenth and early sixteenth centuries. They now occupy three connected regions of the area: Khumbu, the highest, coldest, and northernmost; Solu, the lower, (relatively) warmer, and southernmost; and Pharak, a valley running between Khumbu and Solu. There is a system of patrilineal clans, which in modern times primarily regulates (clan-exogamous) marriage. Their traditional economy combines agriculture (now mostly wheat and potatoes); herding (mostly yak and cow); and trade (selling rice from low-altitude Nepal in Tibet, and Tibetan salt in low-altitude Nepal, as well as breeding and selling dairy animals). They live in small villages and sometimes in isolated homesteads. Property in both land and animals is privately owned by families. They practice the Tibetan Buddhist religion, which includes in modern times both the monastic emphasis on merit and rebirth, and the popular emphasis on rites of exorcism and protection. Since the turn

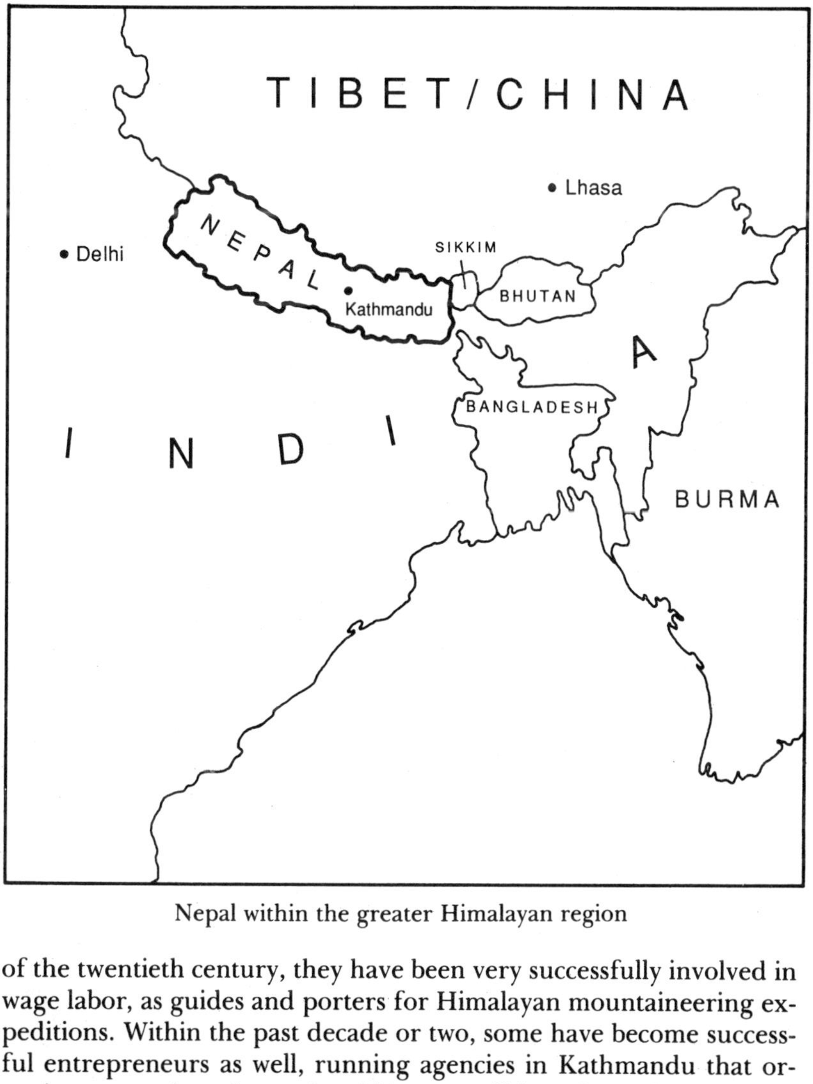

Nepal within the greater Himalayan region

of the twentieth century, they have been very successfully involved in wage labor, as guides and porters for Himalayan mountaineering expeditions. Within the past decade or two, some have become successful entrepreneurs as well, running agencies in Kathmandu that organize mountaineering and trekking expeditions throughout Nepal.

The Sherpas' success in mountaineering was in part due to their physical hardiness and their physical and social high-altitude adaptations. But it was also due in large part—and here one arrives at the question of ethos—to their friendly and outgoing demeanor, and their willingness to work hard, long, and cheerfully for the greater good of an expedition. The Western mountaineers' image of the Sherpa—good-natured, hard-working, loyal, reliable—was echoed by the first anthropologist to work with them (in 1954), Christoph von

Fürer-Haimendorf. For example, von Fürer-Haimendorf began his monograph by saying:

> What I have set out to do is to describe and analyze the type of society in which the Sherpas have developed their spirit of independence, their ability to cooperate smoothly for the common good, their courtesy and gentleness of manner and their values which are productive of an admirable balance between this-worldly and other-worldly aims. (1964:xix)

I first worked with the Sherpas in 1966. At that time, although I too found people to be quite outgoing, and in many ways quite easy to get along with, I also found much strain in social relations, a great deal of intracommunity conflict, and a general unwillingness on the part of the villagers to cooperate for the general welfare. I described Sherpa life as "premised on culturally defined and structurally induced tendencies toward individual selfishness and family insularity" (1978a:162). I also said:

> Without denying that there are structures and processes of "community" in Sherpa villages . . . the point is that such community must be achieved through *overcoming* the basic atomism and insularity of the component family units. (1978a:41)

Much of my monograph was concerned with the way in which popular religion interacted with these structural tendencies in Sherpa society.[1]

There are many things to be said about these sorts of discrepancies in ethnographic observation and description, especially in the wake of the recent Mead/Freeman controversy (for an insightful review of the controversy, see Rappaport 1986). Differences in age, gender, cultural background, and the like all enter into the problem. At first I was inclined to put a great deal of weight on these more "subjective" factors. I now think, however, that the differences are relatively real and objective, and are essentially regional differences: von Fürer-Haimendorf worked in Khumbu and I, initially, in Solu. I later worked in Khumbu as well, and the people of that region did in fact appear more cooperative and community oriented. The reasons for these regional differences cannot be detailed here, and will in any event play no role in the present work. I note them here simply because, after thirty years of varied ethnographic research among the Sherpas, one can no longer give a simple account of their style or ethos.

Fieldwork

The fieldwork for this project entailed five months in the Sherpa regions of Khumbu and Solu, and in the capital of Nepal, Kathmandu, in 1979. I talked for the most part to people selected for having special knowledge of the events surrounding the foundings of the monasteries. (I had already spent seventeen months doing general ethnographic fieldwork in the area in 1966–68, and four months making a film and collecting incidental data in 1976.) I had the impression beforehand that there might be some documentary evidence, but this turned out to play a minor role in the research.[2] Rather, the work consisted almost entirely of asking people for personal memories, and for stories that they might know about the foundings of monasteries and of temples, and other aspects of Sherpa history.

Compared with earlier ethnographic fieldwork, the oral history fieldwork for this present project seemed very easy. In ethnographic fieldwork, as every field-worker knows, there are a range of difficulties in eliciting data, some general to the nature of the process, and some specific to the culture in question. For example, although the Sherpas have the concept of "custom" (as in, "What is Sherpa custom regarding X?"), nonetheless a lot of my questions about "Sherpa custom" seemed relatively meaningless to people, and they cooperated only out of kindness, or because of anxieties about the (imagined) consequences of non-cooperation. Further, the *sequence* of my ethnographic questions often seemed meaningless to informants, as I pursued aspects of a topic that seemed unimportant to them, rather than what they felt was the main point. This was especially the case with "expert" informants—generally lamas—who had their own agenda about what needed to be explained, and in what order, and I was more than once criticized for "jumping around" from topic to topic (from the informant's point of view) rather than allowing the informant to present things in the "proper" order. Moreover, shortly after an interview during which the informant complained about my jumping from topic to topic, the subject of insanity came up with this same informant. I asked him about the causes of insanity, and he listed several items, including—pointedly—jumping from topic to topic.

The fact that there were indeed "experts" on certain matters (again, usually religious matters) in Sherpa society presented a different set of problems as well. Many lay people were uncomfortable acting as informants on religion, and told me to ask the lamas. My research assistant several times told me to stop asking "small" people about religion, as they didn't really know anything. I protested that I wanted to know what a range of people knew and thought about such matters, but this did not make much sense, either to him or to others. (There was a subproblem connected with this point: I was told it was not nice to ask many different people the same question, as this implied that one hadn't believed the first informant. The first time I was told this, it made me feel utterly despairing about the fieldwork. I simply had to ignore it in order to proceed.) Even among the lamas, the highest-status ones, from the Sherpa point of view, were not necessarily the best informants from the anthropologist's point of view. I learned to take my informants in status order, even if it meant "wasting" a few interviews until I could get to the individual who could articulate what I needed to know.

All of these reactions were, of course, revealing in themselves, but it did mean that, to some degree, the anthropologist's needs for certain kinds of information, and the Sherpas' sense of what constituted meaningful information were frequently at odds. Although as time went on I learned to fit my needs better to Sherpa senses of the sensical (although I wonder now about the questions—having become somewhat Sherpaized—that I stopped even conceiving to ask), nonetheless I always felt to some degree that general, wide-ranging, ethnographic fieldwork was like the proverbial pulling of teeth.

The difference between the earlier ethnographic work and the oral history work for the present project was dramatic. For one thing, the whole project—described as "a history of Sherpa religion"—made sense to people. To a great extent, Sherpa history *is* a history of their religion. With a few exceptions, the only historical stories they have are connected with the foundings of religious institutions, and with the lives, miracles, and social relationships of the founders. Further, although the earlier fieldwork emphasized religion, it still covered a wide (even unlimited) range of other topics. This inquiry was much more focused. It also concentrated on the past, which I think was a relief to informants, who felt their own present personas were not under scrutiny. For the first time, I was spontaneously praised for what I was doing. As I wrote in my notes: "Everyone here is saying what a good project I'm doing, retrieving all this old information that will soon be gone, on religion, interviewing old people who will soon die, and so forth."

Further, I did in general want to talk with people whom the Sherpas themselves considered "experts"—the people who knew the stories, or who had been personally involved in some of the events, or who had other reasons for being particularly well informed. Compared with the first project, the information seemed to flow from informants with relatively little effort on my part.

There were also historical reasons for this change in the fieldwork experience. Between 1966–68 and 1979 many Sherpas had become interested in their own history. Although there had already been some impact from mountaineering and tourism before my original field trip in 1966, this impact had been accelerating dramatically in the intervening period. The cumulative effect of this, and of other forces impinging on the Sherpas (including, it must be said, the virtually continuous presence of one or another researcher—anthropologist, Tibetologist, Buddhologist, linguist, and others—asking the Sherpas a lot of questions about themselves) was clearly an increase in Sherpa collective self-consciousness.

Based on fieldwork done in the 1950s, the ethnographer von Fürer-Haimendorf had written that the Sherpas displayed "scant interest in the past both of the Sherpa people as a whole, and of individual groups" (1964:144). By 1971, on the other hand, a Sherpa lama from the Solu region had written a religious history of the Sherpa people. The lama, Sangye Tenzing of Sehlo monastery, wrote this of his project: "I myself have had a strong desire to set down this religious history, shining forth like the splendid light of the moon" (1971:63). The lama not only wrote the book, he did fieldwork for it. In one of our conversations in 1979,

> Sehlo lama was kind enough to praise my project. For himself he stressed that he did not do his out of his own head, but that he spent his own money, he went around examining *chayik* [the founding charters of temples and monasteries], talking to old men, and so forth.

According to the lama, the book represented two years of labor, most of which went into collecting the information—the writing itself, he said, was easy (see also MacDonald 1980b).

Other individuals made a point of claiming that they had historical interests as well. One man boasted that he had compiled a Sherpa clan history four years before the Sehlo lama, and that the Sehlo lama had looked at it when writing his book. Others whom I interviewed, who felt unsure about some point, said they planned to check on it with some more knowledgeable individual—not for me, but for their own interest. The Sehlo lama's book was also being read by other literate Sherpas, both lamas and laymen.[3]

In sum, I found the fieldwork to be relatively painless. Not only was it fairly easy to elicit the information; it was fun. The process had a certain detective-story quality about it; one tracked down clues, made fortuitous discoveries, found heroes and villains, and had a

Sangye Tenzing, head lama of Sehlo monastery and author of a history of Sherpa religion, 1976.

sense of really "solving" something that had begun rather as a mystery.

But if the fieldwork was easy compared with earlier fieldwork, the writing seemed doubly hard. It was precisely the narrative, mystery-story quality that caused the problems. In the first place, I simply found it difficult to assemble the narrative account of what happened in the foundings of the monasteries. I had bits and pieces of stories, and different versions of the bits and pieces, and different dates (or no dates) attached to the different versions. It took me about two months simply to construct a narrative account of the foundings of the first two monasteries. My anthropological training simply hadn't prepared me to put together stories of this sort, and I found it all quite frustrating. (I also developed a lot more respect for narrative history.)

But there was a second, and more serious, difficulty with the writing: trying to interrelate the narrative on the one hand and what I would normally think of as "analysis" on the other. The two forms of writing and thinking kept getting in each other's way. The story would have a certain momentum of its own, and it often seemed awkward and artificial to break into it and "do some analysis." Yet the story could never speak for itself, could never tell its own story, as it were, and I had to intervene. The secret of the problem, of course, is that what I thought of at that point as "analysis" was essentially static, a matter of understanding what things mean and how they hang together, rather than a matter of understanding how things generate other things, or derive from other things, and so forth. Which brings me to the theoretical underpinnings of the present work.

Expanding Practice Theory

In the broadest sense, this book is meant to be a contribution to a theory of practice, that is to say, a theory of the relationship between the structures of society and culture on the one hand, and the nature of human action on the other. Practice theory has received significant attention and refinement in recent years, with the works of Giddens (1979), Bourdieu (1977), Sahlins (1981), and others. An earlier version was set forth in Berger and Luckmann's classic work, *The Social Construction of Reality* (1967). Berger and Luckmann enunciate the basic elements of the position, in the form of a triad of seemingly contradictory statements: "Society is a human product. Society is an objective reality. Man is a social product" (1967:61). The theoretical effort is to understand how these three statements can be simultaneously true, how persons and human activity can be constituted through the social process, while at the same time society and history can be constituted through meaningful human activity.

Practice theory is at the moment scattered across a rather diverse body of work. For purposes of the present discussion I will approach it via four keywords: practice, structure, actor, and history.[4] The book as a whole will represent a theoretical and methodological fleshing out of these four terms.

Practice. In a 1984 paper, "Theory in Anthropology since the Sixties," I said that any form of human action or interaction would be an instance of "practice" insofar as the analyst recognized it as reverberating with features of asymmetry, inequality, domination, and the like in its particular historical and cultural setting. The emphasis on the centrality of asymmetry or domination is one of the primary elements distinguishing current practice theories from older theories of social action, interaction, and transaction. Thus human activity regarded as taking place in a world of politically neutral relations is not "practice." To this minimal definition I would add the following: Practice is action considered in relation to structure; that is, in contrast with the position taken in "symbolic interactionism," say, structure is not bracketed analytically, but is central to the analysis of action or practice itself. Practice emerges from structure, it reproduces structure, and it has the capacity to transform structure. Human action considered apart from its structural contexts and its structural implications is not "practice." And finally I would add an optional third dimension: history. History is optional in the sense that Bourdieu's *Outline of a Theory of Practice* is certainly an instance of practice theorizing (one could say he wrote the book on the subject), yet it is not historical. But I think it is only in historical contexts that one can see the relationship between practice and structure fully played out. Most current anthropological work utilizing practice theory is in fact historical, and this book is no exception.

One other general point about "practice theories." A practice approach can be used to analyze quite a wide range of problems. In terms of published examples, it has been used to analyze statistical conformity and nonconformity to cultural rules, as when Bourdieu used it to explain the range of variation of conformity to marriage rules in Kabyle society (1977). It has been used to analyze an existing configuration of a cultural system, as when I used it to explain the pattern of gender beliefs in traditional Polynesian society (1981). And it has been used to analyze structural transformation, as in Sahlins's analysis of Hawaiian history (1981). Whatever the specific purpose of the analysis, however, the general line of questioning is the same: to try to understand something the people did or do or believe, by trying to locate the point of reference in social practice from which the beliefs or actions emerge. This is not just a question of locating the actor's point of view, although that is a part of it. It is a question of seeking the configuration of cultural forms, social relations, and historical processes that move people to act in ways that produce the effects in question.

In the present work I am using a practice approach to analyze historical innovation—the founding of the Sherpa monasteries. Situating actors within a structural and historical field of problematic relations—relations of rivalry and inequality—I ask how they came to perform these impressive historical deeds.

Structure. "Structure" as a symbol appears to be the most hotly contested term in the set. It is almost as if the term "practice" could exist only in mutually exclusive relation to structure, such that if one talks about the importance of practice, one could not possibly have any appreciation of the presence, and the constraining force, of structure. In fact, however, my notion of practice is inextricably tied to a notion of structure. If I may quote once from my 1984 paper:

> The newer practice theorists . . . share a view that "the system" does in fact have very powerful, even "determining," effects upon human action and the shape of events. Their interest in the study of action and interaction is thus not a matter of denying or minimizing this point, but expresses rather an urgent need to understand where "the system" comes from—how it is produced and reproduced, and how it may have changed in the past or be changed in the future. As Giddens argues in his important recent book (1979), the study of practice is not an antagonistic alternative to the study of systems or structures, but a necessary complement to it. (Pp. 146–47)

This point requires some elaboration here. In general my position is that any of the standard notions of structure can be used in conjunction with a practice approach, but they will tend to undergo certain changes. Specifically, I would say that the image of structure, of what structure would look like if one could see it, changes in the context of a practice perspective. Where in earlier representations structure looked like a building or a machine or an organism, or like one of those geometric spaces in *The Savage Mind* (Lévi-Strauss 1966), now it appears in forms that themselves contain a dynamic assumption. Probably the clearest example of this point is Bourdieu's notion of *habitus*. Habitus is, at one level, structure in the Lévi-Straussian sense, as is clear from those diagrams in *Outline* depicting the interlocking oppositions between wet and dry, up and down, in and out, male and female. Yet at the same time the image of structure in habitus is profoundly transformed by its theoretical linkage with practice. Thus it is structure that is doubly practiced: it is both lived in, in the sense of being a public world of ordered forms, and embodied, in the sense of being an enduring framework of dispositions that are stamped on actors' beings. I made a similar point in the 1984 paper when I contrasted Foucault's (1980) notion of discourse (which assumes a context of multiple unequal interactions) with established notions of culture, which assume an actor's point of view but do not assume the actor to be involved in any particular kind of interaction. Discourse is culture in motion, as it were, both communicationally (within a certain kind of social/political field) and also historically, in the sense that discourses come and go more readily than does what we think of as culture.

The present work will utilize a similarly active notion of structure, or actually two interrelated ones. The first is a concept of structural contradictions—conflicting discourses and conflicting patterns of practice—that recurrently pose problems to actors. The second is a concept of cultural "schemas," plot structures that recur throughout many cultural stories and rituals, that depict actors responding to the contradictions of their culture and dealing with them in appropriate, even "heroic," ways. Here again structure (or culture) exists in and through its varying relations with various kinds of actors. Further, structure comes here as part of a package of emotional and moral configurations, and not just abstract ordering principles.

The point in these examples is that—contrary to the assertions of Bloch (1987), Gibson (1987), and others—practice approaches have very robust notions of structure, and of structural dynamics, forces, constraints, and outcomes. But the way in which structure is imaged, represented, and conceptualized is itself changing, as a result of its being conjoined with an equally robust notion of practice.

Actor. I will repeat first that the focus on actors in the context of contemporary practice theory is not a new form of either voluntarism or transactionalism. The actor is not viewed as a free agent, engaged in unconstrained creativity on the one hand or manipulation on the other. Rather, the actor is recognized as being heavily constrained by both internalized cultural parameters and external material and social limits. Thus the central problem for practice theory is, as all its practitioners seem to agree, precisely the question of how actors who are so much products of their own social and cultural context can ever come to transform the conditions of their own existence, except by accident.

In the 1984 paper I complained that much of practice theory today, including some of my own work, tends to fall back on an interest-theory view of actors: actors are rational strategists, seeking to maximize or at least optimize their own advantage. I said then, and I would still say now, that while such rational calculation is always a part of actors' intentions, it is never exhaustive of those intentions, and in many cases it is not even the dominant part.

One response to this (for example, Gibson 1987 and Stephens 1987) has been to argue that anthropologists must attend more to the ways in which actors are culturally constructed in different times and places. While I do not think that this fully resolves the theoretical problem, I agree very strongly that the historical and comparative study of the cultural construction of persons, and of the stuff (like motive, will, interest, intention) that moves persons to act, is an enterprise of major importance. Indeed this entire book is, from one point of view, organized around the question of how various individuals in Sherpa society arrived in various ways at a certain configuration of felt need and active will at a certain moment in history. That is, this history of the founding of the Sherpa monasteries is framed as a question of the social, cultural, and historical construction of "interest" (see also Sahlins 1981).

Yet at the same time I think it must be recognized that an emphasis on the person as entirely a cultural product poses problems that are merely the inverse of the overly Westernized actor. It evades the problem of adequately theorizing the actor, and leaves the scene to reductionist theories in which people are either overly rationally calculating or overly propelled by biological or psychological drives. It also has the potential for falling into what might be called the Talcott Parsons (for example, 1951) effect, in which the only actors capable of changing the system are either deviants or geniuses. I will return to this point shortly.

Before moving to the final keyword, "history," two more general comments should be made about the practice enterprise as a whole. The first concerns the question of whether there is really anything new here (see Bloch 1987). The second concerns the question of whether the theory is already outmoded (see Stephens 1987).

On the first point, it is clear that an interest in the relationship between human action and social transformation can be traced back quite a long way. It can be traced back clearly to both Marx and Weber, though I will not review their positions here. But I do not think that there has been a serious attempt in modern social science, until this current body of so-called practice theory, to reraise the issue. Instead there have been, as Bourdieu (1977, 1987) emphasizes, oscillations between overly structural and overly actor-focusing frameworks. The arguments (as represented in Lévi-Strauss 1966) between Lévi-Strauss and Sartre are of course paradigmatic here. Thus while I think one could construct a syllabus on the problem of action and structure, I do not think one could say that people have been consistently and self-consciously working on a synthesis in which, as in the present case, the two terms are given equal power.

On the second point, concerning whether practice theory may already be outmoded, Sharon Stephens questions "the possibility and desirability of developing a unified, general theory of practice at all"

(1987:2). Instead she proposes that anthropologists rethink the concept of culture, "in order to explore and systematically compare very different modes of making and unmaking humanly constructed, historically developing worlds" (pp. 2–3). Now it may be mischievous of me but it seems to me that this formulation, with its emphasis on "making and unmaking," is already paying some dues to a practice perspective. But more generally, as I indicated a moment ago in the discussion about actors, I would resist what I hear as a call, albeit a very sophisticated and eloquently argued call, for a new form of cultural particularism. I agree that different cultures construct actors, structure, and history very differently from our own, and that a large part of anthropology's project is to understand this. But I disagree with the suggestions that "a general theory of 'the system' and its relation to 'practice' [will] obscure rather than illuminate" (p. 3) these relations. On the contrary, it seems to me that the examination of cultural constructions of persons, of social life, and of history, on the one hand, and of theories of "agents" and "structures" on the other, take place most fruitfully in dialogue with one another. This brings me to the final keyword in the present discussion:

History. Maurice Bloch (1987:6) has said that it is "in the rapprochement between anthropology and history that the really exciting things seem to be happening." The present book constitutes my wholehearted agreement with this point. But the general area of historical anthropology also contains at the moment one of the sharpest oppositions in the field: that between the so-called political economy approach (as exemplified most recently in the work of Eric Wolf [1982], Sidney Mintz [1985], Richard Fox [1985], and others), and what I think some people are starting to call structural history but what I will simply call ethnographic history (this would include works by many of the practice theorists discussed earlier, but also works like Geertz's *Negara* [1980], Bloch's own recent book on Malagasy history and ritual [1986], Kelly's *Nuer Conquest* [1985], and so forth). In the political economy approach, the analytic emphasis is on impingement of external forces on the society in question; for the ethnographic historians, on the other hand, the emphasis is on internal developmental dynamics of the society. In the 1984 paper, I called attention to the opposition between these two contemporary schools, and in some quarters the opposition has been getting sharper since then. Since the present work is situated right in the middle of this opposition, it is worth exploring it a bit more fully here.

There are certain historical reasons for the current oppositional relations between the two schools. The relationship is in many ways a continuation of that between symbolic anthropology and cultural ecology in the sixties, even including many of the same key players. But there are also many more terms of shared perspective between the two schools than there were twenty years ago, and in the contemporary context this needs to be noted first. In particular, there is a wing of the ethnographic-historical camp (for example, Bloch 1986, Comaroff 1985, Dening 1980, Dirks 1987, Sahlins 1981, and including the present work) that takes a good deal of its inspiration from Marx, as do the political economists, and here the similarities between the two schools are at least as striking as the differences. Their parallel shifts from synchronic to historical perspectives of course form one point of commonality. Further, the ethnographic historical side is much more interpretively and analytically critical than it used to be, whether in a strict Marxist sense, or simply in the sense of attention to more broadly defined structures of domination. And finally, it seems to me that the ethnographic historians have largely accepted the necessity for considering the impact of external political-economic forces on a society's history and culture. This is a real shift from the sixties, when the external forces in question were those of the natural environment, in which most of the people now involved with ethnographic history were largely uninterested.

The ethnographic historical anthropologists, however—again including myself—still seek much more extensively to show the way in which the impact of external forces is internally *mediated*, not only by social structural arrangements (acknowledged as important by the political economists as well) but also by cultural patterns and structures of various kinds. This strong emphasis by the ethnographic historians, both Marxist and non-Marxist, on the importance of the cultural mediation, reinterpretation, and transformation of outside forces is probably the main point of difference between the two schools at this time, and it brings us back to the old subjectivist/objectivist controversies of the sixties, complete with the old familiar name-calling. The political economists accuse the ethnographic historians of "culturology" (Fox's [1985] term), of a form of idealism or mentalism that does not recognize the impact of the real world (see also Wolf 1982), while the ethnographic historians accuse the political economists of ethnocentrically projecting their notions of agency and social action into other times and places.

For better or worse, I have come to the conclusion that this opposition may never be mediated, or at least not with the prevailing concepts of mediation. In the worst case, mediation appears as merging or synthesis, which everyone opposes since all would lose their identities (Stephens [1987] also made this point). In the intermediate case, mediation appears as a dual perspective, in which both sides accept the fact that the world is *both* subjectively and objectively constituted. This is a noble ideal, but I do not believe it can be sustained, since the underlying opposition is posed precisely as an opposition, an either/or relation.

Instead of trying to mediate, then, I urge *acceptance* of this opposition, but *within* a controlling theoretical framework. And here I return to practice theory, which is in itself a theory of translation between an objective world and a subjective one, between a world constituted by logics beyond actors' perceptions, and a world constituted by logics spun by thinking and acting agents. Practice theory always has two moments, one largely objectivist and one largely subjectivist. In the first, the world appears as system and structure, constituting actors, or confronting them, or both, and here anthropologists bring to bear all their objectivist methodologies. But in the second, the world appears as culture, as symbolic frames derived from actors' attempts to constitute that world in their own terms by investing it with order, meaning, and value.

Practice theory in fully developed form attends seriously to both of these moments. But its special contributions lie in the ways in which it operates on the interface between them, examining those processes by which the one side is converted into the other. Thus one observes actors in real circumstances using their cultural frames to interpret and meaningfully act upon the world, converting it from a stubborn object to a knowable and manageable life-place. At the same time one observes the other edge of this process, as actors' modes of engaging the world generate more stubborn objects (either the same or novel ones) that escape their frames and, as it were, reenter the observer's. Here subjective and objective are placed in a powerful and dynamic relationship, in which each side has equal, if temporary, reality, and in which it is precisely the relationship between the two that generates the interesting questions. This book is situated on this subject/object cusp, and is concerned with these inside/outside translations. The Sherpa monasteries were built by actors who creatively used a world that was using them. I now turn to that history.

CHAPTER

II

The Early History of the Sherpas: Fraternal Contradictions

IN THE present chapter I discuss what is known, and what can reasonably be postulated, about the earliest period of Sherpa history. I also argue that there is a fundamental contradiction in the Sherpa social and cultural order, between an assumption of the naturalness and desirability of (male) equality, and an assumption of the naturalness and desirability of hierarchy. This general contradiction takes many specific forms or manifestations. One is seen in the discourses and practices of the brother relationship, and will be discussed in the present chapter. A second, which appears in patterns of political stability and succession, and a third, which appears in the larger order of relations between what the Sherpas call "big" and "small" people, emerge more fully in the next period of Sherpa history, and will be discussed in the next chapter. These are not of course the only areas of contradiction in Sherpa society—one immediately notes the omission of questions of gender, for example—but they are the ones that appear, with analytic hindsight, to have the greatest relevance for understanding the foundings of the monasteries.

Theoretical notions of "contradiction" in one form or another have cropped up throughout the history of social science thought. One may say that they all represent notions of what Giddens calls "immanent change" in a society, even if—as in the case of Talcott Parsons's idea of "strain"—the whole thrust of the analysis is to show how societies overcome such internal tendencies and keep themselves homeostatic. I take some notion of contradiction to be central to a historical anthropology that seeks to place a significant part of the historical dynamic *within* a society's own organization. It will thus be useful to review, extremely briefly, some of the available theoretical positions on contradictions, and their relation to historical change.

Marx essentially opened the debate on the subject. Although there is a fair amount of disagreement about what Marx meant by contradictions, the generally accepted interpretation emphasizes the co-presence of principles of relationship (specifically economic relationship) appropriate to different modes of production (Giddens 1979:ch. 4). In the classic formulation, contradictions are incompatibilities between the "forces" and "relations" of production, usually between an emergent economic formation (the "forces" of production) and the historically evolved structure of social relations appropriate to the dominant economic formation (the "relations" of production). In the Marxist view, contradictions render any given social formation implicitly unstable, producing certain inherent tendencies toward (evolutionary) change, and also in principle making the system vulnerable to challenge and revolutionary transformation.

Parsons is the virtual antithesis of Marx in most respects. His theory is concerned with the "functional prerequisites of society," that is to say, the things society somehow "needs" in order to function stably and enduringly—particularly its needs for people to play certain kinds of roles. Parsons's equivalent of the notion of contradiction is his notion of "strain," which emphasizes the incompatibilities between social requirements and individual desires, or rather the incompatibilities between the needs and patterns of the social system on the one hand, and the needs and patterns of the "personality system" of the individual on the other (see for example 1964:180–99). In terms of the implications of strain for historical change, Parsons insists that strain is not a "prime mover" in such change (1964:493), although it may play a role in some cases: "the progressive increase of strains in one strategic area of the social structure [may] finally [be] resolved by a structural reorganization of the system" (ibid.).

A recently developed contradiction-based theoretical frame is to be found in Raymond Kelly's *Etoro Social Structure* (1977:ch. 9). Kelly's interest is in explaining the relationship between behavioral patterns (including so-called deviant patterns) and social rules. Behavior does not of course always conform to (explicit) norms. Kelly argues that the lack of fit is itself structured, and emerges systematically from the operation of contradictory structural principles (some of which are unarticulated) in the culture. Although not directly concerned with historical change, Kelly does suggest ways in which structural contradictions may give rise to progressive, structurally ordered transformations, essentially by forcing actors to make certain behavioral choices and compromises that in turn may give rise to new rules (1977:289).

My own perspective is an amalgam of these three approaches. In general I share Kelly's and Marx's views, which I take to be quite similar at one level: both are concerned with contradictions at the structural level. The two contrast with a Parsonian perspective, which sees the structural level as largely coherently integrated, and places the locus of strain in the relationship between the actor and the structure. As between Kelly and Marx, I place myself closer to Marx, since I am interested primarily in contradictions founded on problems of inequality and domination, whereas Kelly's contradictions are more generically social. I do retain one bit of Parsonian heritage, which is the emphasis on the actor's point of view. (Kelly has this too.) Although in theory Marx might not deny that contradictions must ultimately manifest themselves in actors' experiences, he does not regularly consider the impact of contradictions on actors. However wrongheaded Parsons is in most aspects of his social theory, and indeed in his theory of actors and action, he does maintain the actor as the analytic reference point, and I will do so as well. Ultimately, contradictions are only analytically significant insofar as one can show how they impinge on actors' experience, and force actors to respond to the problems they pose. That is the way in which they will be examined throughout this book.

Time Frame

The book will proceed in more or less chronological order, although different pieces of the chronology will be used to reveal different aspects of the problem. I will begin each chapter with a simple time chart, showing the time period to be covered in the chapter and the main dates of that period. A composite chronology of Sherpa history, for the entire span of time covered by the book, will be found preceding chapter 1. Most dates are only approximate.

1480	Sherpas leave Kham and settle in south-central Tibet
1533	Sherpas cross into Nepal and settle in Khumbu
1553	Settlement of Solu
1667	Founding of first temple at Pangboche

The Sources

There is very little in early Sherpa history that can be known with any certainty. Although, as I will describe in a moment, the Sherpas migrated into Nepal in the early sixteenth century, no observations of their society by outsiders prior to the nineteenth century have come to light.

The earliest British travelers in Nepal, Kirkpatrick in 1793 and Hamilton in 1802–1803, did not travel to the east or west of the trail leading north from India to the Kathmandu valley, or beyond the Kathmandu valley itself (Kirkpatrick 1811; Hamilton 1819). Hodgson, who held various posts up to, and including, British resident in Nepal between 1820 and 1843, trekked eastward from Kathmandu to Darjeeling but swerved south of Solu-Khumbu (Hodgson 1848; Hunter 1896). Hooker, the great British naturalist living in Darjeeling between 1848 and 1851, trekked westward into Nepal shortly afterward, but stopped at the Arun valley, immediately east of Solu-Khumbu (Hooker [1854] 1969). Most Western exploring and (later) mountaineering expeditions operated out of Darjeeling until 1953; the mountaineers approached Mount Everest from the Tibetan side, which they reached via the Jelap La (or Jelap Pass) from Sikkim.

The first account of a visit to the region by an official of the Nepal state is dated 1805 (Stiller 1973:265; Regmi Research Series 1979b).[1] As high-caste Hindus, the Gorkha kings (who ruled Nepal from 1768 to 1846), had promulgated a law banning the slaughter of cows throughout the country.[2] The Sherpas were evidently not abiding by the law, and a delegation of "judges" was sent to Solu-Khumbu to try to enforce the ban. Although the crime was theoretically punishable by enslavement or death, the Sherpa defendants, who not only readily confessed but implicated all their neighbors as well, were merely fined. The writer of the report realistically notes that "if this crime is to be punished with death or enslavement, many people [in the regions] will be put to death or enslaved." But the writer, who was doing a bureaucratic job and not "exploring" or otherwise making "objective" observations, offers no description of the region, the villages, or the people.

The first visit to the region by a foreign observer appears to have been that of the Indian explorer Hari Ram, working for the Survey of India in 1885–86 (Survey of India 1915b).[3] Hari Ram provides the first known descriptions of Solu-Khumbu. He enters the region at Jubing and works his way up the Dudh Khosi (Milk River). He has little to say about the villages or the people—much is said about the depths of the rivers, the widths of the bridges, and the quality (from "bad" to "very bad") of the roads—until he gets to "Nabjia" village, which the Sherpas call Nauje (currently known as Namche Bazaar). Here he says that:

> This is the largest of twelve villages which comprise the Khumbu patti [district], and is the chief resort of traders both from the north and south. The village consists of 50 houses, and the in-

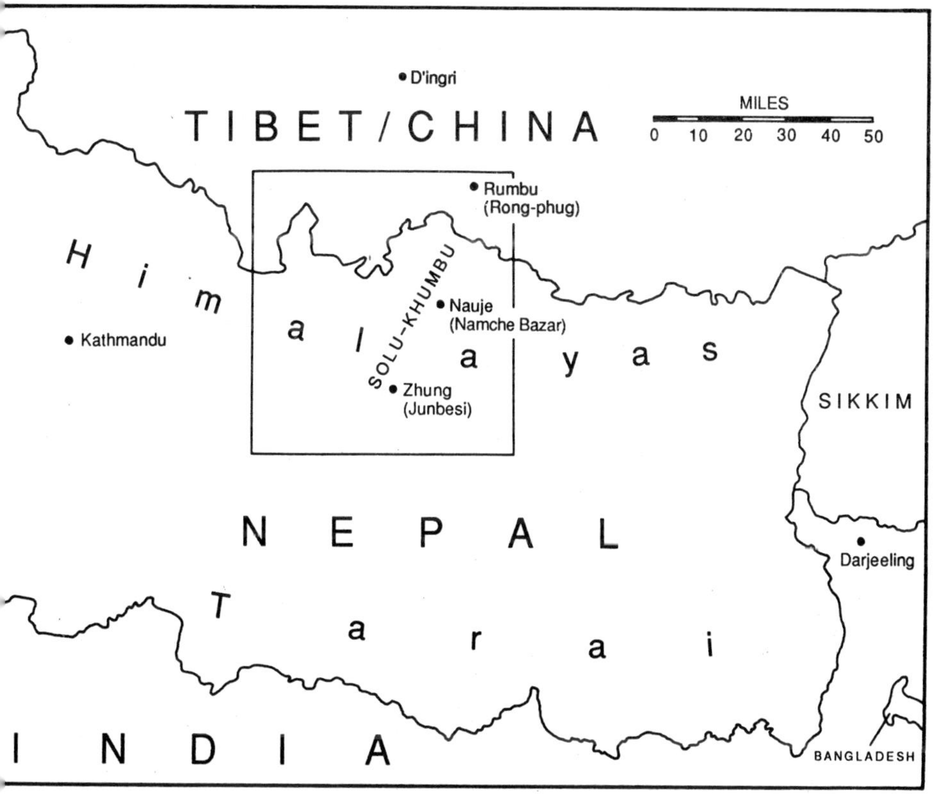

Eastern Nepal, showing the Sherpas' home area of Solu-Khumbu in relation to their primary points of regional travel

> habitants are more well-to-do than those of any village that the explorer passed through from Dagmara thana [on the India-Nepal border] to Ting-ri [in Tibet]. . . . About two miles north of Nabjia and on a flat part of a spur, is Khumbu Dzong [in modern times, Khumjung], the residence of the Governor of the Khumbu district. This official is a Tibetan [Hari Ram calls the Sherpas "Tibetans" throughout; there is little question that he means "Sherpas"], and has held the post for the last 30 years: he receives no pay from the Nepal Government, but is allowed 15 percent of the nett [*sic*] revenue of the district. The explorer was told that he pays an annual visit to Katmandu. (1915b:385)[4]

It appears that the first Westerners to visit the Sherpas' home region were the members of the Houston-Tilman expedition, who passed through Solu-Khumbu in 1950 (Tilman 1952). But the Sherpas as a recognized ethnic entity turn up a bit earlier in Western sources, around the turn of the twentieth century in various publications emanating from the Darjeeling district of India. Although the Sherpas had probably been in Darjeeling in gradually increasing numbers since around 1800 (Oppitz 1968:109), they were evidently classed within a general category of "Bhutia," or peoples of Tibetan stock. In the early twentieth century, however, they were "discovered" by British mountaineers in Darjeeling, because they established themselves as outstanding climbing guides and porters on the increasingly popular mountaineering expeditions (Mason 1955; see also R. Miller 1965). It soon became the norm among Western mountaineers to use (Solu-) Khumbu Sherpas exclusively as guides, and nearly exclusively as porters, on their expeditions. From that time until the 1950s, then, one can find in the various expedition accounts highly colored (and generally very positive) sketches of Sherpa "character," as well as anecdotes about individual Sherpas who accompanied the expeditions.

As for Sherpa sources, these are of three types. There are first of all the *chayik*,[5] or charters, of Sherpa religious institutions. At the time of the founding of a temple of any sort, one of these charters is drawn up, detailing the rules of conduct of the participants (whether monks, noncelibate lamas, or lay people) in the religious life of the institution. Chayik are dated (using the Tibetan calendar) and signed by the founder(s), and so in theory provide precise information on the dates of the foundings of all the temples in the region. (This precision is somewhat compromised by the fact that most chayik are acknowledged to be copies, the originals having been lost to fire or to water damage.)[6]

The richest source of information on early Sherpa history is a body of oral folklore. These tales are almost entirely connected with the foundings of temples, although they provide hints of a broader picture of Sherpa society as well. I collected versions of as many of these as I could in the course of the 1979 fieldwork, and other versions of most of them appear in Oppitz (1968), von Fürer-Haimendorf (1964), and Sangye Tenzing (1971). Such folklore is also the most ambiguous source, since there is no way of dating its origin, and no way of observing the changes it may have undergone over the years (assuming that there have been years) of retelling. I will rely heavily on the tales in the discussions that follow, although I am well aware, and in turn caution the reader, that any history derived from this material must be taken as very tentative.

And finally, there are written clan genealogies, or *merap*. One of these is held (in modern times) by the senior member of each group that considers itself to be a lineage, and traces the line of the clan through the one individual in each generation who was a direct ancestor of the present lineage. When two lineages diverge from one another, it appears (at least for those of any substance and prestige that bother with genealogies at all) that each of the two branches will have its own merap, and each will differ starting at the point of divergence. In other words, lineage A will list as its ancestor brother A of a group of brothers, while lineage B will list brother B. No one except an anthropologist will have a complete genealogy that maps all the lineages of a clan down to all the present-day descendants (although some individuals within the society clearly have a better overview than others). The merap also tend to begin with some sort of legend about the origins of the clans, and so provide additional, if still ambiguous, material for historical work. The most extensive work with these clan documents has been done by Michael Oppitz, who has used them to reconstruct the migration and demographic history of the Sherpas, and some other features of pre-modern Sherpa social organization (1968, 1974).

Special mention should also be made here of the work of the Sherpa lama and historian Sangye Tenzing, who drew upon all three types of sources in writing his illuminating history of Sherpa religion (1971).

In the present chapter, which covers the period between the Sherpas' settlement of Solu-Khumbu in 1533 and the founding of the first noncelibate temples in 1667, I will rely primarily on the merap as translated in Oppitz (1968), and on related (or sometimes identical) genealogical accounts as chronicled in Sangye Tenzing (1971). These are really the only sources for the earliest period; the oral folklore pertains mostly to the temple foundings in the later seventeenth century, and to subsequent events.

It is worth stressing once again just how speculative most of the historical reconstructions are, particularly concerning the earliest period of Sherpa history in Nepal. There are many reasons why they could be wrong, including the possibility that the texts from which they are drawn are actually modern compositions (see, for example, MacDonald 1980b). But I am using these texts in two ways: first, I do try to reconstruct early Sherpa history, since it seems to me that a tentative reconstruction, which might be modified by later evidence, is more useful than none at all; but second, I use the texts as sources from which to elicit the structural contradictions and cultural schemas that will be important for analyzing the foundings of the monasteries in the twentieth century. Even if the historical reconstructions are wrong, the structural and cultural analyses could remain accurate as interpretations of more recent conditions, and relevant to the analysis of the foundings.

Migration, Settlement, and Subsistence

According to Oppitz, from whose valuable work (1968) I draw most of the information in the present section, the Sherpas' ancestors came from different localities in the Salmo Gang district of the Kham region of eastern Tibet, between 1480 and 1500. Their reason for leaving was apparently to escape the turmoil of war being carried on by the Mongols in eastern Tibet (Oppitz 1968:75).[7] They settled for a while in Tinkye, in south-central Tibet, apparently planning to stay, but decided to move on again in 1533, because of rumors of an invasion from the west. Sangye Tenzing makes no mention of the Sherpas' ancestors fleeing from a rumored invasion, but simply says they "were of different families, different ways of thinking, and different life styles" (1971:154).

According to Sherpa folklore, the Solu-Khumbu region was known in Tibet as a wilderness, and was used for meditation retreats by Tibetan hermits before it was settled by Sherpas. According to an oral account, the area was first discovered by accident:

> Khumbu was opened by Kira Gombu Dorje. He was a hunter, with dogs, and his dogs were chasing a blue sheep. He chased after the dogs [and shot the sheep], and now people still call the place La-dze; "La" means (he shot the sheep at the) pass. Afterward he came down into Khumbu; he saw it was a nice place, and told many other people. After that [though not immediately] many Tibetans came to live here, and then villages were built.

The party from Tinkye crossed the Nangpa La (Nangpa Pass) in 1533 and settled first in the upper Khumbu, in Pangboche and Dingboche, which were already sites of meditation retreats for Tibetan lamas.[8] Oppitz reckons that the original immigrant group contained between twenty-five and fifty persons, and that 90 percent of the Sherpas in modern Solu-Khumbu are descended from that original group. His figure for the Sherpa population of Solu-Khumbu in 1965, not counting Khambas (recent Tibetan migrants/refugees and descendants thereof) and "outcasts,"[9] is 14,100, of which 13,300 are members of the clans derived from the original migrants.[10] The whole of Solu-Khumbu was wild and uninhabited, although at least some of the southern portions belonged to the indigenous Rai, and were bought from them by the Sherpa settlers.

The migrants apparently had a reasonable amount of wealth when

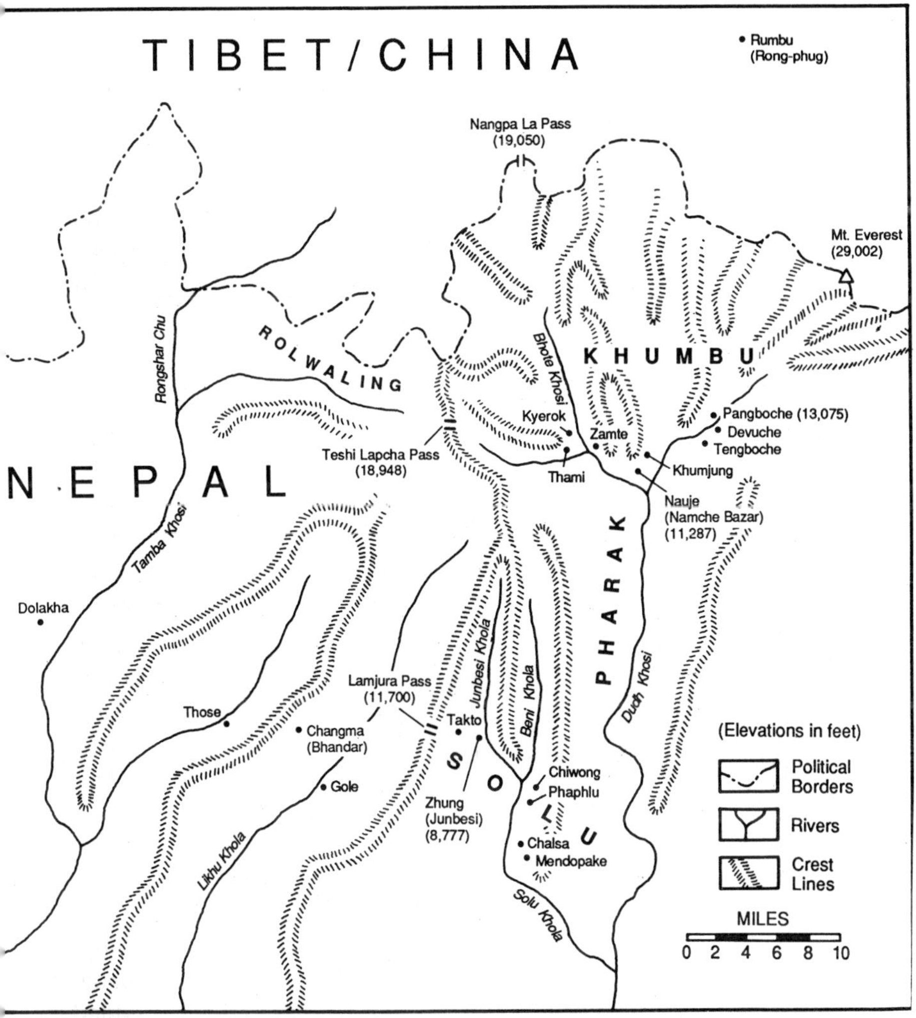

The Solu-Khumbu region

they were in Tibet, as the clan-history texts speak of their carrying gold and silver objects, riding horses, sponsoring religious ceremonies, and making substantial contributions to monasteries in the course of their travels. Nonetheless, the early situation in Nepal was evidently quite primitive, and the early settlers in Solu-Khumbu are described as living as hunter-gatherers when they first arrived, staying in caves and rude bamboo shelters and eating mushrooms, bamboo shoots, and wild millet.

Fifteen or twenty years after their entry into Khumbu, the mi-

Khumbu vista: view southeast along the Bhote Khosi, 1976.

grants moved down to Solu, with its more hospitable climate. This move was made, as indeed was the original move from Kham, on the basis of a vision:

> A few years later Chak Pön Dudjom Dorje had a dream one night in which the figure of a woman in a bluish aureole appeared and spoke the following prophetic words to him: "The time has not yet come for you to remain. You both have to look for a wilderness for yourselves which is situated many passes and valleys away from here between India and Tibet. . . . There in front of a mountain similar to a lion is another mountain which looks like a burning jewel. There you and your following should go, there you should carry out your daily work in order to improve your situation and obtain well-being." On the basis of this prophecy both lamas and their following traveled through many valleys and over many passes and finally arrived at the promised location. (Oppitz 1968:45–66)

In Solu, in turn, various individuals had more visions, and went off to live in various parts of the area.

The migrants apparently settled the area by clan, that is, a set of related individuals claimed a large tract of territory for themselves as clan co-members (Oppitz 1968, 1974) and established one or more homesteads within the area. Small settlements of descendants of the original household(s) grew up around the homestead(s), and these became the original clan villages. Modern Sherpas believe that many of the present-day clans got their names from the original sites of these villages.[11] New settlements, and in some cases new clans, were established by individuals who left these original clan areas, again (according to the merap clan-history texts) under the influence of visions directing them to make the move (Oppitz 1968; Sangye Tenzing 1971). The clans (which are patrilineal) regulated marriage, presumably being strictly exogamous, as they still are today. In addition, they presumably had, as they still do today, distinctive (mountain) deities who served as their protectors, and at least some collective rituals dedicated to those deities (Oppitz 1968:96; Funke 1969).

Shortly after the move down to Solu, it appears that some settlers moved back up to Khumbu. The texts suggest that the Khumbu settlers tried to maintain the same pattern of clan villages and clan land (Oppitz 1968:90), but at some point in time, and for reasons that can only be guessed, this pattern broke down, and today there are no pure clan villages in Khumbu.

The mode of subsistence of the early settlers is not described. One assumes an early differentiation, for ecological reasons, between Solu and Khumbu subsistence modes. Solu is much more conducive to agriculture, being warmer and also (slightly) more gently sloping. The early crops in both areas would have been wheat and barley; the potato, which is today the staple Sherpa food, was not introduced until the nineteenth century, and corn, which is now grown in many parts of Solu, was not introduced until the twentieth.

But the greater warmth of Solu, though better for agriculture, is not hospitable to the traditional Tibetan domestic animals, yaks and cow-yak crossbreeds called *dzo*. It is actually rather difficult to understand why some of the Solu settlers moved back up to the colder and less fertile Khumbu not long after the settling of Solu, unless it is assumed to be part of a strategy of maintaining traditional patterns of yak and dzo herding.[12] These herds have tremendous economic value. They produce dairy products that the Sherpas consume as food and use in religious offerings. More important, they play major roles in trade: the butter is an important trade commodity, the animals carry loads, and the animals themselves are bred and reared for sale. I will have more to say about trade later in this chapter.

Family and Inheritance

Modern Sherpas live in nuclear family households. Each family owns its own land and herds, and works largely as an independent unit. Although the clan has certain residual rights to a family's land, nonetheless a family has strong rights to transmit its property to its children. Sons get land and herds, while daughters normally get movable household goods and jewelry. Beyond the family, there are mutual aid groups that can be called upon for help at certain times of need (at certain times in the agricultural cycle; for house building; for help at weddings and funerals when a family must do a lot of entertaining), but by and large the family is economically self-sufficient and operates on its own much of the time.

There are no indications that family organization was radically different in the early Sherpa period in Nepal. It seems safe to assume that the basic unit was a nuclear family group privately owning and transmitting its own productive property. One can, however, perceive some variations within this larger continuity. For example, the texts reveal that people got married at much earlier ages than they do now—around age fourteen or fifteen. This would have been consistent with the need for more people in that time of low population, both for labor and general sociability. The emphasis in the genealogical texts, however, is specifically on the production of sons, and on the founding and perpetuation of lineages and clans, which is after all what the texts are supposed to be about. Women appear only as wives who bear sons, although there are some female figures in supernatural and magical roles.

Parent-child relations appear to have been harmonious, and this too (if true) would represent a difference between early and more recent times. In any event, there are no instances of parent-child conflict depicted in the texts, and there is one extended case of warm and positive relations between a grandfather, a father, and a son. This case forms the core of the text called *Ruyi* (The account of the clans). The text begins with a man called Minyag Donka Ringmo (or Donka Ringmo for short) having a vision, to which I will return later. It continues (in summary) as follows:

Donka Ringmo had two sons, the younger of whom was called Chak Pön Sangye Paljor, or Chak Pön for short. Chak Pön went off to central Tibet and became a powerful lama. He returned to his home area in Kham and conducted the rituals for naming his older brother's new son. He got married and went off to central Tibet again where he began to found a temple. His wife bore two sons, the younger of whom was called Dudjom Dorje.

Chak Pön's reputation continued to grow and reached his family in Kham, where his father, Donka Ringmo, decided to pull up his roots and join his now famous son. After the father came to join him (with a large number of relatives), Chak Pön gave his father religious instruction. Eventually Donka Ringmo died, and Chak Pön performed his funeral rites.

The action then shifts to the relationship between Chak Pön and his younger son, Dudjom Dorje. Although this point does not emerge until later in the text, it seems that Chak Pön trained and empowered his son as a married lama. But there were threats of invasion in the region where the family was living. A lama came to study with Chak Pön, and Chak Pön asked the lama to accompany his son to Khumbu, presumably to remove the son from harm's way. He gave his son a sacred relic for his protection and sent him off to Khumbu, where he became one of the first clan founders of the Sherpas. The text goes on to chronicle Dudjom Dorje's activities in leading the settlement of the region (condensed from Oppitz 1968:32–49).

The story illustrates, as I said, positive relations between fathers and sons: Chak Pön's father follows his son; Chak Pön gives his father religious instruction and performs his funeral rites; Chak Pön trains his son as a lama and sends him off, well protected, to save him from possible harm. This picture of father-son relations may well be idealized, in part because such is the ideal, and in part because it is the business of genealogical texts to portray the orderly transmission of patrilineal bonds. Nonetheless I am inclined to think that the ideal may have been more frequently realized in this early period than was the case in more recent Sherpa history. My primary reason for thinking so is that the texts are not at all reticent about portraying other forms of social conflict; the silence on fathers and sons therefore seems significant, possibly representing a genuine absence of strained relations.

The main problem in family relations seems to have lain elsewhere, in the relations *between* sons/brothers. The Sherpa brother relationship is supposed to be one of "natural" hierarchy. Terminologically, one must always distinguish between older and younger brothers; there is no generic term for brother that does not mark relative age. Elder brother has both "natural" authority and "natural" status superiority over younger brother, and descendants of elder brother have status superiority (though not authority) over descendants of younger brother. These status patterns are displayed at all public events in village life, as men must sit and be served in the order of precedence derived from their positions in a sibling, and sibling-derived (lineage), order (Ortner 1978:ch. 4).

At the same time, brothers have jural equality with respect to the inheritance of property. In modern times, there is a rule that all sons should inherit equally, and this rule was evidently in effect in early Sherpa history as well. One early text indicates that this was so, and also shows that the inheritance process did not necessarily work harmoniously for brothers:

> According to the express desire of the parents, each of the sons was to have inherited some of the property; all three of them, however, favored the female servant, and so they agreed to settle the matter with a game of chance. The youngest son was very cunning . . . [and brought in a Brahmin to help him. Eventually] the elder son won the house. The youngest son won the maid. Then some years passed [and the three sons moved to three different villages]. (Sangye Tenzing 1971:159–60)

This little vignette from the early genealogical texts shows both the assumption of equal inheritance ("each of the sons was to have inherited some of the property") and the competition between brothers that surrounded the inheritance process. The competition was petty (over a servant), yet intense: the younger brother even had recourse to trickery to get what he wanted.[13] And in the end the three brothers split up, all going to live in different places.

A second example again shows the competition between brothers, and also a more seriously unequal outcome:

> [A certain man] also had three sons: Ngampa, Ngoni, and Darben. These three had as a habit to always pray to the gods at home. By the power of such prayers the household of Darben flourished more than ever before. *He received the most land.* Ngampa settled in a place by the name of Lhabsang Gangme . . . Ngoni settled in a place by the name of Trashing Chewa *but half of it belonged to his brother Darben.* (Oppitz 168:60, emphasis added)

Fraternal conflict continues throughout Sherpa history, and indeed plays a major role in the foundings of the monasteries in the twentieth century. It emerges, I would suggest, from the contradictory nature of the brother relationship, at once hierarchical (in the natural superiority and authority of elder over younger) and egalitarian (in the rule of equal inheritance). This contradiction is more general to the Sherpa social order than the brother relationship, and must be discussed here in a broader way before continuing with the examination of early Sherpa history.

EGALITARIANISM AND HIERARCHY: THE CORE CONTRADICTION

The Sherpas explicitly say that all unrelated men are equal. (The specification that *unrelated* men are equal is necessary because, as just discussed, kinship produces relative inequality among kin, as a result of birth order differences.) Sherpa egalitarianism is very much like the American variety, in the sense that it is an egalitarianism of opportunity. There are no status differences given by birth, and every individual in principle has the possibility of achieving whatever forms of success are available, to whatever level he[14] is able to achieve. Indeed there are very few forms of higher achievement available in traditional Sherpa society. One form of such achievement is to take training and become a religious specialist, or lama. Another lies in building wealth and becoming "big," an influential and respected person. Big people in turn may achieve certain political positions (*pembu*), to be discussed at length in this book. But none of these achievements is automatically heritable. Neither the status of lama nor the position of pembu can be passed on to a son as a matter of course, although such transmission may take place under certain circumstances. Given the equal inheritance rule for property, even material wealth is only theoretically hereditary, since it will tend to disperse in the course of a few generations. Each generation must thus rebuild its own fortune and status.

A major dimension of the Sherpa ethic of egalitarianism and achievement is a strong streak of competitiveness in the culture.

Given the theoretical equality of all men, the fact that in reality some do better than others is a source of resentment and renewed striving. Modern Sherpas very consciously recognize this competitiveness in their own culture. Here are some excerpts from field notes:

> N[a thirty-five-year-old, middle-status man] was a little worried about having gambled today. He said there is some sin accruing from this or any game, from competing. You are thinking symbolically of killing your opponent, and eating his money.

> [A fifty-five-year-old man of middle status was talking about two guests at a dinner party.] There was some question about whether KC would get along with Z, who were both invited to dinner. [The informant] said rich people always fight with one another, smart people always fight with one another, the idea apparently being that the more you have the more competitive you are. I said, well, everybody fights, poor people fight too. Yes, he said, but that's for food, for survival. That's different. [A twenty-five-year-old man] had said something similar a few days earlier. I asked him, why do people steal? First, he said, for competition: to keep up with their neighbors. And [only] second, need.

More generally, there is an elaborate vocabulary pertaining to competition, envy, rivalry, and so forth.

> I was asking [a thirty-five-year-old, middle-status man] about the fight between Z and U. What was the fight about? He didn't know exactly, but anyway they were both sardars [expedition leaders] and they were competitive. When one sees the other going higher he can't stand it. There are at least three different words for competition: *balabenzin* [a Nepali word] is like a dance competition, or a running race; it's not very serious, it's good, it's fun or play, if you lose it doesn't matter. Then there's *tatok.* This is bad. It doesn't necessarily involve fighting, but the parties wish each other ill. If something bad happens to one, the other's happy, if something good happens, the other's depressed. *Tatok* is always trying to have as much as the other, can't stand to see the other get ahead. Like Lama Sangwa Dorje and Zongnamba [early figures in a tale to be told shortly]. It occurs between gods, between lamas, between big people, between little people. There is also a notion of "triumph"—*nosu shetu,* as when the one who wins a race dances around with glee.

Yet other terms appear in these other examples:

> [A Solu monk was talking about the founding of Chiwong monastery in the twentieth century by a man named Sangye:] Sangye built Chiwong out of competition with his brother (*sheka-shek*; there are two kinds, one involving arguing with words, the other just having bad thoughts). Maybe there was a bad fight. One brother does a big thing and the other doesn't, so maybe the other feels shamed.

> [The forty-year-old head lama of a monastery said:] the sponsors of Tengboche [the first monastery] were [Solu people]. . . . One of them was the older brother of the Chiwong sponsor. People get *ngargyal*—competitive, angry, like jealous. Then he said (and here the lama imitated his tone—very strong, aggressive) "I'll build a monastery too."

At one level, the competitiveness of Sherpa society is a direct manifestation of Sherpa egalitarianism. Indeed it is the primary manifestation, in terms of Sherpa self-awareness. People do not talk much about equality and about egalitarian ideals. But they talk a great deal about competitive feelings and competitive relations, about—in the informant's words—not being able to stand seeing others get ahead.

But Sherpa egalitarianism, as a dominant discourse/practice of social relations, does not stand alone. There is also in Sherpa culture a hierarchical discourse that accords "natural" authority to some individuals over others, and that makes submission to certain kinds of authority in certain contexts a proper and positive thing to do. The hierarchical discourse will be discussed more fully in the context of examining political relations; for now it is enough to note that the contradiction between egalitarian and inegalitarian discourses was beautifully illustrated by the brother relationship. On the one hand there is the equal inheritance rule, which treats all brothers as equal individuals. But at the same time birth order distinctions between brothers give "natural" authority to older brothers over younger, and form the basis of enduring social rankings. The overall effect of this contradiction—of an egalitarianism that is permanently unbalanced by a ranking principle, and a ranking principle that is permanently countered by an egalitarian rule—is a chronic fraternal rivalry that reappears throughout Sherpa history. Indeed it is likely that the acute competitiveness of the culture, discussed above as a manifestation of egalitarianism, is generated precisely by the fact that there is a contradiction, and that the egalitarianism is always threatened by contrary discourses and practices.

INHERITANCE, ECONOMY, AND INEQUALITY

Returning to early Sherpa history, the equal inheritance rule was apparently instituted very early (if not indeed brought by the original migrants from Kham), and was enormously consequential for other aspects of Sherpa social and economic relations. Put very simply, the rule is, in practical terms, unworkable over time. Assuming an expanding population (and the evidence for this is clear; see Oppitz 1968:part 3), if all sons inherit equal shares of a given amount of land, it will not take very many generations before each person's plot is too small to support a family.[15] Left to its own devices, in other words, the inheritance rule will produce a declining standard of living for the group as a whole.

There are three possible responses to the problematic consequences of the inheritance rule: (1) reduce the number of cuts in an existing estate by not having all sons inherit; (2) augment the land under cultivation through opening virgin land; or (3) augment land-based wealth with income derived from other economic activities. A few words may be said about each possibility.

Strategies for reducing the number of cuts in an estate could have included fraternal polyandry, in which all the brothers shared a single wife and set of children, thus maintaining the father's land as an undivided common whole; and monasticism, in which one son went off to a monastery and did not take his share. Both of these strategies are common in twentieth-century (but pre-Chinese) Tibet, although one does not know how common they were in the sixteenth and seventeenth centuries. In any event they were not much used by the early Sherpas. There is only one case of polyandry in the genealogies of this era. Nothing is said about young people going off to Tibet to join monasteries, but it is doubtful that there was very much of this either. The Sherpas' biggest need in the early years of settlement was labor, which both of these strategies would have reduced rather than augmented.

Then there was the possibility of opening virgin land. In the early years of settlement of the region, land was in plentiful supply, and this possibility was presumably widely available. It is also the case, however, that opening virgin land is a lot of work, and that people would rather have an already tilled field if they can get it. This is where the contradictions in fraternal relations manifested themselves. If all brothers could not inherit without pulling down the standard of living of all, but if they were not willing to enter into some sort of collectivist arrangement (as in polyandry), then someone had to get more and someone had to get less. This is the frequent outcome in modern times, and it apparently happened in early times as well, as was seen in the example of Darben, who wound up with his own share and half the share of one of his brothers.

The final possible approach to the land parcellization problem is to augment land-based wealth with income derived from other economic activities. In the Sherpa (as in the Tibetan) case, this essentially meant trade.[16] The Sherpas were involved in trade from their earliest days; some of the original migrants are described as merchants. Speaking of how the early settlers gradually raised their standard of living, one of the texts says: "They destroyed most of the forests and changed the landscape in cultivated regions to fieldcrops and in the meadows for cattle. *Then some of them went to India and Tibet in order to import and export various goods*. Several also went to Tibet in search of the teaching of religion and disseminated the Buddhist doctrine. The Sherpas became more prosperous and better" (Oppitz 1968:52, emphasis added). The Sherpas became regional middlemen, moving grain up from the Nepal lowlands to Tibet, and salt down from Tibet to southern and eastern Nepal. The significance of trade for the early Sherpa settlers is conveyed in this folktale, which purports to explain why the Sherpas can speak Nepali and the Nepalis can't speak Sherpa, but which also shows the Sherpas accepting a polluted status within the larger Hindu Nepali caste system, in order to stake out a position as traders within the system:

> The early settlers went hunting down below Lukla, at a place called Buo that the Nepalis call Surkye. They had no flour [that is, grain products], only salt. They met some other hunting people coming north, who had no salt, but who did have flour. The Tibetan people gave the salt, and the Nepalis gave the flour. The Nepalis got angry, saying that the Tibetans took their flour but only gave them in return sand, or ash, or mud.
>
> Actually, the two groups did not really meet. The Nepalis had only left the flour somewhere, and the Tibetans found it while hunting, and they took it and left the salt. This happened three times. The third time the Nepalis were very angry. They climbed a pine tree to watch and see what was happening. The Tibetans came to take the flour, and the Nepalis said, "We found the people who have been stealing our flour," and descended on them with *khukuri* (Nepali curved daggers).
>
> The Tibetans said, "Please don't kill us, try our stuff, it's very good, taste it on your tongue, don't kill us, we'll make friends." The Nepalis in the tree said, "Open your mouths and we'll spit

> in them, and then we can make friends." This was all done in hand language, since they couldn't understand each other. The Tibetans were afraid, and so they opened their mouths and ate the spit. Now people say it's because the Tibetans ate the spit that Sherpas can learn the Nepali language very easily, but the Nepalis can't learn Tibetan/Sherpa very easily.

The overriding value of trade—besides providing nonlocal subsistence goods of various kinds—is that it generates new wealth from the outside and thus allows a man to overcome the chronic and structurally self-defeating inheritance problem.[17] With trade profits a man can do any number of things—buy out a brother's share of land, hire labor to open virgin territory, make good marriage matches for his children (a daughter of a wealthy family may bring a field or two in her dowry), send a son to a monastery, and so forth.

More generally, trade is the primary source of large-scale wealth. The traders make up the bulk of what the Sherpas call "big" people—wealthy and influential members of the community. Trade thus plays a major role in large-scale political dynamics, as will be discussed at length in the next chapter.

Leadership and Power

It is commonly understood that politics has two poles. On the one hand there is "leadership," where an individual is consensually granted the right to make decisions for the group, and where such decision making in the group's interest is the primary function of the position. On the other hand there is power and domination, where an individual controls (and makes decisions for) others largely in his own interests, and where his position is not based on consensus but on threat of force. Both types of political roles appear among the Sherpas, although in the early texts the "leadership" of political figures is dominant.

The primary role of the early leaders was to lead migrations and to establish new settlements and clans. They are not shown, for example, collecting "taxes" (goods and services) from the villagers. The basis of a leader's right to make decisions for the group, and of his wisdom for doing so, was largely his seniority in a patrilineal clan (which in the early years was probably not much bigger than a single lineage). Leaders are specifically portrayed, as was seen in the case of Chak Pön, as nonviolent, and as being followed quite voluntarily by their kin and neighbors. The general pattern of leadership seems to have been that the leader had some sort of vision or supernatural experience that encouraged him to move to a particular place, and on the basis of this vision, his "family and followers" voluntarily went with him. The most fully spelled out instance of this pattern is seen in the *Ruyi*, or (the Account of the Clans). Here Donka Ringmo, the ancestor of one of the original Sherpa clans had an encounter with a supernatural bird that offered to become both his personal tutelary and that of his lineage. The bird stressed its own place in a set of kin relations: "This white cliff is my father. The black cloud of the south is my mother. The entire family of bird brothers and sisters is my retinue" (Oppitz 1968:35). Although the bird did not actually suggest the move that began the migration, its relationship with Donka Ringmo clearly gave the latter a certain authority when he suggested the move to people later on.

The vision can be interpreted in several ways, but in this context it reinforces what was initially a form of authority based largely on kinship seniority. This is clear a bit later, when Donka Ringmo actually initiated the migration from Kham. He at first merely intended to leave with his immediate family, and sold all of his immovable property to "cousins and relatives" (ibid., 37). But then "his relatives changed their minds and decided to move with him" (ibid.). There appears to have been no coercive dimension to Donka Ringmo's leadership. He had a certain positive authority, based on his kinship position and the visions that seem to reinforce it, and people—mostly his own relatives—followed because they felt that his decisions were good.

The portrayal of early Sherpa leadership as generally peaceful and nonviolent is also underscored by another passage in the texts. Speaking of the six original clan leaders/founders who migrated from Kham, one of the clan texts says: "These six [men] came to the agreement never to fight with one another, but always to lead a cooperative life as the lions of the Himalaya, and always to behave correctly to one another, as if they were weighing out butter or gold" (ibid., 57).

The picture of early leadership as based on benign and collectively accepted authority is an instance of the (positive) hierarchical discourse of Sherpa culture. But there is another image of early Sherpa leadership lurking in the texts. It appears only in fragments but it foreshadows a pattern that will appear much more strongly later, in the period depicted primarily in the oral folklore. This is a pattern of violent, strongman politics, based not on kinship seniority, passed on in orderly fashion through patrilineal succession, but rather on the ability, and the willingness, to seize positions of dominance through threats of force.

The politics here pertain to the position called *pembu*, often translated as "governor." The dynamics of pembu politics will be discussed in more detail in the next chapter, but here it may simply be said that the pembu was not primarily a leader in the sense of a figure with collectively agreed upon authority, but rather an individual who was largely in political business for himself. His main purpose was to collect "taxes"—goods and labor—over a given area.

The origins and early functioning of pembu tax collecting are unclear. One possibility is that it arose from nonkin co-residence relations. That is, if an individual had "ownership" rights to an area, and individuals unrelated to him resided in the area, he probably had the right to charge such unrelated individuals some form of rent. As noted above, the original settlement pattern probably involved claims to large areas of the region by co-clan members when they first settled in Solu-Khumbu. The senior kinsman would have represented the ownership claims of the group. If unrelated individuals—either new immigrants from Tibet, or Sherpas moving from other clans—came to live there, they may have had to pay some sort of recurrent fee in goods and labor to the senior kinsman for the right to settle on the land. Thus the senior kinsman would have evolved into a landlord in a contractual, rather than a kinship, relationship with at least some people on his clan land. In Khumbu in particular, it appears that clan co-residence patterns broke down at some point, and most contemporary Khumbu villages have members of more than one clan. This would have facilitated the emergence of the pembu role along the lines just suggested. (Eventually, when the Sherpas came under state control, the regional landlord would have been deputed to collect taxes from everyone in the region, kin and nonkin alike. This would represent the final transformation of the role.)

Alternatively, an individual unrelated to the people living in a particular territory may have come in and claimed "ownership" of that territory, with the same effect: the residents would not have been his kinsmen, and would have had to pay some sort of rent or fee to remain on "his" land. There are several instances of such individuals coming down from Tibet to Khumbu and making such claims, which were clearly illegitimate and were backed largely by threat of force. Here is an example, apparently from the earliest period; another will be given in the next chapter.

> Lama Zangpo came over the Nangpa La to Khumbu. At his arrival in Khumbu he encountered three persons by the name of Shuwa, Ngampa and Dapa. . . . He remained in Teshubuk in a small tent. From this place he set out flying to Phurte. He looked around himself and wrote "The land above Lartsa extending to

> the high mountains of the Himalayas belongs to me." He married a daughter of the Shuwa. Shuwa, Ngampa, and Dapa became his enemies. On the basis of this hostility he returned to Tibet and remained there with Lama Nyeme Thokda for three years. After that he returned to Khumbu. He received the land claimed by him. He also received three bars of gold. (Oppitz 1968:58)

This story illustrates one of the sanctions at a pembu's disposal: supernatural power, as seen in the lama's ability to fly around Khumbu. Many of the early pembu were lamas credited with such magical powers.[18] Secular pembu, too, could conceivably have access to supernatural power; in modern times it is suspected that secular individuals hire shamans to send sorcery against their enemies, and this option may have been thought to be available in earlier times as well.[19] In addition, secular pembu used threats of physical force, and both kinds of pembu also offered more positive incentives for their clients' continued cooperation. In particular, they offered the kind of paternalistic protections that had traditionally been made available by senior kinsmen—loans; ritual contributions of various kinds; protection against the possibility of domination by other (and by implication, less indulgent) pembu; and later, mediation between the individual and the state.[20]

As pembu positions became more materially valuable, and as individual occupants of the positions became less able to claim the "natural" legitimacy of kinship seniority, the evidence of competition, and sometimes violent competition, for the positions increases. This will be particularly visible in the examples given in the next chapter, but even in the example of Lama Zangpo, the fact that Shuwa, Ngampa, and Dapa became his "enemies" suggests that they may have been his political rivals rather than merely his subjects.

Pembu politics represent a transformation of the same contradictions that cluster around questions of inheritance. Pembu dominance is not "hierarchy," and is not in itself consistent with Sherpa cultural values. But insofar as the pembu role is historically rooted in claims of kinship seniority, and insofar as individual pembu attempt to instantiate those claims through paternalistic and "protective" behavior, then the pembu position taps into the discourse of (legitimate) hierarchy in Sherpa culture, as did the clan leaders of old. At the same time, the egalitarian ethic is also at work within pembu politics. There is no fixed rule of succession, and anyone with the necessary qualifications can in principle succeed to the position. The absence of hereditary rights is analogous to the equal inheritance rule in the domain of fraternal relations, but with even more possibility of intense competition, since there can only be one winner. Pembu conflict is thus the arena of greatest violence in Sherpa culture, as will be copiously illustrated in the chapters that follow.

Religion before the Temples

The texts show that the early Sherpa migrants and settlers practiced religion much as they do today. The migrants gave donations to monasteries along their route and sought rites and instruction for their protection; they circumambulated religiously sacred and powerful sites for the same purpose; and they passed on religious instruction and empowerments through both descent and teacher/disciple relationships.

The early Sherpa lamas are shown performing life-cycle rites (naming of new babies, funerals) and also founding *gompa*—which I will translate in the present context as "chapels"—for the purpose of worshiping their gods.[21] Most of the settling of habitation sites was accompanied by the founding of a gompa, and some of the moves are phrased in terms of finding better locations for gompa. It is almost certain that the gompa in question were located in conjunction with private homes, probably those of senior clan members, and that the relatives and followers of the senior family would gather at the private gompa when rites were held of relevance to this larger group. Public gompa, or gompa established outside private homes explicitly drawing a non-kin-based clientele—which I will call "temples"—were apparently not established until the late seventeenth century.

Gompa are desirable because they provide an especially favorable context for contacting and worshiping the gods. Although sacred precincts for worship may be constructed as well in private homes, or indeed in any locale at all, a gompa provides, as the Sherpas say, a "house" for the gods, in which the gods may be entertained in the best possible manner and so will be more likely to respond favorably to the desires of the worshipers. There is also a certain coercive aspect to a gompa in relation to the gods connected with it. The physical temple structure, the statues, and—when it is constructed for particular rites—the altar, all serve to "hold" the gods to some extent and make them more available to receive the worshipers' petitions (see Ortner 1975, 1978a; Waddell [1894] 1959). The gompa in effect materializes the relationship between specific gods and the specific group of people who are associated with it.

A few words may be said here about the nature of Sherpa religious practice, and specifically about the way in which the relationship between humans and gods is expected to work as a result of the performance of rituals. The basic idea is that the world is full of negative forces taking the form of demons and other nasty creatures, of which the Sherpas (and their relatives, the Tibetans) conceive a large variety. In a general way, the gods are protective of people, but this protection does not come automatically; it must be petitioned and renewed through ritual. Thus the essential act of ritual practice is to make offerings to the gods, to flatter them to some extent, and to request that they continue their protection of humanity against the evil forces of the world. While these rites are not described in the early texts, it is virtually certain that they were as central to Sherpa ritual practice at the time of the early settlers as they are today. They form the unspoken, because fundamentally assumed, rationale for the thing that *is* repeatedly mentioned in the texts, the importance of the founding of gompa.

Ordinary people can pray to the gods on their own, and in certain circumstances—especially if the individuals have demonstrated unusual faith and piety—the gods will hear them and help them.[22] Normally, however, the gods can only be contacted through the mediation of duly trained and duly empowered specialists, or lama.

The texts of the early period show that there were essentially two kinds of lamas operating in Solu-Khumbu, or perhaps better said, that the lamas of the period operated in two distinguishable modes: as village or clan lamas, who conducted the routine rituals (both life-cycle and calendrical) for others, and as hermits or tantric adepts, who were mainly involved in raising their own spiritual powers. The founders of the Lama, Takto, and Paldorje clans were all what I have called clan lamas, who performed rites for others and founded gompa for the social worship of gods. The stories in the early texts of the lamas who sought to meditate in Khumbu in deep isolation, as well as the stories of lamas with mystical powers who flew about like Lama Zangpo, are stories of lamas in the hermetic or tantric modality. Modern Sherpas refer to married lamas in lama lineages as *gyudpi* (lineage, or descent) lamas, while hermits and lamas actively engaged in mystical practices are referred to by a variety of terms—*tolden* (yogi) and *ngawa* (black-hat), among others.

At one level, the two types of lamas should not be contrasted too sharply. Hermits were themselves duly ordained lamas, while ordinary lamas in turn were required to undertake periods of hermetic retreat for meditational and mystical practices. Moreover, there was no clear-cut superiority in one or the other form of the role: a gyudpi lama from a long descent line of lamas might have just as much religious power (concentrated in him through descent) as a hermit who had meditated intensively and acquired many mystical skills. And finally, hermits often settled down and founded lama lineages, thus cycling back into the descent system, as was indeed the case with most of the early hermits in the genealogical texts.

The contrast between the two modes of religious specialization, and the interrelations between the two, are similar to the contrast and interrelations between authority based on kinship seniority and strongman politics, discussed earlier. This is not at all surprising since there was little if any distinction between the realm of politics and the realm of religion at this stage of Sherpa history, and indeed for a long time to come. Many of the early lamas were also political leaders, whether in the senior-kinsman leadership mold of the early clan-founding lamas like Chak Pön, or in the violent power-asserting mold of Lama Zangpo, who flew around Khumbu, claimed the land and the gold, and got his way.

In the next chapter I examine the first major "events" in Sherpa history after the early migrations and settlement of Solu-Khumbu: the foundings of the first (non-kin-based) temples in the late seventeenth century. These events emerge in part out of the dynamics of fraternal rivalry discussed in this chapter. In addition, I will use the stories of the foundings to explore much more fully the contradictions surrounding pembu politics, in terms of violent competition between pembu, and in terms of domination of big people over small.

CHAPTER

III

The Founding of the First Sherpa Temple: Political Contradictions

THE earliest Sherpa religious institutions—temples run by married lamas that conducted rituals (and still do) for the benefit of a hereditarily attached clientele—were founded in the late seventeenth and early eighteenth centuries, about 150 years after the Sherpas migrated into Nepal. The events are heavily folklorized; indeed, the tales of these foundings constitute the bulk of Sherpa folk history. They are told with great relish in modern times, partly because they historicize the current religious landscape (not only the temples, but various miraculous imprints in rocks and so forth), and also because they are powerful stories—by turns violent, awe-inspiring, and spiritually uplifting.

Four temples were founded in roughly a fifty-year period, between about 1670 and 1720. One can only speculate as to why there should have been a spate of temple foundings at this time. In terms of the influence of larger regional forces, there are virtually no clues at all. In Nepal, it was a time between an earlier period of state formation (the twelfth through the sixteenth centuries) and the later foundation of the Gorkha state (in the late eighteenth century). Perhaps the relevant point about Nepali history at the time, in relation to the temple foundings, is precisely that nothing much was going on, and the area was broken into numerous small and relatively weak princedoms (Stiller 1973:ch. 2).

On the Tibetan side, there was more activity, but it is not clear what impact, if any, this had on Sherpa religious developments. In 1642 there was a momentous event: the first ruling Dalai Lama (thought of by Tibetans as the fifth reincarnation in his line) was placed on the throne in Lhasa with Mongol backing (Richardson 1962). But the

Sherpas had relatively little contact with Lhasa, which was quite far to the east of Solu-Khumbu. To the west, the kings of Ladakh were threatening to expand eastward across southern Tibet, as they had done in the early sixteenth century when the Sherpas came into Solu-Khumbu (Francke 1907). There was thus a great deal of military activity across southwestern Tibet, and this may have affected local politics and economics in regions bordering on Solu-Khumbu. But again it is virtually impossible to link these developments with changes in Solu-Khumbu and the foundings of the first temples. One is pushed as well as inclined, then, to look largely at internal Sherpa developments.

It is almost as difficult to be clear about what was going on in Solu-Khumbu at the time, but one may point to a cluster of factors that may have been at work. For one thing, there would have been population growth. The Sherpa population by this time could have reached about four hundred people.[1] For another, one guesses that the Sherpas' middleman role in trans-Himalayan trade might have been paying off nicely by this time, producing some of the wealth that would have gone into founding and sustaining the temples. Most of the clan-history texts discussed in the last chapter emphasize that the Sherpas grew more prosperous over time.

And, finally, it appears that the shift toward a more violent pembu political system may have come to fruition in this period. Virtually all of the temple-founding stories are concerned with pembu violence, whether in terms of competition between pembu and their rivals, or (in some cases) in terms of threats of violence on the part of a pembu vis-à-vis his clients.

Whether such a shift really took place, or whether it simply appears so because of differences in textual conventions between the merap clan-history texts (which formed the basis of most of the discussion on the earliest period) and the oral folklore (which forms the basis of most of the discussions for the temple-founding period), cannot be known. But there is a certain logic to the proposition that the shift really took place. If the region was more prosperous, it would have made the pembu positions more attractive objects of competition among big men. And if the kinship basis of local residence patterns, and therefore the kinship legitimacy of local leaders, had by this time broken down to some extent, this would again have encouraged challenges and competition for the positions, since succession to these positions would increasingly have been a matter of "achievement." In turn, the suggestion that the kinship basis of both co-residence and leadership/politics was relatively weakened is supported by the fact of the temple foundings themselves. One of the distinctive features of the temples is that they draw their clientele on a voluntary basis from a given geographic area, and kinship criteria are irrelevant for membership.

All of this is, again, largely speculative. The only thing known with any certainty is that the tales of the early temple foundings situate the foundings in large part within the context of violent pembu politics. In the present chapter I will use the stories of the early foundings to explore the contradictions surrounding such politics: the competitive struggles among pembu for dominance, and the relationship between the economics and politics of the pembu system on the one hand, and larger patterns of inequality on the other.

Time Frame

1553	Sherpas enter Nepal
1667	Founding of Pangboche temple in east Khumbu
1667–77	Founding of temples at Thami (west Khumbu) and Rimijung (Pharak region)
1720	Founding of Zhung temple (Solu region)

The Novelty of Noncelibate Temples

The first Sherpa noncelibate lama temple was founded in northeast Khumbu at a place called Pangboche.[2] This heavily folklorized event seems to have taken place between 1667 and 1672. The dates are derived from assertions by Ngawang Samden, the senior monk of Thami monastery. In the course of searching for the original charter of Thami gompa, he came up with a claim that "Thami is 302–5 years old [in 1979], and Pangboche is 5–10 years older than that. Old people remember the dates from the old [but now destroyed] charter."[3] The date agrees with Snellgrove's comment that the Sherpas "received Buddhism" at the end of the seventeenth century (1957:213), although Snellgrove does not give the evidence for arriving at this date, and although, despite his phrasing, there is no evidence that the Sherpas were not already Buddhists.

Von Fürer-Haimendorf places the foundings in the early sixteenth century, and some Sherpa informants with whom I spoke also gave figures of "four hundred to five hundred years ago."[4] Von Fürer-Haimendorf based his estimate on human and reincarnate generations in the lineages of the lamas involved. This was a reasonable procedure, but he did not have access to Oppitz's migration reconstructions, which show the Sherpas first arriving in Nepal in the early sixteenth century. All of the dating is of course highly uncertain, but the late seventeenth century makes somewhat more sense, if only for reasons of population growth and wealth accumulation just suggested. Three other temples were all founded shortly after the founding of Pangboche—Thami, Rimijung, and Zhung. The Thami and Rimijung foundings are closely connected with the founding of Pangboche and will also be discussed in this chapter.

There is some debate as to whether Pangboche was originally founded as a *labtsang*, a celibate monastery. Most people said it was not, but a few claimed otherwise. The current Pangboche head lama (a Tibetan émigré with the high religious rank of *geshi*) stated that Pangboche was a labtsang at the time of its founding, as did Au Chokdu, a very senior and highly respected Tengboche monk. According to one bit of folk etymology, the syllable *pang* in Pangboche derives from the verb *pangup*, which means "to renounce," and therefore the name of the area suggests that the gompa originally founded there was a celibate one.[5]

Some of those who claimed the temple had been part of a celibate establishment offered explanations for why it had declined into a married religious community. The Tengboche monk Au Chokdu said that the problem was that the early monks began to engage in agricultural production. They planted a few potatoes and a few turnips, and when they saw how nicely the vegetables grew, they planted more and more and gradually became involved in worldly work.[6] Another man offered a strange and elaborate tale in which the celibate monks of earlier times were all wiped out in a fire as a result of contact with "zombies" (*roblang gyaup mi*; see appendix 1 for the text).

Even if the early temples were not celibate monasteries, they nonetheless represented the emergence of a novel form of religious institution on the Solu-Khumbu scene.[7] For one thing, they were founded apart from settlements and did not relate to any particular kin group or clan. Although the lamas were married and provided their own subsistence, their ritual activities were supported by hereditarily attached clients who were obligated to make contributions on a recurrent basis. How the clients were initially attracted to the temple is unclear, but one guesses a voluntary commitment based on a perception of the greater ritual potency of such establishments. The temple rituals—oriented primarily toward gaining the protection of the gods against demons and other evil forces—in turn were performed for the benefit of the contributing clients (as well as, in a residual way, for all sentient beings), regardless of social affiliation.

The temple's relation to its "congregation," then, was somewhat like a pembu's relation to his clients. The congregation was hereditarily obligated to contribute to it, and in turn received its protection.

The basis of the relationship was not kinship but the personal forcefulness and supernatural powers of the lama. This parallel of political and religious structures will be echoed by other political-religious homologies and will be central to later discussions.

The Stories of the First Founding

The stories of the founding of Pangboche are in many ways the *mythes de référence* of Sherpa religious (and even secular) history, and the founder of Pangboche, Lama Sangwa Dorje, qualifies as the preeminent folk hero of early Sherpa culture. Other stories and tales from long, long ago (*tangbo, tangbo*) tend to become linked with this tale, with their protagonists being styled as kinsmen, disciples, or descendants of disciples of Lama Sangwa Dorje, or being related in some other way to the key figures in the tale. For example, as discussed in chapter 5, the first submission of the Sherpas to a king of Nepal is blamed on the descendants of the arch-rival of Lama Sangwa Dorje. Similarly, the reincarnate lama who was one of the most important figures in the founding of the first celibate monastery in the twentieth century claimed to be a reincarnation of Lama Sangwa Dorje. Moreover, all the Dumje festivals—the big annual exorcisms—in the Khumbu temples today are said to be Lama Sangwa Dorje's *gongdzo*, memorials of his death. (See Sangye Tenzing 1971:11–23 and von Fürer-Haimendorf 1964:127ff. for other versions of the tales.)

There is some debate over whether Lama Sangwa Dorje was a Sherpa or a Tibetan. The most common belief is that he was born in Mo'ung, a small Khumbu settlement that was primarily a meditation retreat for lamas.[8] There is also a notion that he was the son of one Lama Budi Tsenjen, a lama of Mo'ung village who was a member of the first party of settlers who migrated into Khumbu.[9]

Lama Sangwa Dorje, in some accounts, did his basic religious training in Mo'ung, but then went back to Kham for further study and for his *ong*—his empowerments or initiations. It is said that when he received his ong from his teacher in Kham, the lama told him—in a standard formula—"Now you can do anything."

When he returned to Khumbu, he studied further with Lama Rena Lingba, one of the ancestral Sherpa lamas.[10] He is said to have been a very bright and able student and to have learned very quickly. He became very *khamu*, very expert, at his work, including not only text reading and ritual performance, but religious curing as well. He is said to have been a skilled *amji*, or religious doctor. Although it is now claimed that he is in a long line of reincarnate lamas, ultimately traceable back to a god (see Sangye Tenzing 1971:22), this is never men-

Lama Sangwa Dorje, founder of Pangboche temple in the late seventeenth century; from a mural at Pangboche.

tioned in any of the stories of his life. The point about his learning religion easily, however, implies reincarnation, since if he had been a lama in a previous life, he would already have acquired all the relevant training and knowledge, which training in the present life would simply reactivate.

Returning from Kham to Khumbu, Lama Sangwa Dorje did two things recorded in Sherpa folklore; he became a pembu, and he founded Pangboche temple. Which came first is not clear. But there are essentially two sets of stories about him, one set concerning his conflict with another pembu, and one set concerning his founding of Pangboche. The temple-founding set, in turn, has several subtales. I will examine these first.

In one of the subtales about the temple founding, the emphasis is on fraternal rivalry. Here, the founding of Pangboche temple is linked with the foundings of two other early Sherpa temples, the one at Thami, on the west side of Khumbu, and the one at Rimijung, in the Pharak region between Khumbu and Solu. These two are said to have been founded by two brothers of Lama Sangwa Dorje (who was the eldest and most powerful): Thami by Ralwa Dorje, who was the middle brother, and Rimijung by Kemba Dorje, who was the youngest. The three foundings are linked by a story of how each of the brothers performed an astonishing feat in order to outdo the others: Lama Sangwa Dorje hung his lama cloak over a sunbeam, Ralwa Dorje took an iron rod and twisted it into a knot, and Kemba Dorje stood seven grains of barley on top of one another, and stood an idol of the goddess Drolma on top of them.

There is some dispute as to whether the three lamas were actually brothers, or whether they were simply contemporaries who were political competitors. The most common assumption is that they *were* brothers, but that they were also political rivals. As one informant said, merging the two dimensions, "All the big founders were brothers. They were like kings [that is, they were pembu]. They were brothers and they were competitive. They spoke nicely but inside they felt tatok (rivalry, jealousy)."

This merging of fraternal rivalry and political rivalry is in part real and in part metaphoric. It is real because the competitors for a political position could well be brothers—sons and patrilateral nephews of a pembu fighting over succession to the position. But it is also metaphoric because the relationships have such similar qualities—they are intensely competitive, involving what is felt to be a zero-sum game in which only one person can win.

The other story directly concerned with the founding of Pangboche (as opposed to the more purely "political" Lama Sangwa Dorje tales) makes no reference to fraternal/political rivalry, and is highly "spiritual" in tone. In it the lama establishes a relationship with a tutelary deity who helps him build the temple. He also displays a wide range of supernatural skills. The significance of his relationship with his protective deity—an expression of the hierarchical side of Sherpa culture—will be discussed in the next chapter. Here I use the story as a vehicle for exploring Sherpa notions of personal potency, magical and otherwise.

> Lama Sangwa Dorje was a Sherpa from Khumbu. He went to Kham, where he stayed a long time, doing much religious work. He then came back to Khumbu and began looking for a place to

build a gonda [gompa]. He flew first to Purte, in the Thami area, and from Purte to Saranasa where he left two footprints in a rock. From there he flew to Tengboche and thought to build there, but he slipped on a rock, again leaving a print. Because of having slipped, he felt that Tengboche was after all not a good place, although he thought that in some future time it might be a fine place for a temple. [Tengboche was to become the site of the first Sherpa celibate monastery.] From Tengboche he flew to Pangboche, and he sat on a rock which now has a print of his bottom. You can still see the rock with the imprint today [the teller said to the ethnographer], if you shine a light into the recess behind the paneling in the main altar.

Just as Lama Sangwa Dorje was looking around for where to build the gonda, a god in the form of an idol flew from India and sat down in front on him. The god/idol was very bright, and Lama Sangwa Dorje was a little afraid. The god was Gombu [Skt., Mahakala]. And Gombu said, "Don't be afraid, I am your *yidam*, your tutelary deity." And so the gonda was built, and the Gombu idol [which was a material manifestation of the god's *sungjen*, his words or voice], became the first of all the gonda's *nangden*, its treasure.[11]

This other story in which Lama Sangwa Dorje is involved in the founding of Pangboche emphasizes his magical/religious potency: he flies about Khumbu, he leaves imprints on rocks, his meditations are powerful enough to bring the god to him in person and to make the god want to stay as his personal protector. Here, as in the story of his hanging his cloak over a sunbeam, Lama Sangwa Dorje is what the Sherpas call a *tsachermu* lama, a lama with great magical powers.[12] The notion of tsachermu potency is one of a large set of Sherpa notions of personal powers, and the emphasis on these powers is consistent with the emphasis on strongman politics and religion throughout these stories: people's abilities to seize positions of secular power, or to do large and important things like founding temples, is portrayed as dependent in part on their possession of these inner traits.

All of the traits are seen as accidental knacks or talents or propensities that a person might possess. The most innocent sort is called *chuchermu*, which is something like a midas touch, or a green thumb; everything a chuchermu person does will tend to thrive, and such a person will tend to make a lot of money.[13] There is, similarly, *yenden chermu*, which is a talent for learning. Closer to the issues of this book, there is *hamba chermu*, which for the Sherpas seems to mean something like "ruthlessness." One man defined it negatively as having "no fear, no shame, and no pity."[14] But finally there are the two qualities that appear repeatedly throughout the tales of the early temple foundings, and indeed throughout the recounting of events of much of Sherpa history: *tsachermu* and *ongchermu*. Both are forms of personal power. The first, as already indicated, is the magical power that only lamas can have, and then only certain lamas who have the relevant inner qualities. The second, ongchermu, is almost entirely used in describing pembu tax collectors and other politically domineering people. It means a kind of bully-power, or perhaps simply force.

The founder of Pangboche, Lama Sangwa Dorje, is repeatedly described as tsachermu, and this is illustrated by the constant references to his magical and spiritual accomplishments. It is interesting to note on the other hand that his brother Ralwa Dorje was described as ongchermu, and his twisting of the iron rod was seen as part of a display of domination:

> Ralwa Dorje was very ongchermu. The people did not want to obey him. But he said, "Do you need this [to make you obey]?" And he twisted an iron rod into a knot. And people were scared. He said to the people, "Are you sure you're not listening? Is this what you need?" And he twisted the rod. And people were scared.

Both kinds of power, tsachermu magical potency and ongchermu force, are politically effective. Both may be mobilized in competitions between political rivals, and either one may bring about success in a given context. And both may serve to keep followers in line: Ralwa Dorje's threatening behavior cowed his followers into submission, while Lama Sangwa Dorje's magical abilities engaged their loyalty through admiration and a sense of his superior protective abilities.[15]

The Political Rivalry with Zongnamba

There are two sets of stories concerned with the actual founding of Pangboche and the other earliest lama temples in Khumbu. One set places the founding in the context of the competitive relationship between Lama Sangwa Dorje and his brothers, the other in the context of Lama Sangwa Dorje flying about Khumbu and praying to his tutelary deity who helps him found the temple. In addition there is a set of tales about Lama Sangwa Dorje that portrays him as an ordinary pembu, and makes no direct reference to his founding of Pangboche temple at all. (Indeed, these tales' sequential relationship with the story of the founding of Pangboche is somewhat unclear.) They portray him locked in (nonfraternal) political rivalry with another pembu, one Zongnamba, who is said to have come over the border from Tibet. Zongnamba was described by one informant (the one who also told the story about Ralwa Dorje threatening his clients) as a "horrible tyrant, who made his subjects miserable, making them work for him all the time and expropriating all their crops." But in this purely political/economic context Lama Sangwa Dorje was no angel of mercy himself:

> Long ago in Shagar Dzong [that is, Shelkar, near D'ingri, in Tibet], a fine was imposed. A man called Zongnamba committed some wrongful act and he was fined, and so he came down to Khumbu, where he stayed on the Thami side in a place called Tarnga. At that time Khumbu was outside the control of either the Tibetan or Nepali king, and Lama Sangwa Dorje was both pembu [that is, tax collector] and "king" [that is, he kept the taxes] of the whole Khumbu region.[16] Lama Sangwa Dorje lived on the east side of Khumbu, in the Pangboche area, where he owned three large pastures on which no one was allowed to graze their animals.
>
> Zongnamba sought to set himself up as pembu of Khumbu, and to that end he decided to kill Lama Sangwa Dorje. He sent two men to do the job. The lama heard about this plot, and ran away and hid in a cave at Palung. From there, he saw Zongnamba's two men coming from Peruje. He said to himself, "Maybe these two men are my friends, coming with good intentions [*sem*], but maybe not." So he made two *pak*, two dough figurines, one in the shape of a tiger [*tak*] and one in the shape of a leopard [*zik*], and he sent them down to meet the two men.
>
> They met them between Tukla and Pulungkarwa, and asked them where they were going. "We're going to find and catch and kill Lama Sangwa Dorje," they said. Whereupon Taki [the tiger] grabbed one man and Ziki [the leopard] grabbed the other, and they smashed them against the rocks and killed them. And you can still see the red rocks, like blood, in that place between Pulungkarwa and Tukla. And you can still see at Pangboche the rock where Lama Sangwa Dorje fed Taki and Ziki; their clawprints are on the rock. Then the lama came to Pangboche.[17]

Despite Lama Sangwa Dorje's apparent victory over Zongnamba, however, he evidently no longer felt safe in Khumbu. He hid in various places—in Lowuje, Zongtan, and Nanga Dzong[18]—but the Zongnamba people pursued him. And so he fled (in one account, flew) over the border to Rumbu, where he lived a long time. He died in a place called Chowuk, near Rumbu, where he had been invited to visit by another lama. His funeral was attended by miracles: "His body was not cremated; it evaporated in the form of a rainbow, and only his eyes, tongue, and heart remained" (von Fürer-Haimendorf 1964:128; see also Sangye Tenzing 1971:22).

Lama Sangwa Dorje's remains were kept in Chowuk, where the local people made a reliquary for them. This reliquary was later stolen by a group of Pangboche and Khumjung people, who felt that Lama Sangwa Dorje was *their* lama. It now rests in Pangboche gompa, where it is among the gompa's important *nangden*, or treasures.

The lama was noncelibate, as was true of all Sherpa lamas at that time. Nonetheless, he left no lineage in Khumbu, having had only two daughters. He is said not to have wanted more children, and to have exercised yogic control over the ejaculation of his semen toward this end. One of his daughters is said to have married a son of Lama Rena Lingba, with whom Lama Sangwa Dorje had studied.[19]

The Lama Sangwa Dorje cycle of tales continues with further exploits of the lamas's rival, Zongnamba, and his descendants, and I will return to the cycle in chapter 5. At this point, however, it is appropriate to consider the contradictions of Sherpa society in part reflected in, in part constituted by, these stories.

Contradictions of the Political Order

At the broadest level, there is only one contradiction in the Sherpa social order, which is that between an egalitarian ethic and a hierarchical ethic. Within the domain of the family, this contradiction appeared in the form of an equal inheritance rule on the one hand, and a rule of birth order authority on the other, each destabilizing the other and producing chronic competitiveness. Fraternal competition in turn often produces a situation in which one brother winds up with more (or all) and another with less (or none). Further, these differential outcomes feed into the larger social divisions between what the Sherpas call "big" and "small" people. The equal inheritance rule, in other words, is both contradicted by a hierarchical discourse/practice, and is directly implicated in the production of microinequality (between brothers) and macroinequality (between big and small people).

The same contradictory dynamics underlie the political dramas of the temple-founding stories. What follows is essentially a model based on sketchy information, rather than an analysis of detailed descriptive material. The Sherpa political/economic order has never been systematically studied, in part because of the theoretical interests of the ethnographers who have worked there, and in part because the pembu system in full-fledged form was abolished before the first ethnographer arrived on the scene. Nonetheless a model can be constructed that helps make sense of both historical and ethnographic material (see also Samuel 1978, 1982). The first order of business is to look more closely at why pembu positions seem to have been so valuable and thus so violently contested.

In the first place it is clear that the positions were directly generative of at least some wealth. A pembu had the right to reallocate the lands of a client who died without heirs, and he often kept such lands for himself. One pembu in the 1950s is described as having acquired significant holdings in this way. Further, since pembu were also allowed to take free labor from their clients, such labor would allow them to cultivate holdings larger than a family could normally handle. Concerning the individual just mentioned, von Fürer-Haimendorf notes that "the service of his 189 clients made it possible to cultivate all this land without great expenditure on labor" (von Fürer-Haimendorf 1964:122–23).

In addition, as tax collector the pembu took a portion of people's crops. When the Sherpas came under the control of an external state (about which more in chapter 5), the pembu had to turn at least some of the taxes in goods over to the state, but he still kept some. He also gained all the benefits of the free labor and enjoyed at least partial exemption from the taxes. When the Sherpas were not under state control, as appears to have been true for the entire period discussed thus far, or when (later) state control was not strong enough or organized enough to collect what the pembu had collected, then he simply functioned as a one-man "state" unto himself, in the sense that he kept the taxes. For this reason pembu are sometimes also referred to as *gyelwu*, or kings.

The taxes probably also played a significant role in underwriting trade. I have already indicated how crucial trade was for the Sherpas, in terms of bringing in new wealth to the system and thus allowing a man to overcome the limitations of an inadequate inheritance. The trading sector as a whole constituted what the Sherpas call the "big" people, and it was from among these people that the pembu always arose. Trade was capable of generating a great amount of wealth, and of doing so in a way that did not entail any direct exploitation of others—an important point in the context of the egalitarian ethic. Many traders, those perhaps who did not have the ongchermu (strongman) leaning, thus never sought to be pembu. But pembu tax collecting could have a very positive effect on trade in a variety of ways: the corvée could take care of much of the pembu's agricultural activities, and could free him to spend more time on trade; the taxes in goods provided him with a cushion of wealth and capital in case his trading ventures should fail; and so forth. Tax collecting could thus have a multiplying effect on trade profits, producing greater returns.

And finally, there was the subjective sense of power and of having a big name. A pembu was the dominant figure in his area. In some cases he was actually liked and respected, but in most cases he was at least feared and deferred to. It will be clear in the next set of tales that pembu became very invested in their reputations, and experienced great shame upon losing their positions.

One can even go further, however, and suggest that pembu tax collecting not only enhanced the wealth and power of particular individuals but was directly implicated in the reproduction of the structural divide between big people and small. The taxes in themselves may not have amounted to very much. In the late nineteenth century the explorer Hari Ram reported in the Survey of India that the pembu in "Nabjia" collected 15 percent of the people's crops. One of my twentieth-century informants said that people had to give five free days of labor per year on the pembu's lands.[20] Let us say, simply for the sake of argument, that these were the numbers in earlier times as well. They do not appear very high. But they must be considered in conjunction with the inheritance problem. The taxes would here have had a compounding effect. I have said that trade was the major solution to the inheritance problem. I have also said that, for pembu, collecting taxes could compound the profitability of trade, and indeed in some circumstances could create the conditions for trading at all (by having tax clients farm the pembu's land, and by providing seed capital after a failed venture).

The reciprocal points may now be made for the small people. Giving up their taxes and labor to the pembu would have prevented them from trading and hence from circumventing the inheritance problem. The taxes thus would have had a *negatively* compounding effect for the small people. They took away both the goods (beyond subsistence) and labor (beyond subsistence production) that could have been the small people's resources for engaging in trade.[21] Taxes thus played a major role, in conjunction with the inheritance problem, in keeping the small people small.

Tax collecting thus violates Sherpa egalitarianism more deeply even than fraternal inequities. Whereas fraternal rivalries produce individual inequities, they do not repeatedly hinder the losing individual in his efforts to reestablish parity. Tax collecting, on the other hand, places a permanent (though not totally insurmountable) obstacle in the way of small people's attempts to build up resources and pull themselves above the subsistence level. At the same time it gives the pembu a permanent (for as long as he holds the position) advantage, protecting him against risks and thus against the slide to smallness. Further, since as a result of rivalries and challenges, the pembu positions move around among the big people, they protect the big people as a whole. Pembu tax collecting thus comes close to creating a class system, in the sense that it creates an actual structural barrier—though again not an insurmountable one in *either* direction—between big people and small, and systematically contributes to the reproduction of the division between the two sectors. Not surprisingly, then, the pembu had very little legitimacy.

But this structure of inequality continues to operate against a backdrop of the Sherpa ethic of equality. The egalitarian ethic is expressed in the fact that pembu positions are rarely transmissible from father to son. Rather, there is constant competition for these positions among big people. This was seen to be the case with Zongnamba and Lama Sangwa Dorje, and competition marks other accounts given later in this book.[22] The small people in turn could take advantage of these rivalries, by supporting whichever figure seemed to promise them a less exploitative and more "protective" relationship.

The foregoing seem a long way from whatever "religious" meanings and values may have been involved in the founding of Pangboche temple. Yet it is clear that the Sherpa texts have led in that direction. The Lama Sangwa Dorje tales run the gamut from the purely political, in which the lama and Zongnamba engage in mortal struggle for the pembu position that would allow them to collect taxes from the people, to the highly spiritual, in which the lama performs miracles, communes with his divine protector, and founds a temple. The gamut is visible even *within* the tales, as when Lama Sangwa Dorje's feat of hanging his cloak over a sunbeam serves at once to best his brothers for prestige and to create a sacred treasure for the newly founded Pangboche temple. It appears that the two categories, which for Westerners are largely distinct and even contradictory, are very closely intertwined in Sherpa culture. In the next chapter I will consider, among other things, how to understand this cultural juxtaposition.

CHAPTER

IV

The Meaning of Temple Founding: Cultural Schemas

THE foundings of the early temples, like the foundings of the monasteries, are both events and symbols. As events, they move the narrative of Sherpa history along in time, and have further event-ual effects. As symbols, they convey meaning—they can be read expressively as well as instrumentally. Indeed, one may say that their eventness, their capacity to reorient the direction of Sherpa history, in part depended on their meaning, their capacity to say something significant to Sherpa actors.[1]

I have argued in the preceding chapters that Sherpa society is founded on a contradiction between an egalitarian and a hierarchical ethic. The contradiction between egalitarian discourses (as seen in the statement of male equality, the equal inheritance rule, the equal opportunity structure of political succession), and hierarchical ones (as seen in the rule of birth order seniority, the authority of senior kin, the status gradations of the village) expresses itself in a chronic competitiveness in both fraternal and political relations. Individuals are sensitive to loss of parity, are quick to compete for whatever resources are available, and tend to compete on a winner-take-all basis.

These points are not merely analytic constructs. The Sherpas recognize the chronically competitive quality of both brother relations and relations between "big" men. Moreover, this recognition is, as it were, culturally formalized, in the sense that important cultural stories both depict such competitive relations and show the ways in which they may be resolved. In the present chapter I will examine another story cycle, pertaining to the founding of the noncelibate temple at Zhung, in Solu, around 1720. I will argue that the stories collectively embody what I will call a cultural schema. The notion of "cultural schemas," in one form or another, has a certain pedigree in anthropology, which I will survey briefly here.

Cultural Schemas

In an earlier paper (1973a, based in turn on a 1970 dissertation), I sketched a concept of "key scenarios." These were defined as preorganized schemes of action, symbolic programs for the staging and playing out of standard social interactions in a particular culture. The point was that every culture contains not just bundles of symbols, and not even just bundles of larger propositions about the universe ("ideologies"), but organized schemas for enacting (culturally typical) relations and situations.

I argued further that these schemas often take on an ordering function, achieving a degree of generality and transferability across a variety of somewhat disparate social situations. Thus I showed that the Sherpas use a scenario of hospitality to structure a wide variety of social encounters: ordinary social interactions in which the host or hostess is simply "being social," pressure transactions for the purpose of getting a favor, shamanistic séances for curing the sick, rituals of offerings to the gods for community well-being. In all these contexts, the interaction is structured as a hospitality event, with Ego defined as the host, Alter as the guest(s), and food and drink served as if the event were a party. Hospitality here is an ordering schema, shaping these interactions in particular ways, endowing them with particular meanings, and setting them up to unfold along more or less predictable lines (Ortner 1970).

The same general idea appeared in other works in that same era. In *The Sorrow of the Lonely and the Burning of the Dancers* (1976), Edward Schieffelin explored a "cultural scenario" of reciprocity and opposition among the Kaluli of New Guinea, and showed the degree to which the scenario orders a range of social and ritual interactions. Another work centered on this sort of idea was *Dramas, Field, and Metaphors* (1974), in which Victor Turner showed the persistent force of what he called "root paradigms" (such as martyrdom in Christianity) in various religious traditions.[2]

The whole idea of cultural schemas went dormant for a while, but it has recently resurfaced in a number of specifically historical studies, with the argument that the events of history may be structured by cultural schemas in much the same way as social behavior across synchronic contexts. In both Geertz's *Negara* (1980) and Sahlins's *Historical Metaphors* (1981) one finds the notion that there are cultural patterns of action, cultural dramas or scenarios, that reappear over time and that seem to order the ways in which people play out both conventional and historically novel social encounters. In *Negara*, Geertz talks of the reconstruction of forms and the "transcription of a fixed ideal." He shows the way in which the shape of the Balinese state was fixed by a cultural schema over a period of nearly six hundred years:

> Over larger periods of time or over larger stretches of space, major shifts in political fortune could and did, of course, take place. . . . But for all that, the characteristic form seems to have reconstructed itself continually, as Balinese theory claims that it should; new courts model themselves on vanished ones, re-emerging under different names and in different places as but further transcriptions of a fixed ideal. . . . The scale of things varied, and their brilliance, but not, so far as I can see, between, say, 1343 and 1906, what they were all about. (1980:134)

As for Sahlins, he writes of "structures of the long run" (Braudel's phrase [1980]), and of the replaying of "a cosmological drama." He specifically sets about showing that a cultural script, embodied in myth and ritual, ordered the ways in which Hawaiians dealt with certain novel historical events:

> At the great annual Makahiki festival, the concept of political usurpation is set in the context of a cosmological drama. The lost god-chief Lono returns to renew the fertility of the land, reclaiming it as his own, to be superseded again by the ruling chief and the sacrificial cult of Ku. Now Captain Cook's second visit to the Islands coincided with the annual return of Lono, and the treatment Hawaiians accorded him corresponded to the prescribed sequence of ritual events in the Makahiki Festival. (1981:17)

Neither Geertz nor Sahlins discusses why cultural schemas have the kind of durability they seem to have. I would argue that there is an important reason for this: they depict actors responding to, and resolving (from their own point of view), the central contradictions of the culture. In the Sherpa case, as I will show in this chapter, there is a cultural schema that portrays a hero playing out, and "winning," the fraternal and political rivalries that are recurrently reproduced out of the contradictions of the social/cultural order. The first order of business in this chapter will be to establish that there does appear to be such a schema in Sherpa culture. I will do this by examining another temple-founding story, this one pertaining to the founding of Zhung temple. The Zhung tale will also facilitate a rereading of the more ambiguous Pangboche stories of the last chapter in a clearer way, and I will show that the Pangboche stories after all embody the same schema.

The Founding of Zhung Temple

The story of the founding of Zhung temple[3] is loosely linked with the Pangboche set of tales, in that the founder of Zhung temple is said to have been the son of another lama who was either a "friend" or a "disciple" of Lama Sangwa Dorje. If this is the case, it also suggests a date for the founding: taking Oppitz's proposal of a twenty-five-year generation span for the Sherpas (1968:69), and given a date for the founding of Pangboche of about 1670, the founding of Zhung temple can be placed in either 1695 or 1720.[4]

When the story begins, the pembu of the Zhung area of the lower (Solu) valley was a lama called Lama Gombu, described as "rich and famous." Living in the region was a certain Lama Pakdze, who had built a shrine at Senghe Puk, a local holy site, and who had a son named Dorje Zangbu. Young Dorje Zangbu was not very rich, but he was very clever. After the father, Lama Pakdze, died, the pembu Lama Gombu felt politically threatened by the young Dorje Zangbu and decided to kill him.

> Lama Gombu made a plan. He went to talk with Dorje Zangbu: [He said,] "Straight below [the modern site of] Chiwong temple there is an eagle's nest. If you don't remove it you will have a problem, but if you do remove it, you will find a wealth-producing gem (a *norwu*) inside it which will help you. But you and I must remove the nest together. One alone will not succeed."
>
> Dorje Zangbu said [to Lama Gombu], "All right, I will open it, but you must not touch the rope [on which Dorje Zangbu would be lowered] and you must not carry any kind of weapon. You must promise." If the rope were cut Dorje Zangbu would fall all the way down to the bottom of the gorge. Lama Gombu thought a while and said he would not [do these things].
>
> So Dorje Zangbu let himself down on a rope from the top of the cliff carrying a magical dagger (a *purwa*) in his belt. Lama Gombu, knowing he could not touch the rope or use any kind of weapon, struck his flint and put the spark to the rope. Dorje Zangbu smelled smoke. He pulled out his purwa and stuck it into a hole in the rock, wrapped his belt around it and hung there against the cliff. The rope burned and fell down but Dorje Zangbu was safe. He then made another spike, wrapped the rope around that, recovered his purwa, and let himself down.[5]
>
> Lama Gombu meanwhile cheered when he saw the rope break. He felt he had triumphed, had been made high (*temba taru*).

Dorje Zangbu then left the area, both to escape from the murderous intentions of Lama Gombu and to gather his own powers against such assaults:

> Dorje Zangbu thought, "He tried to kill me." That night, Dorje Zangbu went home, took some blood from his gum, and wrote in blood on the center pole of his house, "I haven't died. If someone comes to kill me, I've gone to another place for a few months."
>
> He went to Tsilo on the other side of Khari Khola, and cut down a banana tree inside of which a small shoot was growing. Meanwhile, Lama Gombu heard that Dorje Zangbu was still alive, and went to follow him. He got to Tsilo and saw the shoot growing, which made him think that Dorje Zangbu must have passed many days before. Nonetheless, he decided not to go back, but to follow Dorje Zangbu to Khumbu.
>
> Above Namche Bazaar, Dorje Zangbu arrived at his father's sister's house. He said, "There are people following me, don't tell them I'm here, I'll hide in this box and you lock it." Lama Gombu arrived as if coming to trade, and asked, "Did anyone come here?" [The aunt said,] "Nobody came here."
>
> A friend of the aunt was watching her sheep, and Lama Gombu asked him if he saw anybody. The shepherd said that two or three days before, he had seen a lama going through on his way to Tibet. The shepherd was actually Dorje Zangbu. "Now," said Lama Gombu, "I can't follow him to Tibet." And so the *mingen*, the wicked man, went back down to Solu.

Dorje Zangbu then went to Kham (the Sherpas' area of origin in eastern Tibet), where he spent a number of years studying and practicing religion. Returning to Solu-Khumbu, he came by way of a holy place in Tibet called Tsibri, where a reincarnate lama gave him an extremely sacred idol, the Kutsap Ternga, of which there are only five in the whole world. In giving him the idol, the high lama said, "You have been attacked many times. Now that you have the Kutsap Ternga, you can triumph" (he used the same term for "triumph" that Lama Gombu had used when he thought he had succeeded in killing Dorje Zangbu: "temba taru"). Dorje Zangbu stayed three years in Tsibri, and then returned to Solu.

> He arrived at the house of his mother's brother, his *ashang*. The ashang was very rich. Ashang asked him, "Where have you been

to do religion? How much power to transform things [*tutang nuwa*] do you have?"

"I did religion in Kham," he said, "and I have a Kutsap Ternga."

Ashang said, "Let me see it." And he looked at it, and a rainbow appeared over the house, and he couldn't see anything, he was momentarily blinded.

"Who attacked you?" he asked Dorje Zangbu. "Lama Gombu." What is ashang thinking? "Dress yourself in poor clothes," he said, "and I will call Lama Gombu." And he did.

Lama Gombu and his servant came and did *lokpar*, an exorcism ritual. Dorje Zangbu sat in the lowest status position and pretended he was a beggar.

And Lama Gombu sang and danced and beat his drum but did not have any success in visualizing/actualizing [*miwa*] the gods. Then ashang said to him, "You're supposed to be such a powerful lama, but you can't do anything, shame on you. Whoever is more *dukta* [magically/spiritually effective?], you or a certain Lamaserwa person [that is, Dorje Zangbu, of the Lamaserwa clan], only under him will we place ourselves."

This comment, that he and others will submit as clients to whoever wins the magical contest, is a good example of political dominance/clientship by virtue of the greater personal powers of one or another would-be pembu. The story continues:

Then he said, "Lama Gombu, you sit down, and now you, beggar, get up." Lama Gombu did not know that the beggar is the Lamaserwa person in question. "Who has a bad soul [*sem*], and who has a good one, today we will find out," said Dorje Zangbu. Then he began dancing. And the *lokpar torma* [the dough pyramid that effects the exorcism] danced with him [he had so much power]. Then Lama Gombu recognized Dorje Zangbu, and was ashamed, and ran away with all his retinue.

Then Dorje Zangbu threw the lokpar. He said, "I have not done anything wrong before, but Lama Gombu has a very bad soul." And he threw the lokpar from Pankongma [his mother's brother's village] so hard that it hit and split a tree near Sehlo [several miles away]. The print of the lokpar is still there at that place.

Now Dorje Zangbu was elevated [again, temba taru] and Lama Gombu was brought low [*temba nuwup*]. Before this Dorje

> Zangbu was not very famous. But because of making the lokpar dance, and doing many other supernormal feats, his reputation became great, like the moon or sun. Lama Gombu could no longer stay in the Zhung area, he felt great tatok [resentment/jealousy]. Today his lineage is found in villages to the west of Zhung, in Changma and Gyama. And because he actually left, Dorje Zangbu's reputation became greater.

Dorje Zangbu then moved down from his father's village, and went to Zhung and built the temple.

Since this is supposed to be the story of the founding of Zhung temple, one would expect it to stop here. Like the Pangboche story, however, it goes on to further, and more violent, episodes in the relationship between the two protagonists.

Lama Dorje Zangbu did good religious work and eventually died in Zhung. His cremated remains were placed in a reliquary, and a *chorten* was built to house the reliquary. His powerful ritual dagger (the one that saved him on the cliff) was also placed inside.

> On the day of the consecration of the chorten, flowers rained from the sky. Thereafter, on days of the full moon and other religiously important days, one could hear temple music coming from within the chorten. Lama Gombu heard the sound of the music, and he thought he had to fix that chorten. [Here my assistant, who seemed to find the story every bit as wild as I did, breathed an aside: "Ah, what goes on between lamas!"]

Lama Gombu decided to pollute the chorten, pollution being the primary way of destroying magical or supernatural powers of any kind (see Ortner 1973b):

> He sent seven widows to place their underpants on the chorten, and the music was silenced. But one of the widows fell down and died beside the chorten. Five more died near Takto, on the way back, vomiting blood. The last one arrived at Lama Gombu's house in Gyama. She told him what had happened, and then she too died vomiting blood.

> Lama Dorje Zangbu's son meanwhile understood what had happened, and he set out to do harm to Lama Gombu. He sent a curse against his lineage, and many of them died of bloody diarrhea. Lama Gombu in turn understood what happened, and sent a curse against the Lamaserwa clan. Their people did not die, but many of them now inherit an affliction of the right eye.

View of Zhung houses and fields, with *chorten* containing Lama Dorje Zangbu's relics, 1967.

The Schema

There are many echoes of the Pangboche tale in this story. In both cases the founding of a temple is embedded in a narrative of violent political rivalry. This in itself suggests the presence of a culturally standardized frame of some sort, and a common plot—what I am calling a cultural schema—underlying both sets of stories. I will take the elements of the schema in stages, showing their presence not only in the tale of Zhung temple, but retrospectively in the Pangboche folklore as well. Following the discussion of the various stages of the schema in the temple-founding tales, I will show that it informs the organization of much of Sherpa ritual action as well. The point here is simply to demonstrate that there *is* a cultural schema of great pervasiveness at work. The implications of its presence will be discussed afterward.

The schema may, for convenience of discussion, be broken into stages.

Rivalry and competition. In the Zhung tale, as in the Pangboche cycle, the whole drama opens with and hinges on a violent rivalry between two politically dominant (or would-be dominant) individuals. The stakes of the rivalry are indicated: material wealth (in the right to collect taxes) and reputation, or "name." In the case of Pangboche, Lama Sangwa Dorje was the established pembu and Zongnamba sought to displace him through violent means. In the case of Zhung, Lama Gombu was the established pembu, and he initiated the violence in order to prevent Dorje Zangbu's rise.[6] Either way, the tales are full of violent attacks and counterattacks. In the Pangboche cycle, Zongnamba first sent assassins against Lama Sangwa Dorje, and Lama Sangwa Dorje's supernatural helpers then killed those assassins by dashing their heads against the rocks. The violence of the encounter was underscored by the statement in the tale that the rocks remain red from the blood to this day.

In the Zhung tales, Lama Gombu first attempted to kill Dorje Zangbu. Although he did not succeed, he continued to chase Dorje Zangbu, to Pharak and then to Khumbu, and only gave up when Dorje Zangbu crossed the border into Tibet. Dorje Zangbu ultimately returned and humiliated Lama Gombu by outperforming him during a ritual. More violence, bloody and disgusting (to Sherpas as well as—I presume—Western readers) followed.

Before going on to further stages in the schema, it is worth recalling that the kind of rivalry seen between big pembu in each of the folklore cycles is also typical of relations between brothers in Sherpa culture, although it is usually not as violent. As described in chapter

2, brothers are portrayed in some of the earliest clan-history texts as competitive (usually over inheritance), and this pattern persists into modern (ethnographically observed) Sherpa society. It is thus interesting to note that there are alternative versions for both sets of tales (about the founding of Pangboche and the founding of Zhung), in which brother rivalry, either instead of, or in addition to, political rivalry, is catalytic for the actions of the protagonists. In the Pangboche cycle, as previously noted, Lama Sangwa Dorje is portrayed in certain episodes as the elder brother of two other men, each of whom founded a temple in part out of sibling rivalry and competition for prestige with the others. Similarly, there is an alternative version of the Zhung story in which Dorje Zangbu left the area not because he was being chased by Lama Gombu, but because of some sort of dispute with his brothers:

> Of the sons of Serwa Yeshi Gyeldzen one of them left his home in search of the teaching of religion *after he had come to differences of opinion with his brothers*. . . . He cultivated a special association with Lama Loben Raechen whom he offered the hair from his head. From him he received the ordained name or initiation name Ngagchang *Dorje Zangpo* [Dorje Zangbu].
>
> His spiritual deity Shinje Tsedak encountered him in a vision and touched his right eye whereupon he became half blind. Therefore so it is said, *it is supposed to still occur frequently among his descendants that they suddenly partially lose their vision*. After completing his spiritual progress he returned to his home where he . . . erected a gonpa [that is, Zhung temple] in the middle of the valley. (Oppitz 1968:46–47, emphasis added)

The two layers of meaning, the political and the fraternal, are not as far apart as may appear at first glance. Since a pembu may have several sons, but can only pass on his office to one of them (if he is in a secure enough position to control its transmission at all), competition over political dominance may well occur between brothers, and indeed is quite likely to do so. More generally, however, political and fraternal rivalry stand in an enduring relationship of mutual metaphorization with one another.

Departure of the hero and acquisition of a protector. In both the Pangboche and the Zhung stories the eventual hero, beleaguered by his antagonist, leaves the area. In exile, he may acquire certain practical aids toward his eventual triumph (a lama will study and gain greater religious skills). But the most important thing he acquires is a protector, a figure of greater charisma, power, and authority, who enables him to return and defeat his rival.[7]

In the Zhung cycle, Dorje Zangbu went to Kham to study for many years. Upon returning he acquired not one but three protectors: the high reincarnate lama in Tsibri, the Kutsap Ternga sacred idol, and the rich mother's brother—and all of these together helped him defeat his rival, Lama Gombu. In the Pangboche tales, Lama Sangwa Dorje went symbolically into exile by hiding and meditating in a cave. While there, he acquired the Gombu god-idol, who voluntarily (in one version) or upon request (in another) became the personal protector of the Lama.

The figure of the benign protector, to whom the hero submits and who helps the hero defeat his rivals, is a strong expression of the hierarchical principle in Sherpa culture. In this context hierarchy is positive, helpful, and noncontradictory. The implications of this point will become clear when the stories are interpreted for their deeper cultural meanings.[8]

Defeating the rival and acquiring his subjects. Despite the fact that "winning" is represented largely as a function of the powerful high-level protection the hero has garnered, it also clearly hinges on attracting or keeping a following of clients and supporters. In maintaining or switching their allegiance, people affirm the greater legitimacy of one or another pembu's dominance over an area. In the Zhung tale, the popular basis of pembu legitimacy emerges with particular clarity. When Dorje Zangbu and Lama Gombu had their ritual/magical contest, Dorje Zangbu's mother's brother said that he and others would place themselves under whoever won the contest.

The dynamic is not as clear in the parts of the Lama Sangwa Dorje cycle discussed thus far, although it may be noted here that Zongnamba's defeat of Lama Sangwa Dorje by threat of brute force (by being ongchermu) would not have had cultural legitimacy, and the continuing loyalty of Lama Sangwa Dorje's subjects is represented in their subsequent theft of his reliquary from Chowuk temple. In a later episode of this cycle, this particular transformation of the basic structural component will be seen again. Zongnamba will kill another rival, thus maintaining his power through illegitimate ongchermu force. But the rival's subjects will remain loyal to their original pembu (a lama with legitimate tsachermu potency) and they in turn will—finally—kill Zongnamba.

The loser leaves the area and settles elsewhere. A pembu defeated in some sort of face-to-face contest will almost invariably leave the area. He may well attempt to set himself up in political or religious business elsewhere, and he may succeed such that in his new context he is a winner rather than a loser, but from the point of view of the original rivalrous relationship, he is a loser, and he leaves. This is very clearly spelled out in the Zhung tales, as Lama Gombu leaves the Zhung valley and moves westward, founding his lineage elsewhere.

Again the Lama Sangwa Dorje cycle is less clear. One could take the Lama's flight from Khumbu as the departure of a political loser, analogous to Lama Gombu's departure from Solu. This creates cultural problems, however, since from another point of view—that of the founding of Pangboche temple—Lama Sangwa Dorje is a winner and a cultural hero. It is possible that the chronology and sequencing of the Pangboche cycle is so fuzzy precisely because the image of Lama Sangwa Dorje as a political loser does not accord well with his cultural importance as the founder of the first Sherpa temple.

One may suggest that the tendency of the loser to leave the area, as well as the extreme violence of pembu relations in general, is related to the cultural view of political success as based on an individual's inner potencies (ongchermu, tsachermu, and the like) and not on social dynamics. The pembu is a person, not an office. His leadership/dominance is embodied in his total self, in the total range of powers that he can mobilize. To defeat a pembu, therefore, one must destroy him utterly, either through physical death (as will eventually happen to Zongnamba) or through social death (causing him to leave the area). The other side of the coin is the defeated pembu's sense of personal humiliation. He has not simply lost an election. The value and integrity of his whole self have been undermined. He feels that he has no choice but to leave. The extreme violence and the extreme shame are two sides of the competitive nature of pembu politics. Since success is self-made in the first place, defeat is the undoing of the self.

Founding a temple. In the Zhung tale, as in the Pangboche tale, the hero founds a temple. Indeed, the foundings of the temples are in principle the main reasons for the crystallization and transmission of the tales in the first place. Thus in Pangboche, Lama Sangwa Dorje founds the temple apparently—although the chronology is unclear—after fending off the assassination attempt by Zongnamba, and magically killing (with his dough helpers Taki and Ziki) Zongnamba's emissaries in the process. In the Zhung case, Dorje Zangbu founds the temple after humiliating Lama Gombu and causing him to leave the area. In both cases the foundings appear to represent expressions of triumph in the rivalrous political relationship.

In both cases, too, the foundings represent an institutionalization of the various hierarchical relations involved in the victory—with the protector above and the followers below. In the case of Pangboche the institutionalization of the relationship between the lama and the protector is clearly represented: the Gombu god-idol encouraged the lama to build the temple and offered to stay and lend his continuing power to it. Similarly in the case of the Zhung temple, the temple is thought to derive its power in part from the presence of the Kutsap Ternga god-idol, one of the original sources of the founder Dorje Zangbu's protection.[9]

The institutionalization of the relationship between the lama and his clients is not as clearly set forth as that of the relationship between the lama and the protector. The fact is, however, that the founding of a temple represents the crystallization of a set of permanent and hereditary relationships between the temple and its congregation, the latter being obligated to support the temple's rituals (through paying the lamas and providing ritual materials) in perpetuity. Thus the foundings of the lama temples emerge as both expressions of political triumph and consolidations thereof, as (among other things) both a statement and a continuing instrument of personal superiority on the part of the founders.

The main steps of the schema may now be summarized: The tales begin with a political or fraternal rivalry, or both. The protagonists struggle back and forth, often quite violently, and the rival appears to gain the upper hand. The hero then departs for remote places, and acquires a powerful protector. He returns to the conflict and, with the aid of his protector, defeats the rival. He acquires the rival's subjects. The rival is humiliated and leaves the area permanently. The hero founds a temple, an act of great virtue.

The argument about the pervasiveness of the schema may be extended beyond the folklore. It can be shown that, although in these cases the schema is embedded in Sherpa stories of the foundings of Sherpa temples, it also underlies a large spectrum of religious practice and religious history over a much wider region. Specifically, with only minor transformations, the same schema can be seen to underlie the most basic rituals of Tibetan Buddhist practice, the rites of making offerings to the gods in order to gain their protection (see also Ortner 1975; Ortner 1978a:ch. 6). An examination of these rituals will indicate the extraordinary cultural generality of this story line, and come closer as well to revealing its meaning.

RITUALS FOR GAINING THE PROTECTION OF THE GODS

Offering rituals (usually *kurim*) are performed with variations with great regularity in Sherpa communities—in households, village temples, and (in the twentieth century) in monasteries. They are performed at both prescribed calendrical times and on occasions of life crises, especially and extensively at death. They are part of fundamental Tibetan Buddhist practice, common to the whole greater Tibetan area, and were performed by Sherpas as much when the early temples were founded in the seventeenth and eighteenth centuries, as when the monasteries were founded in the twentieth.[10]

Offering rituals are held on almost any significant occasion. They must be conducted by trained and ritually empowered lamas, and involve the chanting of texts and the enactment of ritually prescribed sequences of behavior on the part of the specialists (the congregation, which supports the rituals financially, is largely passive during the enactment). Different gods are chosen to be appealed to on different occasions, and depending on the nature of the occasion, the texts (and, in certain minor ways, the offerings) vary with the different gods. Nonetheless, all the rituals have an invariant minimal sequence, in which the gods are first invited to the ritual, then plied with offerings and petitioned for their protection, then sent back to their heavenly abodes until the next ritual.

With very slight reorganization of the stages, the rituals may now be shown to embody the schema seen in the temple-founding tales:

Rivalry. Cosmologically, the assumption of the rituals (as of the religion as a whole) is that people are constantly encroached upon by demons and other evil forces that wish to harm and even destroy the world. Thus the rituals begin by assuming a relationship of chronic antagonism between people and demons that is at least loosely analogous to the relationship between the hero and his political rival in the tales of the early temple foundings.

Acquisition of a protector. The rituals further assume that people can only defeat demons by acquiring powerful protectors—the gods. The solicitation of the gods' protection is the very core of the work of the ritual, as the people, through the mediation of religious specialists, lavish the gods with offerings in order to bring them into battle against the demons on the side of humanity.

Defeat. Since the demons are intrinsically bloody and violent, the gods must adopt violent tactics as well, and when this part of the scenario is fully dramatized (rather than merely recited), the gods, through the vehicles of the lamas or monks, violently stab, eviscerate, and chop up effigies of the evil forces. At the end of the ritual, the demons have been temporarily defeated.[11]

Departure of the loser. The demons cannot actually be killed or wiped out because they are part of the eternal order of worldly existence. Thus they are simply forced to leave the area, only to infiltrate again later and so to require further ritual struggles.

Here then in the rituals is the basic schema found in the tales: an initial relationship of enduring antagonism, the acquisition of protection that allows the good side to triumph, and the departure of the loser. It can even be shown that there is a link with the last step, *temple founding*, in these rituals, as there is in the case of the oral folklore. The link is present in two ways. First, the altar of the offering ritual is constructed on the same cosmic plan (the mandala) as the space of a temple. Indeed, the altar is said to be, among other things, a temporary temple (also palace and heaven) for the gods called in for the occasion. Thus every performance of the ritual, involving the construction of a new altar for each performance, is also a symbolic temple founding.

Perhaps more important, offering rituals are said to have originated in the context of the founding of a temple. Thus it is told in another tale, widely known among both Tibetans and Sherpas, that the ritual was originally taught to people when they were trying to build Samye, the very first Buddhist monastery in Tibet, in the eighth century.[12] According to the version of the legend that I heard from a Solu lama, the people would work hard all day on the building, but at night the demons would come and tear down all their work. The people appealed to Guru Rinpoche, the founder of Tibetan Buddhism, for help. He replied (as the lama put it), "Of course you are having trouble. You are just spending money, but you have not got the gods on your side." And so he taught them how to make the offering rituals to acquire the gods' protection, and then with the gods' help the demons were kept at bay, and the monastery was finished very quickly (Ortner 1978a:85–86). Once again, then, the offering rituals, structured on the same cultural schema as the temple-founding folklore, are also themselves legendarily connected with the founding of a temple.

The tale of the founding of Samye monastery places the rituals and the temple founding in a cause-and-effect relationship with one another, although it is a circular and paradoxical one: Temples and monasteries are founded in order to provide environments in which people can perform the rituals that bring them into contact with their gods. At the same time, people can only build temples, or indeed do anything whatsoever in the real world, if they have the help and support of the gods as gained through those rituals.

The circularity of this relationship is resolved when one looks at the two processes as standing in a relationship of metaphor with one another, rather than a relationship of cause and effect. Thus, founding a temple is a vast act of giving offerings to the gods, providing them not merely with a single act of worship, but with a context for the production of repeated acts of worship. At the same time, an offering ritual is in effect a tiny temple founding, for the altar is constructed, and construed, as a temporary "abode" for the gods, a replication of their heavenly palaces. In the final analysis, both temple foundings and offering rituals are transformations on a common underlying structure, which takes the form of a schema for encountering and overcoming hostile forces, for expressing the triumph of that encounter, and for routinizing the relations that make that triumph possible.

"GROUNDING" THE SCHEMA

Several points may be drawn from this brief discussion. First, the parallels between the "plot" structure of the rituals and the plot structure of the temple-founding tales strongly supports the claim that there is some sort of generalized cultural schema at work here.

Second, the performance of the rituals may be taken as one of several ways in which the schema is "grounded" in practice, that is to say, in real sensuous activity. Of course, the telling of the tales of the foundings of the ancient temples is itself a form of practice. Yet one must perhaps privilege the rituals over the storytelling, as a major locus of reproduction, for several reasons. First, the rituals are far more frequently and regularly performed than the stories are told. Second, the rituals are more materially consequential, in the sense that if the rituals are not done, bad consequences (crop failure, illness, and so forth) may follow, whereas if the stories are not told, no consequences are thought to ensue. And finally, the rituals are often (though not always) performed under circumstances of heightened emotional sensitivity—during funerals, for example, and during festivals. For all these reasons, then, one must take the rituals as one of several crucial loci of the reproduction of this very general—and apparently very durable—cultural schema.

There are of course other major sites of reproduction of the schema in practice. In particular, the two sets of rivalrous relationships, fraternal and political, discussed in the preceding chapters must be seen as contexts in which the schema is in part reproduced. At the same time they must be seen as contexts that are themselves in part constituted by the schema. Let me expand on these points briefly.

Chronic rivalry is clearly a continuing feature of both fraternal and political relations in Sherpa society. All brothers, according to inheritance rules, are supposed to get equal shares of the parental estate—land and herds. When followed rigorously over time, this rule tends to produce excessive land fragmentation, with parcels so small that they cannot support a family. Thus in some cases a brother simply has to go away and start over again. Moreover, the equal inheritance rule creates many opportunities for fraternal friction, even when there is enough land to go around. It is difficult to give each brother precisely an equal share, and there are frequent occasions for a given (usually middle) brother to feel less favored. Once again, then, the solution has been for the discontented brother to go away, both to make a better stake for himself and to escape the strained fraternal relationship. The practice of fraternal relations, then, would in many cases give actors an experiential base from which the cultural schema of rivalry seen in folkore and ritual would appear as a meaningful account of the world.

A similar pattern was seen in Sherpa political relations. Succession to political position was (and still is, to a great extent) a kind of do-it-yourself affair. Individuals (from among the "big" sector) competitively sought to set themselves up as pembu with rights to collect gifts, labor, and taxes. Although an existing pembu might try to pass his position down to his son, and might succeed in doing so if there were no serious contenders, patrilineal succession was not in general a well-established principle, and anyone could mount a challenge who felt he had the power to succeed. Thus the political order, like the kinship/inheritance order, was inherently generative of competition and rivalry. Moreover, the key to success was, more obviously than in the case of fraternal relations, gaining the backing of a powerful protector. For lamas who became pembu, the protection of tutelary deities was crucial in helping them defeat their rivals. Later in Sherpa history, as will be seen in the next chapter, would-be pembu will seek the backing of the state for their protection. The supernatural or secular protection that allowed a pembu to defeat his rival in turn allowed him to claim that he was offering his clients superior protection from whatever ills they feared—worse pembu, worse state officials, worse gods.

One can say then that most of the components of the temple-founding narrative—recurrent rivalries, protectors who help the hero to triumph, defeats that cause the loser to leave the area—are grounded in recognizable practices of ordinary social life. The organization of fraternal relations, particularly surrounding inheritance, produces inequities and rivalries for which the best solution appears to be the departure of the losing brother. The organization of political relations also produces chronic rivalry and competitive challenge, and here again losers tend to leave. Political actors also count heavily on the acquisition of protectors, both for support in defeating a rival and for buttressing claims of their value to their clients.

But if these practices can be said to "ground" the cultural schema of political/religious triumph, they must be seen at the same time as shaped by that schema. In the case of both inheritance and succession, alternative arrangements were possible and were part of local knowledge. Brothers could have shared property: in the Sherpas' home region of Tibet, fraternal polyandry was a recognized way to avoid the fragmentation of an estate and the parcellization of land. Similarly, political positions could have been (and sometimes were) passed on through patrilineal succession. The particular patterns that have emerged thus reflect choices that have been ordered as much by culture—in this case by the Sherpas' unstable (because contradicted by hierarchy) egalitarianism—as by any material necessity. In other words, the cultural schema is shaping the practices, as much as the practices are constituting the groundings of the schema, and this circularity must be acknowledged.

Merit and Power

There is one more question to be addressed in the present chapter, that of the "meaning" of the schema. While the schema does reflect certain patterns of social life, it also places those patterns within a larger, basically religious, story. It links fraternal and political conflict with the founding of religious institutions, a linkage that is by no means a feature of ordinary social practice. This linkage is the key to its meaning.

My theoretical inspiration for this particular part of the discussion derives from Lévi-Strauss, who has argued that cultural constructions—myths, rituals, folktales—with no apparent practical function can be shown to perform a major symbolic function: the mediation of cultural contradictions (for example, 1969). Later, structural Marxists transformed his point to argue that such mediation is after all "practical" and in fact highly political: it serves to legitimate and reproduce the existing order (for example, O'Laughlin 1974).

I am inclined to think these two points should be kept separate, in the sense that the mediations produced in myth and folklore must be recognized at one level as politically ambiguous. They can be read as politically legitimating for the "big" people, or they can be read as encouraging political challenge on the part of the small, depending on who is doing the reading and under what circumstances. In the present section I am concerned with the ambiguous level, that is to say, with the level of meaning at which everyone, as cultural actors living the contradictions of their society, can locate themselves. Various political transformations on this general meaning will be discussed later.

The cultural schema begins by showing the hero acting in a self-interested manner. The hero engages in conflict for dominance or at least parity. He triumphs over the enemy and exults in that triumph. Founding the temple appears as an expression of that exultation, and in many ways has the quality of an egotistical act. Further, in an instrumental sense, the founding is meant to fix and perpetuate the hero's ascendance over his followers and clients, which again would seem to be both materially self-interested and psychologically self-aggrandizing.

But once again a contradiction arises, since building temples and monasteries, and sponsoring Buddhist rituals, are also acts of great religious merit. Merit (*payin*) is a kind of immaterial quantum of virtue that the individual accumulates in the course of a lifetime, in parallel with the accumulation of sin, or demerit (*dikpa*). The final amounts of merit and sin accumulated by an individual at the time of death will determine his or her fate in the next life. A person with much merit may be reborn wealthier in the next life, or with greater spiritual aspirations and greater religious talents. Similarly, a person with a great deal of sin may be born as a poor and miserable human, or may even be reborn as an animal, or in a hell of constant torture.

Listing the kinds of deeds considered sinful and the kinds considered virtuous would take this analysis too far afield for present purposes. It will perhaps suffice to say here that one of the primary bases of sin is selfishness—doing ill and causing harm because one seeks to enhance and benefit the self. Reciprocally, one of the primary bases of merit (and ultimately, of transcendental salvation) is egolessness—negation of the self and its claims to (among other things) power and glory, selfless identification with the sufferings of the whole universe of sentient beings. The Sherpas well know that selflessness, not in any fancy doctrinal sense (that is, the doctrine of *anatta*, or non-self), but in the ordinary sense of altruism, kindness, and generosity, is one of the foundations of Buddhist virtue.

The Sherpas do not seem to find it contradictory that temple founding is an act of both great ego and profound selflessness. When asked why the wealthy "big people" sponsored the monastery foundings in the twentieth century, people generally said, more or less in the same breath, that they did it to gain merit, and that they did it to gain prestige, name, to make themselves "big."[13]

I would suggest that this contradiction, constructed by the schema as noncontradictory as well as possible and desirable, *is* the meaning of the schema. It is the meaning (apart from any particular meanings attributed to it by particular actors) in the sense of being a statement of relations between two major cultural values, and it says that both are attainable simultaneously, and indeed that each is a condition of the other. It says that one must be altruistic while being powerful and dominant, and reciprocally, that one must be powerful and dominant even when one is subjectively humble and self-effacing. It says, in short, that one must be small as well as big, big as well as small.

The key to this mediation in the schema lies in the submission to a protector. Although it is probably the case that one really needs high-status patrons and sponsors to get on in the (socially and culturally constituted) universe in which the Sherpas live, the submission also has signification—that of accepting that one *needs* such patronage and protection, no matter how "big" one may be in one's own context. The submission in turn—the acceptance of one's smallness—is what gives the hero the power to defeat his rival—to be "big."

This was seen in the tales of temple foundings, where the hero first acquires high-level (human and divine) protection, and only then acquires the power to defeat his rival. It was also seen in the offering rituals, in which the lamas, as agents of the human community, solicit the protection of the gods and thus acquire the power to defeat the demons. The point is further illustrated in a Tibetan version of the story of the founding of Samye monastery. It will be recalled that it was in the context of the founding of Samye that the Sherpas' ancestors were said to have learned the basic rites of offerings to the gods. In the Tibetan version, the story begins with the Guru Rinpoche, the founder of Tibetan Buddhism, performing the offering ritual in the presence of the royal sponsor of the monastery, King Thi-Srong Detsan. As a result of the efficacy of the ritual, Guru Rinpoche was able to subdue the demons, who then assisted with the building of the temple:

> [The spiritual agents of the Guru Rinpoche] caused the Tibetan devils to bring stones and wood from the hills and rivers, and thus the foundation of bSam-yas academy was begun. Human beings built it by day, while the devils worked at it by night, and so the great work rapidly progressed. (Waddell [1894] 1959:266–67n)

The king was surprised to see the demons so pacified, whereupon the Guru Rinpoche performed the ritual again, in such a way as to enable the king actually to see its supernatural effects:

> When the king saw the great piles of gathered wood he was surprised and was awestruck, and asked the Guru to explain. The Guru thereon [did another version of the ritual]. And at that very time the Guru himself became invisible, and the king saw in his stead a great garuda [a mythical eaglelike bird] holding a snake in his clutches and beak; but not seeing the Guru, the king cried out in fear. Then the garuda vanished and the Guru reappeared beside him. (Ibid.)

Here the king is a mere layman, lacking the great powers of that original tsachermu lama, the Guru Rinpoche. The king cries out in fear before the lama's and the gods' powers. And in being so humbled, he, or any other wealthy or powerful person who puts himself in the position of a religious sponsor, makes a statement that he is ultimately one with all other lay people, "small" yet at the same time "big," a powerful king and wealthy patron of a monastery.[14]

The hierarchical notion that no individual, no matter how high, can do without higher backing, is culturally represented in other ways as well. For example, the head lama's throne in any temple stands above the seats of the participating lamas or monks. Yet behind every throne there is always a second throne, for the higher lama who stands above the existing head lama. In contemporary Sherpa temples, there is usually a photograph of the absent higher lama propped up in some way on the throne. Where there is no photograph, there is often a robe that either actually belongs to the absent lama, or that simply represents him. The throne-behind-the-throne structure nicely encapsulates the combination of bigness and smallness at issue here: the head lama is big vis-à-vis the lower lamas or monks, but he is small vis-à-vis his own superior lama, who is indeed his protector.

The ideal of the person who is simultaneously powerful and humble is also part of the way in which people evaluate other members of the community. Wealthy and powerful people who are arrogant and snobbish are disliked; they are the ones who will be labeled ongchermu (bully-powerful). On the other hand, the big individual who will talk to small people as his equals is much admired. In one example, I was talking to a young man of middling status about the big people of a certain village:

> [He said that] AD was a good man, the richest in X village. AD's oldest brother [now deceased] had a bad soul [sem], he drank and smoked a lot. Also, he bought things and then didn't pay for them for several years. But [another deceased brother] was a good man—he talked to you like an equal, had regular folks up to tea, etc.

Most important, high lamas who are seen as religiously powerful (tsachermu) and yet responsive to the religious needs of the humble (as well as the great), are greatly revered:

> [A young, middle-status man, talking about Lama Tenzing of Kyerok:] N said afterwards that Lama Tenzing is a very good lama. He goes to both rich and poor, while some lamas only go to the rich. In fact, perhaps he likes the poor better, N said.

> [The reincarnate head of Tengboche monastery talking about the Deu Rinpoche, a high Tibetan married lama:] The Tengboche Rinpoche has invited the Deu Rinpoche up to do [a certain ritual]. . . . He will stay anywhere people invite him, and do any ceremony people sponsor. [SBO, asking what was known by then to be a productive question:] Will he even go to poor people's houses? [Tengboche Lama:] Yes, he's a really good lama, not like some who only stay with rich sponsors.

> [The head lama of Sehlo monastery, writing about the Phungmoche (Phug-mo-che) married lama:] "Due to predispositions developed in former lives he was friendly with everyone—not only did he never harbor an ill thought, but moreover, he naturally wanted to aid anyone who came along. Although he was the son of a great lama who had a religious heritage and wealth, still he was always friendly and devoid of arrogance or spiteful thoughts." (Sangye Tenzing 1971:100)

One could go so far as to say that such lamas are the models of ideal personhood among the Sherpas. Humility without potency is not respected; the kindness of small people is viewed with suspicion, or simply not noticed. But potency without humility is not respected either; it may generate compliance but never admiration and loyalty. The schema constructs a mode in which power is not egotistical, and in which humility is not impotent.

One may carry this analysis one step further and suggest that the mediation between big and small is in turn a metaphor, in a social (status) and psychological (arrogant/humble) idiom, for the mediation of the most fundamental contradiction of Sherpa culture—that between egalitarianism and hierarchy. The critical element is once again the forging of the relationship with the protector. The relationship itself is pure hierarchy—submission to a person defined as naturally and legitimately "higher." But the hierarchical relationship is used to facilitate egalitarianism, supporting the hero's challenge to illegitimate domination, and allowing his rise in the equal-opportunity structure.

To summarize: The schema of political triumph and temple founding stands in a complex relationship to the contradictions of Sherpa society. From the actor's point of view, it offers a course of action for succeeding in various problematic relations—for defeating one's rivals and coming out on top (in politics), or at least not at the bottom (in the brother relationship and in the struggle with demons). From an analytic point of view, it interlocks with various social practices to form a hegemony, a closed and mutually reinforcing world of social practice and symbolic form in which the two levels constitute, reinforce, and naturalize one another.

Yet to say that the practices and the schema together constitute a hegemony is both true and misleading. As a hegemony, the set of mutually reinforcing elements will obviously play a historically conservative role. Heroic actors in cultural stories resolve conflicts by winning, rather than questioning the structural bases of the conflicts. The linkage in the schema between self-interested political triumph and altruistic temple founding in turn symbolically mediates the opposition between power and merit, bigness and smallness, equality and inequality, thereby leaving fundamental contradictions intact. Yet to emphasize these points too strongly is to distract from other possibilities: that the schema can also be read as a lesson in using one's wits to improve one's life, in challenging illegitimate authority, and even in becoming a genuinely moral person. All of these possibilities will be visible in later chapters, as actors who are constrained by the order in which they live will be seen nonetheless to turn that order to different uses with different long-term and often very positive consequences.

In the next chapter I return to chronological Sherpa history, but also to another methodological dimension of the analysis: the impingement of larger political/economic forces. Specifically, I will consider the way in which the Sherpas came to be linked with the Nepal state following the early temple foundings, and I will suggest that the linkage was generated in large part by the cultural schema discussed in the present chapter.

CHAPTER

V

The Sherpas and the State

IN CHAPTER 1 I discussed briefly the current bifurcation of historical anthropology into what is generally called political economy on the one hand, and structural history or ethnographic history on the other. The political economists insist on the importance of studying the impact of large-scale political/economic forces, such as capitalism and colonialism, on local societies. It is only through such study, they argue, that one can reach an adequate understanding of why a particular society has the particular shape it has at a given moment in time. This is a major point, and it is important to emphasize that many, even most, of the ethnographic historians (or whatever they may wind up being called) would not deny it. The next two chapters of this book will precisely be concerned to show the ways in which the Sherpas became embroiled in an "external" political/economic order—with the Nepal state, and the British raj—and to show the impact such involvement has had on Sherpa society for the past 250 or so years.

Yet the dangers of the political economy position are as significant as its virtues. The external perspective—taking, as Wolf put it, "cognizance of processes that transcend separable cases, moving through and beyond them and transforming them as they proceed" (1982:17)—tends virtually to dissolve the societies and cultures that people thought they lived in, rendering such societies and cultures more or less illusory "effects" of the world system. By the same token the perspective tends to cast the people themselves as relatively passive victims of the juggernaut of those world-historical forces. It is ironic that Wolf castigates anthropologists for taking away people's history, yet the history he gives back to them is not their own, but the West's.

While it thus seems essential to attend to such massive phenomena as colonialism, state domination, and capitalism, as they press upon the people studied, it seems equally essential to interpret the impact of such forces from the perspective of the culture on the receiving end of the impact. This does not mean attending only to things the people themselves perceive. It is the nature of such larger structures that their workings are for the most part not perceivable by, no less fully comprehensible to, any single actor. But it does mean that anthropologists must use the cultural frames and structural contradictions of the local society as a kind of lens through which to view the practices and policies of the larger system, because it is these cultural frames and structural contradictions that mediate both the meaning and the impact of the larger political and economic forces in question. Of course to some extent the political economists do this as well. But the ethnographic historical approach proposed here *starts*, as I have done, at the level of the local society, thereby making it as much a cause as an effect of the larger historical dynamic.

"Real" Sherpa history has facilitated the enactment of this theoretical agenda. The Sherpas appear to have had very little outside contact (apart from trade) for the period of their history discussed thus far. It was only after the foundings of the early temples (Pangboche and the other two in Khumbu, Zhung in Solu) that significant connections were established between the Sherpas and the major political forces in the region—the Nepal state based in the Kathmandu valley ten days' walk west of Solu-Khumbu, and the British empire in India as situated in the Darjeeling-Kalimpong region ten days east of Solu-Khumbu (see map, p. 23).

In the present chapter I will focus on the interactions of the Sherpas with the Nepal state, summarizing what is known of this relationship from the Sherpas' entry into Nepal (in the early sixteenth century) until the mid–nineteenth century. The main point of the discussion will be to show how internal structures of Sherpa society mediated all these interactions. I will show first that the original submission of the Sherpas to the Nepal state seems in large part to have been culturally generated. I then briefly consider the state's agenda in its own terms, or at least in terms (probably somewhere between its and ours) external to Sherpa society. Finally, however, I try to demonstrate that the impact of state policies and practices on the Sherpas is best understood by considering the way in which those policies interacted with the contradictions of Sherpa society, as analyzed in the preceding chapters. The general point is to encompass the political/economic analysis *within* the internal analysis, and to give the Sherpas at least their share of their history.

Time Frame

1533	Migration into Nepal
1667	Founding of Pangboche temple, involving Lama Sangwa Dorje and his rival Zongnamba
1717	Submission of Sherpas to the Sen king, involving Zongnamba's (grand-) sons
1769	Gorkha conquest of Kathmandu
1772	Gorkha conquest of eastern Nepal and apparently peaceful acquisition of Solu-Khumbu by the Gorkha from the Sen
1786, 1791, 1805, 1810, 1828, 1829	Gorkha state documents establishing state policies vis-à-vis the Sherpas
1831	Founding of Khumjung temple
1846	Beginning of Rana regime

The Period before the Temples (1533–1720)

From the time of the Sherpas' entry into Nepal in 1533, up through the foundings of the early temples at the end of the seventeenth century, it does not appear that the Sherpas were under the authority of either the Tibetan or the Nepal state (or indeed under any more local ruler outside of Sherpa society on either side of the border). The Sherpas themselves have conflicting traditions in this matter; some say that their ancestors paid taxes to Tibet, others claim that they were under no external chief or king, and still others maintain that at some periods the Sherpas paid taxes to both Tibet and Nepal. It is possible that Zongnamba, coming over as he did from the Tibetan side (remember, he had committed some "fault" there and left), claimed to be, or actually was, the agent for some Tibetan chief who hoped to hold Solu-Khumbu within his domain. If so, Zongnamba quickly did what most provincial authorities in this part of the world tended to do if they could get away with it: he set himself up on his own.

The bulk of the evidence is in favor of the view that for quite a long time the Sherpas were beyond effective state control, whether Tibetan or Nepali. By the bulk of the evidence I mean simply that there are no convincing accounts in the oral traditions of Tibetan control, and there is one rather detailed account in the oral traditions of the submission to the Nepal state sometime after the founding of Pangboche. As one man explicitly said, "Before [the troubles narrated below] Khumbu had no [single] king and no [single] pembu.

Sometimes it was Lama Sangwa Dorje, sometimes the Zamte lama, and sometimes Zongnamba. No pembu and no king for several hundred years."

According to the oral tradition to be recounted here, the Sherpas came under a pre-Gorkha king by the name of "Makwan Sher" a generation or two after the founding of Pangboche temple, "Makwan Sher" apparently being one of the pre-Gorkha Sen kings.[1] In terms of dating, the folklore suggests the early eighteenth century, since the plot that resulted in submission to the king was inaugurated by Zongnamba's sons or, in most accounts, his grandsons. Since Zongnamba was an adult at the time of the founding of Pangboche in 1667, his grandsons (still assuming a twenty-five-year generation span) could have reached maturity in about 1717, or about fifty-five years *before* the Gorkha conquest.

It is probably not wise to make too much of the Sen conquest of the Sherpas. The Sen kingdom was by that time broken up and relatively weak (Stiller 1973:36), and its capacity to collect taxes from or otherwise assert authority in Solu-Khumbu was probably rather tenuous. Nonetheless, it represented the beginning of Nepal state control, later to be much more strongly consolidated by the Gorkha kings with long-term consequences for Sherpa society. It also represented one of several significant conjunctures between internal cultural dynamics and external forces in Sherpa history. Let us then look at the story of this event.

The Further Evil Ways of Zongnamba

As previously described, Lama Sangwa Dorje founded Pangboche temple around 1667, but was then harassed out of Khumbu by his political rival Zongnamba. After Lama Sangwa Dorje went to Tibet, Zongnamba stayed in Khumbu and was apparently bent on eliminating all possible rivals for dominance over the area. The cycle of tales thus continues with the further political machinations of Zongnamba and, later, his descendants. I will follow it a while from the cultural point of view, in terms of the way in which it continues to permute the basic political/religious schema already discussed. Its main function in this chapter, however, will be to link the cultural schema with external historical forces.

> [After the departure of Lama Sangwa Dorje] Zongnamba also tried to kill a certain lama from Zamte. The Zamte lama went way up to a rock cave, and stayed one month there. He had no food, nothing at all. Zongnamba approached him, saying, "Let's

> become ritual friends [*towu*], come down here." Eventually the lama came back to Zamte.
>
> Zongnamba's people set up a big tent [for the ritual of bond friendship]. Zongnamba plied the Zamte lama with beer and liquor, and the lama got drunk. Then Zongnamba went to kill him. He stabbed him with a knife but it would not penetrate the lama's skin. He tried a spear, and it also would not penetrate. Knife and awl and *kurpa* [a kind of Nepali dagger], nothing would cut.
>
> The lama then said, "Weapons won't penetrate me, but there is a way in which you can kill me. If you take my *dorje,* my ritual thunderbolt, out of my hair, I will die. [He was a *ralwa* lama, one who lets his hair and nails grow long, and wears his long hair wrapped around his dorje.] But first, let me say one *molom,* one blessing." And he said a *molom lokta,* a curse [literally, a backward blessing]: "I will return as a *tsen* [a vengeful spirit, often of deceased lamas] and I will cause you to have a short life." And then he gave them his dorje and he died.[2]

Here one sees an interesting inversion of the basic protection structure of the schema. Zongnamba does not at first call in a protector, and he is therefore initially unable to defeat his rival, the Zamte lama, with his own powers. But then he succeeds. The added power, normally derived from a protector, comes instead from the lama himself, who gives Zongnamba the secret of his own vulnerability. The lama's act is difficult to understand, but is perhaps an example of religious heroism as discussed in the last chapter. It is clear that he is magically invulnerable and hence fully tsachermu. Zongnamba cannot kill him by normal means, because the lama is very powerful indeed. But then, out of his great potency, he gives Zongnamba the key to the means of killing him, denying his own egotistical clinging to life (that is, making himself small) through an act of tremendous courage and power (his bigness). The peculiar death of the Zamte lama may thus mediate the big/small opposition, just as the larger temple-founding schema (of which it is a part) does.

The next segment of the tale introduces the other half of a pembu's source of power—the loyalty of his subjects. Since the Zamte lama did not lose his struggle with Zongnamba out of any apparent decline in legitimacy vis-à-vis his subjects, they remain loyal to him:

> Then the subjects (*misir*) of the Zamte Lama met with one another, saying, "Our lama has been killed by Zongnamba, now we will kill him."

> They made a lot of beer and liquor and took it to Zongnamba's tent. They said, "Our lama and pembu the Zamte Lama is dead, you killed him. Now nobody will help us, so now we place ourselves under you." They gave him *chang* and *arak* [beer and liquor; in one version, they added water from washing menstrual underpants to the chang]. And the Zongnamba subjects believed what they said, and they drank the chang and arak, and they all got drunk.
>
> "Now," said the Zamte people, "we will kill them." And they pulled down the tent pole, and all the Zongnamba subjects were trapped inside the tent. They were all moving around under it. And the Zamte subjects took hammers and hoes and sticks [in other versions, also axes and knives] and beat the Zongnamba people to death. All were wiped out.[3]

The actions of the Zamte lama's subjects demonstrate the point made earlier, that a pembu's legitimacy derives as much from his clients' loyalties as from his divine protection. It is clear that both are necessary. For when a pembu who lacks divine protection, like Zongnamba, illegitimately acquires the Zamte's clients, they do not legitimate him, they kill him.

At this point in the tale the end of the chain appears that will lead directly to the Sherpas' submission to the Nepal state. From the Sherpa point of view, as will be seen, this submission came about largely as a result of *internal* decisions, and decisions that were largely in keeping with standard cultural patterns of action. Specifically, faced with a powerful adversary, certain individuals called in a powerful "protector," who also happened to be the king of (much of) Nepal.

At the time the Zamte subjects killed Zongnamba and his subjects under the tent, one pregnant woman survived. She was (in various accounts) either the Nepali wife, or the daughter, of Zongnamba.

> She ran away to Hungo, then to Pare, then to Kongde, down to Rimijung. She stayed in Kango Kami. There she bore twins. When the twins got older, other people asked them, "Who's your grandfather? Who's your father? What's your lineage?" And then the twins asked their mother.
>
> She said, "Don't ask your mother, if you do I'll get angry."
>
> "If we don't ask you," they said, "many people will keep asking us, and we won't be able to stay here."

"Your grandfather was Zongnamba, king of Khumbu. The people all killed him, and I alone escaped," she said. "Then you two were born to me. Don't ask what to do."

The two sons said they would go to make war against Khumbu. But they weren't enough to fight all of Khumbu, so they went and asked the *rongbi* ["lowland"] king for help.

At this point in the story I probed for more specificity about who this *rongbi* king might have been. The term *rongba* (in the possessive or genitive, *rongbi*) means lowlander, but in modern times it almost always specifically means the ethnic Nepalis or, as they used to be called, the Gorkhalis. But the informant said,

> At that time there was no Gorkha king, just a *dongbi* ["tribal"] king. Maybe it was a Kiranti [a Rai or Limbu]. There were many different kings at that time, and the Sherpas say "dongbi" for any local king.

He will give this king's name later; at this point he went on with the story:

> The dongbi king came to Khumbu and said, "Will you submit to me or not?" And the Khumbu people said, "No, we have our own king." They did not agree, and so there was a war.

What follows, then, is an account of the only known pitched battle in Sherpa history:

> The main center [of the battle] was in Zhorsale. The Khumbu fighters were at Zonglo Topdara Pomdok, the spot down the Namche hill from which you can see Mount Everest. The other side was down in Zhorsale, which the Sherpas call Tumbuk. The lowlanders came up, and the Khumbu people threw down rocks and chunks of wood. The lowlanders spent six months in Zhorsale, but they could not get up the hill, and they wanted to go back.
>
> The two boys went to ask their mother what to do, and although she was very old, she came to show them the road by which she had escaped: from Rimijung to Kongde to Pare and then over the bridge. At that time there was no Namche [reader: file this point for later reference], only Takdzo, and all the lowlanders came around this road. And since there were more of them than

> the Khumbu people, the Khumbu people raised their hands in surrender, saying, "Don't kill us."
>
> Then all the people were under the dongbi king for many years. Prithvi Narayan Shah, [the first Gorkha king, and] the ancestor of our present king, conquered the dongbi king 211 years ago. The dongbi king's name was Makwan Sher, it is said.

As noted above, "Makwan Sher" was presumably one of the Sen kings, a dynasty of which ruled (parts of) Nepal on and off from the time of the Sherpas' arrival in 1533 until the Gorkha conquest in 1769.

These tales strike one as having quite an authoritative tone. Although Oppitz states that the Sherpas probably came under the Nepal state at the time of the Gorkha conquest of eastern Nepal in 1772–74, and although he describes a battle much like the one described here (1968:92), no records have yet been found of the Gorkha conquest of, or treaty with, Solu-Khumbu. It may be suggested that the teller of the tale is right: the Gorkhas simply acquired Solu-Khumbu when they conquered the Sen princedom(s) in the course of their eastern expansion. There is some support for this view in the fact that all the Gorkha documents pertaining to Solu-Khumbu that have come to light so far merely seem to confirm some set of preexisting arrangements.

In any event, after almost two hundred years of local autonomy, the Sherpas had then—and forever after—to contend with foreign overlordship. It is entirely possible of course that "Makwan Sher" showed up with his army on his own initiative, responding to his own internal dynamics and not the Sherpas'. But from an analytic point of view, within a Sherpa frame of reference, the Sherpas' connection with the state was at least in part a product of their own cultural dynamics: a claimant to a pembu position called in the king as a "protector," and the protector did indeed help him defeat his rival.

Yet to say that this event was generated by the Sherpas according to their own cultural frameworks, is not to say that the consequences of it were entirely controllable by the Sherpas. On the contrary, as most practice theorists have emphasized, while culturally constituted intentions may generate events, events—especially involving more powerful actors—have a way of "escaping" those intentions. Thus must history be seen both from the native point of view, and from a vantage point that recognizes dynamics beyond the perspective of any given set of actors. The consideration of the impact of the Nepal state on Sherpa society that follows shows the continuing interplay of internal and external dynamics.

The Gorkha Conquest and Long-Term State Interference

In 1769, fifty years or so after the battle of Namche Hill, an army of the king of Gorkha, in western Nepal, conquered the Kathmandu valley. Moving east, it conquered all of eastern Nepal in the period between 1772 and 1774. Whether by military force, treaty, or simply acquisition via conquest of a local Sen kingdom, Solu-Khumbu came under the Gorkha state. The Gorkhas in turn took a fairly active interest in Solu-Khumbu, not only because of tax revenues, but also probably because of their very keen concern to maintain control of the Tibet-Nepal trade routes, upon one of which the Sherpas were sitting (Stiller 1973; Rose and Scholz 1980).[4]

Once the Gorkhas settled into power, they began establishing the bureaucratic instruments for maintaining it. Although their main interest was in tax collections, they were aware of the fact that their realm was composed of peoples of many different ethnicities and religious persuasions, and that this was potentially problematic for the unity of the realm. They thus attempted to influence the affairs of people like the Sherpas, whom they construed as "lower caste" or "tribal," across a broad front of issues—economic, political, and cultural. (For an excellent discussion of the Gorkha state's objectives, see Burghart 1984.) Again, the state's actual influence in this period (roughly, the tail end of the eighteenth century and first half of the nineteenth) was certainly lighter than in the subsequent Rana period. Nonetheless the groundwork was laid for a number of trends that would both continue and accelerate, and that would make their marks in the long run. I cover here the entire Gorkha period, from the Gorkha conquest of Kathmandu in 1769 to the beginning of the Rana regime in 1846.

The impact of the state can only be understood in terms of the contradictions of Sherpa society already discussed at length in preceding chapters. While one can talk about certain effects on the society as a whole, in general the most significant effects in terms of long-term historical consequences are those involving interaction with existing contradictory tendencies. Such interaction may of course take multiple forms. Contradictions may be exacerbated, or resolved, or sidestepped and rendered irrelevant. In the Sherpa case, as I will now try to show, the contradictions were largely exacerbated.

One needs to recognize as well that the state (or any other "outside" entity) has its own contradictions. In the case of the Nepal state, one of these contradictions derived from the use of local elites as tax collectors for the state. The power/authority of local elites constituted both their virtue and their threat in the eyes of the state, which was forced to play a double game. On the one hand, it supported the big people, since it needed them to act as its agents in the collection of taxes. On the other hand, it had to keep the big people in line, in part because too-powerful local elites were themselves potential competitors with the state, and in part because too-greedy local elites tended to press too hard upon the peasants and cause them to move away (again see Burghart 1984, e.g., p. 114). The net effect of this double game was to heighten the contradictory tendencies of Sherpa society—to reinforce the ascendancy of the "big" sector and at the same time to reinforce the chronic weakness of its legitimacy.

THE ENRICHMENT OF THE BIG PEOPLE

Some time after the submission of the Sherpas to Nepal state authority, the large trading town of Nauje (now known as Namche Bazaar) grew up in a central, though agriculturally unproductive, location in the upper Sherpa region of Khumbu. According to the oral folklore, at the time of the battle of Namche Hill (as I called it) in around 1717, "there was no Namche." But by 1828, there was a spate of state documents (Regmi Research Series 1975:124; Oppitz 1968:62; von Fürer-Haimendorf 1975:61) referring specifically to "the traders of Nauje."

The growth of Nauje represents both a growth in size and a change in quality of the Sherpa trading sector. Nauje is a trading town with little agricultural base. Whereas in earlier times people presumably combined trade with agriculture, and many people would continue to do so up into the twentieth century, the Nauje traders are first and foremost business people, and they are generally quite wealthy. The growth of Nauje is thus a strong indicator of, and contributor to, the growth of the "big" sector of Sherpa society.

The growth of Nauje and the trading sector was probably the result of a combination of factors. On the one hand, Oppitz reports that there was another major immigration movement from Tibet into Solu-Khumbu in the late eighteenth century (1968:94; 1974:234). On the other hand, the Sherpa inheritance structure (as discussed earlier) tends to produce leftover sons with little or no land, and some of these men may have become successful full-time traders as well.

The growth of the "big" sector of Sherpa society had little to do with the Sherpas' connection with the Nepal state. It was a product of dynamics internal to Sherpa society, and to the larger local region that includes Solu-Khumbu and the adjacent Tibetan provinces. At the same time, the state made moves that would have enhanced this growth. For one thing, state authorities created the position of *gembu* (which they called in Nepali *amali*) with authority over all the pembu.[5] The gembu/amali is first mentioned in an 1810 document (Regmi Research Series 1979b), and his appearance suggests in turn that there may have been a proliferation of pembu tax collector appointments in the Solu-Khumbu region. That is, since the state's primary interest was in tax collections, they may have been appointing more collectors, and the gembu was needed to coordinate their collections. But pembu positions were lucrative, and their proliferation would have meant the proliferation of this kind of wealth-expanding opportunity among the big sector.

The state was also more directly supportive of the enrichment of the wealthy trading sector. In 1828 it issued several decrees giving the Nauje traders a monopoly on the Tibetan trade. Claiming to be following existing custom, the decrees specified that Sherpa traders from outside the Nauje region (in one version, specifically the traders of Solu), as well as non-Sherpa traders from the lowlands, were not to trade directly with Tibet, but were to buy and sell to the Nauje traders who would in turn have a monopoly on the trade across the border (Regmi Research Series 1975:125; Oppitz 1968:63, 64; von Fürer-Haimendorf 1975:71). The restriction will be of great consequence later in this history, since the founders of the first celibate monastery in 1916 will all be Solu traders who will establish themselves in various ways in Khumbu in large part to get around (or insert themselves into) the Nauje monopoly.

It is not clear what the state was up to in promulgating this decree. It may have simply been an attempt to rationalize the collection of customs duties by having all trade go through a single place and a single set of people. Although no such duties are ever mentioned, this seems to underlie the restriction, also mentioned in at least one of the documents (von Fürer-Haimendorf 1975:71), that all trade during the peak trading season was to be conducted in the presence of both the gembu and a pembu. Whatever the rationale, however, the net effect of the decree would have been to enrich the individual officials overseeing the trading at any given time and, of much wider consequence, the Nauje traders as a whole, who thus came to enjoy a very favorable economic position in the trans-Himalayan system.

THE FOUNDING OF KHUMJUNG TEMPLE

For some reason, and I will speculate about that reason below, the gembu was initially located not in Nauje but in Khumjung, an agricultural village about an hour's walk north of Nauje. (The location of the gembu in Khumjung emerges from Sherpa oral folklore about the founding of Khumjung temple.) It is possible that Khumjung village was designated as the governor's seat for the region at the same time that the office of gembu was created (according to the 1885 traveler Hari Ram, "Khumjung" is a contraction of Khumbu Dzong, which means "Khumbu Fort" or "Khumbu Administrative Center"—see pp. 22–23 above). In the oral folklore discussed in preceding chapters, the pembu in earlier times were situated in Pangboche (Lama Sangwa Dorje) and Thami (Zongnamba); Khumjung was never mentioned.

Thus, along with the growth of a new center of wealth in Nauje, there is a shift in the center of local power. This shift is, not surprisingly, reflected in a temple founding—the founding of Khumjung temple. According to two different informants, citing the founding charter which I never saw, Khumjung temple was founded in 1831, shortly after the documentary appearance of the gembu (1810) and of the Nauje trade monopoly (1828). Since this appears to be the first major temple founding since Zhung in 1720, and since temple founding is what this book is all about, I will digress a bit here to tell the rather skimpy stories available about this event.

The stories of the founding of Khumjung temple are unlike the stories of the earlier temple foundings in that they do not depict conflict between two pembu. They do, however, refer to intervillage conflict between the people of Pangboche (the seat of the former pembu) and the people of Khumjung (the seat of the new gembu). According to one story, the Khumjung village people had been going to Pangboche for the annual Dumje exorcism festival, but fights kept breaking out between the villagers from the two areas. Finally the Khumjung people decided that they wanted their own temple, where they could stage their own Dumje without constant conflict and fighting.[6]

The fighting between the two groups of villagers in the story replaces the fighting normally seen in the cultural schema between two pembu. The absence of pembu conflict may be related to the fact that there was apparently no longer an effective pembu in Pangboche temple; the line of head lamas of Pangboche seems to have stopped being recorded around the end of the eighteenth century, suggesting a vacuum of religious/political power on the Pangboche side of Khumbu.[7]

The Khumjung gembu does appear in another episode of the tale, however. There was, according to this episode, a lama from the Sakya region of Tibet called Kusho Dongumba, who had a particular piece of ritual authority related to Pangboche temple. This lama was apparently the only person who could authorize the secession of the Khumjung people and the founding of Khumjung gompa.[8] (Whether this had always been true, or was only true at that time because there was no effective head lama at Pangboche, is not clear.) Kusho Dongumba's authority derived from the fact that he was a descendant of Lama Rena Lingba, Lama Sangwa Dorje's teacher. As such, he had the right and the duty to display the Gombu idol, the idol that had spoken to Lama Sangwa Dorje at the time of the founding of Pangboche, and that had become one of the chief treasures of the temple.

According to tradition, the idol could only be shown once every twelve years, and Kusho Dongumba had to come down to Pangboche to show it. As he was leaving to return to Tibet on this occasion, he was approached by three leading notables of Khumjung, who asked him for permission to secede from the Pangboche congregation and for a charter to found Khumjung gompa. One of the three was the gembu of the region. There are several versions of what happened next; in one the lama refused the requests in a joking manner, and in another in a bad-tempered manner. But eventually he did give the chayik, and Khumjung temple was founded.

The Khumjung temple-founding stories are very sketchy, and do not show a neat fit with the cultural schema of temple founding (though they do not contradict it either). Nonetheless, the sheer fact of the establishment of a new temple precisely at the point at which there has been a major shift in wealth, and precisely in the place where a new position of preeminent local power has been created, is unlikely to be an accident. Earlier excursions through Sherpa social, political, and cultural dynamics have rendered this occurrence, as well as its time and place, virtually predictable.

CONTROLLING THE BIG PEOPLE

While the Gorkha state had no objection to enriching the big people, and made various moves that either intentionally or unintentionally facilitated this result, they could not let the big people get too powerful. For one thing, as Regmi (1978) has discussed at some length, local elites constituted potential rivals to the state. If they became powerful enough, they could refuse to transmit the taxes to Kathmandu, reclaim local rule, and set themselves up as autonomous "states" in the region. The Sherpas had been in something like this situation before, and presumably there was at least some possibility that they could revert to it.

The other reason that the collectors had to be controlled was that abusive or greedy collectors tended to drive away their peasants, who would pick up and move elsewhere if the situation became intolerable (see Burghart 1984:104). Sherpa inheritance patterns, and Sherpa cultural notions that an individual might do better economically by leaving and starting over again, would have facilitated decisions to move away from abusive pembus. Such moving was apparently commonplace during the period under discussion, since many of the state documents addressed to Sherpa pembu urge them to encourage the return and resettlement of people who have run away because of indebtedness (for example, see Regmi Research Series 1975; Oppitz 1968:66).

Given the importance, from the state's point of view, of curbing the power of local elites, the gembu position may have been created as much for the purpose of controlling the pembu as for reasons of technical coordination mentioned earlier. (In a later dispute involving a gembu, the ethnographer specifically states that the gembu was trying to control a pembu who had become too "highhanded" [von Fürer-Haimendorf 1964:121].) The decision to locate the gembu in Khumjung may also be explicable as an attempt to separate his office from the dominant Nauje trading group, and to give him some leverage over it.

More direct evidence of state efforts to control the pembu comes from the various documents sent out from Kathmandu during the period in question. Virtually every state document from 1810 on contains some specific restrictions against local officials' overstepping their rights to extract more than their due from the people. A document of 1810 places several restrictions on local officials, including one apparently designed to keep the gembu/amali from exacting excessive taxes or unfair fines: "The *amali* shall collect the prescribed taxes, and dispense justice, in the presence of the headman . . . of the village" (Regmi Research Series 1979b).

A document dated 1825 states that people need not give the tax collectors extra meals, nor do any free portering for them (Oppitz 1968:62). This document is apparently reconfirmed in an inscribed copper plate dated 1844 (ibid., 66).

In 1829 the state exercised its right either to fire or reduce in status a particular tax collector: "Through this document the previous document providing Kiawa Mizar up until this day with sole authority for the entire district is invalidated." The document then goes on explicitly to prohibit local officials from harassing the villagers: "Superintendents as well as government emissaries shall in no way cause trouble for the residents" (Oppitz 1968:64).

There are multiple ironies in play here. Most obviously there is the point that, while the state was supporting the big people in general, and probably also acting as "protector" for individual pembu against their rivals, it was also actively pursuing a policy of weakening the pembu position. Even more ironically, in making these efforts to curb pembu powers, the state portrayed itself as an indulgent protector, but here a protector of the people against the pembu. This theme comes through quite consistently as well. Thus in one of the earliest documents, dated 1791, it is stated:

> You [the Sherpas] are devoted subjects, live loyally. Our [officials] will not harass you. Also our troops will not harass you. Live loyally in your homes. No one will be permitted to plunder your property. In case someone harasses you, come to us, and we will hear the case and punish the harasser. (Oppitz 1968:62)

A much later text, dated 1829, similarly explains that although government officials function to collect taxes and remit them to the state, they also ultimately act for the general welfare,

> so that the animals of the water, the animals of the forests and jungle, the animals of the air and land are watched over, so that the villagers are defended against crime and the rights of the residents [are] protected. (Oppitz 1968:64)

Although the state is clearly in business for itself, its claims of being protective toward the Sherpas are buttressed materially, through tax and corvée exemptions. Thus in the 1791 document in which the state emphasizes that no one will be allowed to harass its loyal subjects, there is a handwritten note on the edge: "The lama membership [here apparently meaning the Sherpa people as a whole] shall not stand under the obligation to perform *hulak* [unpaid portering] services." Other tax exemptions appear in other documents as well (for example, in those dated 1844 and 1854; see Oppitz 1968:66).

The tax exemptions were motivated in various ways. But in some cases they were directly linked to protecting people from the local officials:

> It was customary . . . that you gave the *dware*-s [pembu] food to eat during their visits mornings and evenings, however not at other times and that you rendered no *hulak* services and carried no other cargo. (Oppitz 1968:62)

As explained earlier, it was entirely in the state's rational self-interest that it should seek to curb the pembus' powers. From the people's point of view, however, such moves could appear to represent a more disinterested concern for the people's well-being, supporting the state's own representations about its own protective role. There is thus an interesting kind of "structure of the conjuncture" (Sahlins 1981), in which two historical systems, each operating according to its own principles and for its own reasons, interact with one another in ways that appear to respond to each other's needs or interests. Sherpa big men apparently cast the Nepal state in the role of the culturally defined "protector," the figure in a cultural schema who benevolently and disinterestedly adds his power to that of the hero and thus allows the hero to triumph over his enemies. The Nepal state for its own reasons found it useful to cast itself as a protector, exacting taxes not as an illegitimate tyrant, but as one who defends the people from all forms of harassment. This benevolent claim of protectiveness was partly made in direct statements, but also through various restrictions placed on local pembu, who were thus portrayed as the main sources of "harassment." These restrictions, in turn, served as continuing "evidence" that the state had the people's interests at heart.

But since the restrictions blamed the pembu rather than the state for the woes of the people, the restrictions constituted a continuous process of whittling at pembu authority (if not power) and hence served to undermine the legitimacy of the pembu positions over time. This process continues into the next phase of Sherpa history, and will connect directly with the foundings of the monasteries.

There is one final state policy to be mentioned here that had long-term—and again ironic—consequences. The Gorkha rulers were high-caste (Chhetri) Hindus and promulgated a number of laws based on the Hindu purity code. One of these was a ban on cow-slaughter, which the Sherpas of the early nineteenth century evidently violated. They thus called down upon themselves a judicial visitation, as described in the 1805 document discussed briefly at the beginning of chapter 2. The judge apparently let them off lightly.[9] About this time, however, and over the course of the nineteenth century, various Hindu influences made themselves felt in Solu-Khumbu. According to Oppitz, it was at about this time that the Sherpas stopped doing their own smithing, and Nepali low-caste blacksmiths (*kami*) moved into the region (1968:83). In addition, there is evidence from oral history interviews that certain Nepali religious customs made their way into the region during this period (these will be discussed in Ortner n.d.b).

The religious policies of the Gorkha were intensified later under the Ranas (see especially Höfer 1979) and fed, like the policies undermining the legitimacy of the pembu, directly into the foundings of the monasteries. But the effects ran in virtually the opposite direction. Whereas the policy of weakening the pembu sharpened the cleavage between the big and small people, the policy of pushing Hindu values, and despising the "dirtiness" of ethnically Tibetan peoples like the Sherpas, partly acted to unite the Sherpas around their common Buddhist religion and Sherpa identity. Both the cleavage and the unity manifested themselves in the foundings, to which I now turn.

CHAPTER VI

The Political Economy of Monastery Foundings

IN THE present chapter I continue to look at Sherpa society from the outside in, as it were. I continue to examine the impact of external forces, including not only the Nepal state but also the British raj in India. The period is that of the late nineteenth and early twentieth centuries, roughly from the beginning of the Rana regime in Nepal in 1846[1] to the founding of the first monastery in Solu-Khumbu in 1916.

In the last chapter I argued several points about an external analysis. First I proposed that what appears as external penetration from an analytic point of view may well appear as culturally motivated from an internal point of view. Thus the submission of the Sherpas to the Nepal state has been constructed in Sherpa folklore as a product of their own political dynamics, and given the foregoing observations on Sherpa political dynamics, this is not an implausible construction. Moreover, the submission obviously benefited at least some parties in Sherpa society—the individual pembu who received state backing against their rivals, and groups like the Nauje traders who received state economic protection. One can even say, analytically, that in the long run the state's control (accidentally) benefited the small people as well, since the checks the state placed, for its own reasons, on pembu power had the long-term effect of undermining pembu political domination in the region.

These points will be drawn out further in the present chapter. I will emphasize the degree to which outside forces represented opportunities, as well as pressures, for Sherpas at all levels of society. This is an extension of the point that the "imposition" of state power from the outside was also an active appropriation of such power from the inside. Thus I will show how the Sherpas used both the British in India and the Nepal state in Kathmandu to bring in outside wealth and to achieve certain kinds of success, which in turn were celebrated in the foundings of the monasteries.

The point of all this is to de-victimize the Sherpas (or any other group at the receiving end of world capitalist expansion) as much as possible. Of course the Sherpas (and Nepal) had the luxury of never having been directly colonized, and it is thus easier to make the case for their relative ability to control their own fates. Yet I think it is important for anthropologists, in studying any group of people, to recognize the ways in which people are *always* reinterpreting their situation, acting on it in their own terms, and making the most they can—materially, morally, and in every other way—out of it. This does not mean pretending that they successfully turn every problem they encounter to their own advantage. But it does mean recognizing that they always have their own point of view and their own modes of dealing with the world. To understand this point of view and these modes of action is to understand how they did in fact make their history.

To remind the reader briefly of the circumstances of the establishment of the monasteries in Solu-Khumbu: The founding of the first monastery, Tengboche, was sponsored in 1916 by three wealthy big men, all of whom were traders, and two of whom were (at different times) tax collectors for the Nepal state. The founding of the second monastery, Chiwong, was sponsored in 1923 by a younger brother of the senior figure of the first group. The younger brother made his money initially as an entrepreneur on British projects, and also became a state tax collector. I will begin to introduce these people in the present chapter, and use some specific events of their lives to illustrate the ways in which individual intentions may transform the impact of external historical forces.

Time Frame

1846	Jang Bahadur (Rana) takes office
1850	Birth of Karma, the senior founder of Tengboche monastery
1856	Birth of Sangye, Karma's younger brother and the sole founder of Chiwong monastery
1865	Final establishment of the borders surrounding the Darjeeling-Kalimpong area
1866	Completion of road between Darjeeling and the Indian plains
1885	Birth of Kusang, a Tengboche sponsor

1902	Founding of Rumbu (celibate) monastery in the D'ingri region of Tibet, over the Himalayas from Khumbu
1916	Founding of Tengboche monastery
1923	Founding of Chiwong monastery

Getting Rich with the Raj and the Ranas

In the late nineteenth and early twentieth centuries, there was an extraordinary resurgence of religious activism in Solu-Khumbu. Apart from the founding of Khumjung temple in 1831, there do not appear to have been any temples founded in the region since about 1720. Starting in the 1860s, however, there were old temple renovations, new (noncelibate) temple foundings, and finally the innovative foundings of the celibate monasteries. Pangboche temple was apparently remodeled in 1860, and Thami temple, in 1870 (Fantin 1971, 1974; Sestini and Somigli 1978:19n).[2] Chalsa temple was also apparently built in the second half of the nineteenth century, by a tsachermu lama of great local influence. This temple later burned to the ground, was rebuilt, was destroyed in the 1933 earthquake, and was rebuilt yet again (Sangye Tenzing 1971:81–83). Nauje temple was founded in 1905 by a pembu's son called the Zamte lama. Some time in this same era the pembu Karma, later to sponsor the founding of Tengboche monastery, constructed a beautiful family chapel at his new house at Tewa Gondak, above Zhung (ibid., pp. 73–74). His younger brother Sangye, later to sponsor the founding of Chiwong monastery, sponsored the rebuilding of Zhung temple itself in 1914 (ibid.).

I will have more to say about most of these events and people later on. The point here is that this rash of costly religious work betokens, among many other things, a general rise in wealth of the Sherpas during this period, and particularly—as I will concentrate on in this chapter—a rise in wealth of the Sherpa big people.

THE EFFECTS OF THE BRITISH IN DARJEELING IN THE SECOND HALF OF THE NINETEENTH CENTURY

In the second half of the nineteenth century, the British adopted a policy of much more active economic development in India, including the building of large-scale transport (roads, railroads) and economic improvement (for example, irrigation) systems (Spear 1965). They also began investing in commercial crop cultivation, of which a pertinent example is the development of the tea industry in Darjeeling (English 1985; Dozey 1916).

The more active and expanding presence of the British in the Himalayan border areas worked on two distinguishable levels. Politically, it provoked government reactions in the neighboring Himalayan states. Generally speaking, at this level the British were seen—correctly—as an enormous threat. But economically, British activity in the northernmost Indian regions tended to open up a wide range of opportunities for wage labor, trade, and petty (even grand) entrepreneurship. These either enhanced existing patterns of opportunity, or offered attractive alternatives to existing economic binds. At this level, the effects of the British presence were basically positive, at least in the short run. The Sherpas were little affected by the many political and military conflicts between the British on the one hand, and the Nepali, Tibetan, and other regional states on the other. But they were greatly affected by the economic changes in the region. (For an excellent overview of the impact of the British raj in India on the Himalayan region, see English 1985.)

The British had been in India since the sixteenth century, but the beginnings of the empire are generally dated from 1765, when the British government took control of the British East India Company. At about the same time (1769) the Gorkhas conquered Kathmandu, and in 1772–74 they conquered all of eastern Nepal as well as much of what is now Sikkim. The British in India were concerned about Gorkha expansion, both eastward and westward across the Himalayas. They feared Gorkha control of all the trade routes into Tibet, to which the Company itself sought independent access and control. There was a war between the Company and Nepal in 1814–16, one of the outcomes of which was that the British repossessed the Sikkim corridor from the Gorkhas, who had conquered it, and returned it to the Chogyal, the Religion King, of Sikkim (Rose and Scholz 1980:ch. 1; Stiller 1973:ch. 12).

As a result of the war with Nepal, and despite the fact that they won, the British came to the conclusion that they would not be able to hold and govern the country, with its strong Gorkha fighters and its enormously difficult terrain. But they were still interested in establishing their own trade routes into Tibet, as well as into western China and Inner Asia, and for this reason they took a great interest in the Sikkim corridor, which connected India and Tibet between the two strong states of Nepal and Bhutan, but which was itself a relatively weak state—indeed, it had earlier been conquered by the Gorkha forces.

When the British restored Sikkim's independence after the war with Nepal, the Chogyal ruler became a British dependent (Kotturan 1983:59). Shortly thereafter, the Company decided that the site of a village called Dorje Ling, south of the capital of Sikkim, would make an excellent site for a sanitorium and a summer resort (a "hill station") for company officials, and offered to buy or trade for it with the Chogyal. The Chogyal then diplomatically presented it as a "gift" to the British in 1835 (ibid.).[3]

Various factions in Sikkim were unhappy with Sikkim's dependent status, and after the cession of Darjeeling, relations with the British in the area grew worse. The Sikkimese carried out various raids, kidnappings, and other indignities against the British, and the Company in 1861 sent an armed force to Sikkim and reduced it from the status of an independent state to that of a so-called native state (of India) (ibid., pp. 63–67). The area was rounded out to its present boundaries in 1865, when the British annexed the eastern portion of it, including the trans-Himalayan trade entrepôt of Kalimpong, from Bhutan in retaliation for Bhutanese raids (Dozey 1916:ch. 1; see also Rose 1977).

It was after that time (1865) that local economic development began to accelerate. The first tea plantations had been established in 1841, and the industry was organized in 1856 (Dozey 1916:191–213). But the crucial turning point for the development of the area, for both the local tea industry and the trans-Himalayan trade, rested on the building of the infrastructure of mechanized transport—roads and railways in this very steep, hilly region cut by numerous gorges and rivers. A road connecting Darjeeling with the Grand Trunk Road on the plains of India was completed in 1866 (ibid., p. 4), and a road from Darjeeling north to the Tibetan border at the Jelap pass was completed in 1877 (Kotturan 1983:71). In addition, railroad connections between Calcutta and Darjeeling were constructed between 1855 and 1878 (Dozey 1916:8–10).

It is in this period that Sherpas from all levels of the society began going to Darjeeling to make money. The founder of the second Sherpa monastery, a man called Sangye, made the beginnings of his fortune in Darjeeling, and his story illustrates well the way in which many (big) Sherpas were able to capitalize on British economic opportunities and turn them to their own interests. This was true (as will be discussed in chapter 8) for many of the small people as well. The British effect on the Sherpas was largely favorable; their material situation improved while they were never dominated politically. I will tell Sangye's story here as a way of illustrating this process, and also of introducing a major figure in the twentieth-century monastery foundings with which this study is concerned.

Sangye was born around 1856,[4] in Zhung village in Solu, site of the noncelibate temple founded amid violence and miracles in 1720. Sangye was the third of four sons of a man called Karma Chotar, who was both a married lama and the local pembu. Sangye had classic middle-brother problems. His older brother, also called Karma, would inherit their father's government position, while his younger brother would, in accordance with Sherpa inheritance norms, inherit the best part of the parents' estate. In particular, the youngest brother would inherit the parental house and household effects, and one of the main problems of the other brothers was simply to establish an independent place to live. It is evident that the father did not have enough houses for all four sons. The eldest brother Karma would later build (or rebuild) a fine house at a site called Tewa Gondak, just up (straight up) the hill from Zhung village, and Sangye would later build a magnificent house in another location in Solu.

Sangye's older brother Karma went into trade with great success. Sangye may have traded together with Karma for some time; they are known to have cosponsored some religious work in Tibet, and their joint presence across the Himalayas in Tibet suggests they were trading together. But when he was in his early thirties, Sangye decided to try his luck in Darjeeling. He had been married to a woman seven years his senior, and together they went to Darjeeling around the time of the British-Tibetan clash in Sikkim in 1888. This was evidently a daring move, since at that time (and up to the 1930s), Sherpas who spent time in Darjeeling were defined as polluted vis-à-vis their home community, and had to be purified before they could reenter the village (B. Miller 1958:238). (This seems to have been a state Hinduism policy, rather than an indigenous Sherpa rule, but apparently the Sherpa pembu were enforcing it locally. See chapter 8.) But Sangye and his wife were willing to risk some trouble, given the enormous money-making opportunities for anyone with the enterprise and skill to take advantage of the situation. Sangye set himself up as a labor contractor for two road construction projects in the Darjeeling area.[5] With the aid of his wife, who is described by informants as hardworking and clever in financial affairs, and who had a great deal of influence over Sangye, he made a substantial amount of money.

Sangye stayed in Darjeeling for three or four years, and then returned with his wife and money to Solu. He was in his late thirties. At this point he had the resources to launch an independent career, apart from, and eventually in competition with, his brother Karma. He did some trading in Tibet, in Nepalese paper and iron. For a while he had a contract for delivery into Tibet of iron mined and smelted in Those, a small Nepalese village west of Solu (von Fürer-Haimendorf 1975:62). But his main activities increasingly centered on the gains to be made through government employment, in the pembuship, and also in other government positions that were becoming available under the Rana regime.

A great deal more about Sangye will follow. At this point it should simply be noted that Sangye used the British in Darjeeling, at a certain stage in his life, precisely as a first attempt to get around the inheritance problem, to generate new resources for himself, and to launch what would be a brilliant economic career. According to one of his descendants, he never actually took *any part* of the family inheritance to which he was due, a classic instance of the situation in which, despite the equal inheritance rule, some brother(s) wind up with all, and some wind up with none. In the course of his lifetime, the Darjeeling money would be parlayed into probably the largest fortune in Solu-Khumbu.

TRADE AND PROFIT: THE FURTHER ENRICHMENT OF THE BIG PEOPLE

While Sangye (and probably other big people) began to amass a fortune by taking advantage of novel economic opportunities in British India, the other three major sponsors of the modern monastery foundings made their money largely through trade. Trade was the more traditional route to wealth, but its profitability apparently increased dramatically in this period, again as a result of British economic activity. In this section the possible sources for the increased profitability will be sketched. The sketch will be quite tentative, since a substantial analysis of the regional economy as it affected Solu-Khumbu would extend far beyond the space limits of this book.

The economic effects of the British presence in India in the second half of the nineteenth century are vast, complex, and also contradictory. Simply within the microregion of the Sikkim corridor, contradictory economic trends can be seen. On the one hand, the British were trying to establish trade routes and trade monopolies that would in some cases compete directly with the Sherpa traders' means of earning their wealth. For example, some Sherpa traders had been carrying iron for trade from Those over the Nangpa La into Tibet. After the completion of the road between Gangtok/Kalimpong and the plains, in the 1870s, this trade began to decline, and it dried up completely by the 1930s (von Fürer-Haimendorf 1975:62). It is possible that Sangye gave up his trade in Those iron in the 1890s because it was becoming unprofitable.

On the other hand, Sherpa traders (and particularly the monastery founders) are known to have done extremely well in this period, and the best guess is that this success was in large part the result of favorable economic conditions created by British development activity in the region. British road and railroad building created various local

Sangye, founder of Chiwong monastery; early-twentieth-century photo.

(and probably temporary and shifting) booms in various parts of southern and eastern Nepal. One of the most significantly affected areas was the so-called Tarai, an extension of the Ganges plain along the southern border of Nepal (see Tucker 1979). The Tarai was one of the end points of the Sherpa traders' routes; it was there that they sold Tibetan horses and ponies, and it was one of the places in which they bought rice and other lowland grains for sale in Tibet.

The Tarai experienced tremendous economic growth in the late nineteenth century. As M. C. Regmi tells us:

> The latter part of the 19th century also witnessed a big spurt in economic activity in northern India, mainly because of the development of railway transport facilities. This inevitably had spread effects on the Tarai region of Nepal. By the end of the 19th century, India's railway network had touched the Nepal-India border at several points. The construction of railway tracks led to an increased demand for construction materials, such as timber and boulders, which were readily and abundantly available in the Tarai region of Nepal. Of greater importance was the fillip the new transport facilities gave to the production and export of such agricultural commodities as rice and jute from the Tarai region. These developments opened up unprecedented prospects for agricultural expansion in the Tarai region (1978:140).[6]

There were other sources of economic improvement on the traders' routes. Sherpa traders sold most of their Tibetan salt in the middle hills regions of the districts to the east of Solu-Khumbu, and brought back from these regions, as from the Tarai, the warm-weather grains they traded in Tibet. These were the regions from which most of the tea plantation and other construction labor in Darjeeling and Kalimpong was drawn (see, for example, Caplan 1970; Kotturan 1983; Nakane 1966). Although many of the people from these regions who went to do labor actually emigrated permanently, it would also seem likely that some of them either brought or sent back some part of the wages they earned, thereby providing the local people with more resources with which to buy the Sherpa traders' goods. There was also significant Brahman migration *into* these regions, and the Brahmans seem to have been quite successful economically (Caplan 1970). Their economic success may also have enhanced trade conditions for the Sherpas.

At the Tibetan end of the traders' routes, the region of D'ingri, adjacent to Khumbu on the other side of the Himalayas, was also apparently enjoying economic growth. It is not clear why this should have been the case, except perhaps that the volume of trade throughout the region was up. In any event, Aziz comments on rapid social/economic expansion in the region since the end of the nineteenth century (1978:33), and one is inclined to think this expansion began a bit earlier, because the founding of a major monastery in the region in 1902 (Rumbu, about which much more later) suggests that significant wealth had already accumulated, and significant population growth (mostly, as Aziz tells us, from in-migration) had already taken place. Thus the Sherpa traders in the late nineteenth century may have found excellent economic conditions at most of the end points of their trading routes, compensating for British competition in iron (and probably in other goods as well), and also compensating for the inflation of prices that the British activity in the area probably produced.

Yet to know that the volume or profitability of trade was up in the region is not to know why and how a particular trader got rich. Opportunities exist, but also constraints; people must have or create the ability to take advantage of the opportunities. Just as Sangye overcame certain restrictions against working in India, and seized the British opportunity, so the other big people who would eventually be involved in the monastery foundings had to surmount certain obstacles in order to take maximum advantage of the trade boom. Specifically, there emerges another (variety of a) structure of conjuncture. It was seen in the last chapter that the Nepal state implemented a trade restriction in 1828, prohibiting traders from the lower Solu region from trading directly into Tibet, and requiring instead that they sell their goods to Nauje traders in Khumbu. These in turn had a monopoly on the final leg of trade over the Himalayas (see also Oppitz 1968:52; von Fürer-Haimendorf 1975:61). Now, all the big people involved in the foundings of the first two celibate monasteries in the early twentieth century were traders originally from the lower region of Solu. They thus would have come under the government restriction against trading in Tibet, and would have had to give up a good part of their profits to the Nauje traders. But for the people ultimately involved in founding the first monastery, it seems that this restriction was taken as a challenge, and means were devised for getting around it. As in the last section, I will take this opportunity to introduce some of these individuals, in this case Karma, the senior sponsor of Tengboche, and his son-in-law Kusang, the only one of the four original founders still alive (in his early nineties) at the time of the fieldwork for this project. The stories of the early careers of these men will illustrate the way in which some Sherpa traders creatively positioned themselves to maximize their profits from British-generated opportunities.

Karma was born in 1850, the eldest son of the lama and pembu Karma Chotar. Like his younger brother Sangye, Karma was born in Zhung village, in Solu. It is assumed by modern Sherpas that the father, Karma Chotar, became reasonably wealthy as a result of his tax collecting work. It was the father, too, who originally made the Kathmandu contacts that were to become so important for this family later. As eldest son, Karma at some point took over the pembu/tax collecting post from his father.

But Karma's major economic activity was long-distance trade. The 1828 restriction on Solu residents trading into Tibet was still in effect, but Karma was evidently unwilling to accept the constraint. His scheme for getting around it was to marry his daughter to a young man who was prepared to challenge the system. The young man—Kusang by name—was from the Solu village of Takto, just around the ridge from Zhung. Kusang was the son of another wealthy trading family, and he had either moved up to the Nauje area already (actually to Khumjung), or he did so at Karma's suggestion, as part of a joint scheme that would benefit both of them. (It can be noted only in passing that, in contrast with the relationship between Sherpa brothers, which is often competitive and strained, the relationship between Sherpa male in-laws is often quite cooperative, and colored with positive feelings.) The marriage of daughters of the main lineages of the Lama clan to prominent Nauje (including Khumjung) men was continued long after the trading restriction was lifted, becoming a common practice that has extended into modern times. But Karma and his son-in-law Kusang apparently started it in the late nineteenth century, and both went on to make a great deal of money from trade in that era.[7] Later in his life, Karma moved up to Khumjung as well, and when the notion of founding the first Sherpa monastery was launched, with Karma and Kusang as two of its three main sponsors, it was sited in the upper Khumbu region despite the Solu origins of these two men.

The Continuing Contradictory Impact of the Nepal State

I have been following the impact of the British presence in north India on the Sherpa big people, as illustrated by the careers of some of the monastery founders. For them, the projects of the raj appeared almost entirely as positive opportunities, ways of earning wealth and thereby resolving their own internal (for example, inheritance) problems. Nor is this only true for the big people; in chapter 8 I will show that the small people used British-generated wage labor the way the big people used favorable trade conditions and entrepreneurial opportunites—to enhance their material circumstances and thereby creatively resolve their structural difficulties. The world system here is thus taken almost entirely on Sherpa social and cultural terms.

But the British were not the only source of opportunity for generating wealth beyond the internal economy; the Nepal state was another. The state in fact played several different, and contradictory, roles in Sherpa history as discussed in the last chapter. That discussion will be continued here for the period leading up to the foundings of the monasteries. On the one hand the state offered, like the British, opportunities for enrichment, and this will be discussed first. On the other hand it had a number of negative effects, including the fueling of rivalries among big people, and the continued undermining of the legitimacy of the big people vis-à-vis the small. The treatment of these issues will again be illustrated with incidents from the careers of the monastery founders.

THE STATE AS A SOURCE OF WEALTH

The normal way in which an individual could gain wealth through the state was to serve as a tax collector, gaining from that position a percentage of the taxes and certain rights to free labor from the villagers. In addition to tax collecting, however, there were other ways in which an individual could derive economic benefit from the state, including acquiring trade protection (seen in the last chapter) and also privileges in the acquisition of landholdings.

One example of this last possibility predates the Rana period under consideration here. The lama who founded the temple at Chalsa, in Solu, is reported to have received a *birta* land grant from the state in the earlier part of the nineteenth century.[8] This lama was reportedly very skilled at rain making and successfully made rain for the king of Nepal. The king was pleased and rewarded the lama with a birta land grant, which his family still holds.

But again the best example of the state as a major source of wealth, and at the same time of the clever utilization of state wealth-generating opportunities, comes from the monastery founder Sangye, the man who as a youth had gone off to Darjeeling and exploited that novel opportunity as well. After Sangye returned from Darjeeling, he did some trading for a while. At one point in his life, he became the steward (*naike*) of a government dairy farm in Solu; later he also became a pembu (or, as it was called in Nepali, *dware*) tax collector. But what Sangye did with these positions was, again, relatively unique, at least for a Sherpa in that historical era: he used his contacts in the Nepali state apparatus to acquire large landholdings in eastern Nepal.

The first parcel was obtained shortly after Sangye was appointed pembu, when the government dairy farm in the Phaphlu area was shut down by the government, and the land on which it was situated went up for grabs. Both Sangye and another man (a Chhetri, a high-caste Hindu Nepali) claimed it, or bid for it. The case went to court, and Sangye, possibly because of his contacts, won the case and got the land. The land was mostly forested, but had good soil, and today much of it has been cleared and turned into a highly productive agricultural estate. The land may also have carried with it at least some tenant families that had been bound to provide the labor on the dairy farm, and that subsequently would have been obligated to provide labor for Sangye's agricultural activities.

Similarly, Sangye acquired a rice-growing village belonging to members of another ethnic group, the Rai, to the east of Solu, with rights to collect rents, taxes, and labor from its inhabitants. The previous landlord had failed to pay the taxes for this village, the government confiscated the area, and Sangye successfully bid to take over the tax collections and payments. In the case of both the Phaphlu lands and the Rai village, he did not actually pay any money; he simply agreed to pay the taxes henceforth, and was given the titles. As one of his descendants put it, "At that time, there was much luck."

Sangye thus used the political system not so much as a backup for his trading activities, which was the traditional pattern, but as a mechanism for acquiring land, the main value of which was the further tax, rent, and labor revenues it generated. It is known that he came to own other low-altitude lands as well, since he is said to have had the tea rations for the Chiwong monks delivered from tea-producing lands he owned in the south.[9]

The state thus made it possible for some people to become very wealthy in this era. These effects of the state joined with the effects of the British to contribute to an apparent overall rise in wealth of the Sherpa big people at this time, much beyond any level that had been achieved before. At the same time, since the state, unlike the British, did have direct political power over the Sherpas, it also had certain more problematic effects. In particular, it put pressure on the Sherpa political order, exacerbating the inherent contradictions of that order. I examined some of these dynamics in the last chapter with respect to the period under Gorkha rule, and I continue the discussion now in relation to the Rana period. Here I will be able to show more directly how some of these pressures manifested themselves at the local Sherpa level, and became linked with the foundings of the monasteries in the early twentieth century.

MORE PEMBU CONFLICT

It will be useful at this point to review the structure and functioning of the pembu political order in Solu-Khumbu. Pembu may be defined as people who for one reason or another claim or have the right to collect some sort of revenues among the Sherpas. In the pre-state period, the revenues they collected may have largely been in the nature of "rents" from nonkin living on land owned by a kin group. Once the Sherpas came under state control, it was probably these individuals who were then appointed by the state to collect taxes from all residents, including their own kin, and to transmit them to the state. The positions generated a certain amount of goods, labor, and power, as well as—potentially—prestige.

I argued earlier that the very existence of pembu political control was contradictory to Sherpa egalitarianism. While senior kinsmen, such as the individuals who led the migrations into Nepal, may be acknowledged to be entitled to some respect and authority (and even here this very much depends on the qualities of the individual), unrelated men are not considered to have any significant power or authority over one another. All claims of such power and authority are thus intrinsically weak, and require a constant process of practical validation and legitimation.

The weakness of pembu claims of authority had several different manifestations. At the level of the "big" people, it meant that individuals were constantly competing with one another for these positions. Since no individual's rights to the position were ever wholly secure and legitimate, another individual could always come along and mount a political challenge. Second, in terms of big/small relations, it meant that a pembu's standing in the eyes of the small people made a difference. Small people could exert leverage in the competition between two big individuals by putting their support behind the more desirable candidate from their point of view. The two levels thus interacted with one another to sustain the general shakiness of pembu domination: lack of legitimacy in the eyes of the small people kept individuals open to rivalrous challenge; lack of security vis-à-vis big rivals gave the small people political leverage. The impact of Nepal state policies on the Sherpas must be understood in terms of their interactions with this structure. I begin with the exacerbation of rivalries between big people.

At least since the period of the foundings of the early temples, Sherpa pembu have competed with one another, and even tried—at least mythically—to kill one another. At the start of the monastery-founding period, stories of major conflicts among pembu, and specifically involving several of the monastery founders, begin to reappear. While pembu conflicts were probably recurrent over the centuries in between, they do not appear to have been inscribed in oral memory. The preservation of the stories about the particular conflicts to be considered here is almost certainly related to the fact that they are tied up with monastery foundings (the same can be said about the stories of pembu conflict leading up to the foundings of the early noncelibate temples in the late seventeenth and early eighteenth centuries). But I am also inclined to think that there was an actual intensification of pembu conflict in this period, for at least two reasons: first, because the overall rise in wealth of the region meant there were more gains to be made from the positions; and second, because the state was destabilizing the positions and making any given pembu weaker and more open to challenge. In any event, there are two cases of pembu conflict of great interest for the story of the monastery foundings, and for the analysis of the dynamics of that process. The first involves the brothers Karma and Sangye.

It will be recalled that their father, Karma Chotar, was both a married lama and a pembu. As eldest son, Karma had inherited the pembu position from his father. Meanwhile, a new government installation was created in the Solu region, a cattle farm that was to supply dairy products to the king. The operation of the farm was to be overseen by a naike, or steward, and the disposition of this position is the subject of conflicting accounts. In some accounts, Sangye held the position first, then Karma took it away from him, then later Sangye took it back. In other accounts, Karma was responsible for getting Sangye the position in the first place, with the implication that he was within his rights to take it over himself later. This latter story is more plausible, since Karma was the elder brother, and was initially the one who had the Kathmandu contacts that would have brought the position into the family.

Sangye went off to Darjeeling to make bigger money, and it was perhaps while he was away that Karma took over the naike position, thus holding both of the lucrative government posts (naike and pembu) in the region. It seems that the conflict between the two brothers began after Sangye returned from Darjeeling, having become independently wealthy. Sangye began to make moves to recoup his political position. He did some trading, but more important, he began to cultivate an independent relationship with Karma's Kathmandu contact, the Rana official (and later prime minister of Nepal) Juddha Shamsher. He thus succeeded in getting the naike position on the cattle farm transferred back to himself. Karma was still pembu (dware), or tax collector, for the region, but eventually Sangye pushed him out of that position as well.[10] According to most informants, Karma and Sangye then had a major falling out, in some accounts culminating in at least the threat of physical violence:

> Karma being *teka* [contractor, tax collector], and Sangye being his brother, and another teka, they were not very friendly, and Karma took the job away from Sangye. Sangye hit Karma [but this same informant said in another interview that there never was any actual physical hitting, just "thinking"]. Sangye had four strong fighting sons, while Karma had only one son and four sons-in-law, so Karma just sat down and didn't fight back. He traveled to many places and ultimately became a sponsor of Tengboche monastery.[11]

The conflict between the brothers strikingly illustrates the ways in which external forces worked into internal structures. (Note the linkage in the quote: "Sangye being his brother and another teka, they were not very friendly.") Both brothers used both the state and the raj as opportunities for gaining wealth. Both were creative in doing so, Karma through affinal maneuvering into the Nauje trade monopoly, Sangye through a kind of entrepreneurial daring that enabled him to flaunt local "purification" rules, and to move confidently into an unknown economic system and make money from it. Sangye's success in turn allowed him to overcome the disabilities of middle-brother status, with respect to inheritance and other less tangible benefits of both the eldest and youngest positions. Yet the relationship between Karma and Sangye was strained by the local operation of these forces. It is known that the brother relationship is latently competitive purely in structural terms. The same informant who described the confrontation between the two emphasized the competitiveness inherent in the fact that they were brothers: "Being brothers," he repeated at another point in the interview, "they did not get along." But external forces added new resources for them to compete over (the naike position is a perfect example). External forces (in the form of free enterprise under the raj) also gave the younger brother a more decisive advantage than perhaps he would have been able to gain before. Thus Sangye reached a position of wealth and power from which he felt able to bully his older brother.

The other major conflict involving a monastery founder concerns the last individual to be introduced, a man called Sherap Tsepal, who became gembu, or head tax collector, for the whole Solu-Khumbu region, and who also committed—allegedly—the only known murder in modern Sherpa history. Tsepal's story revolves around the office of gembu. It will be recalled that the gembu position was apparently created in the early nineteenth century by the Gorkha state. The original creation of the gembuship appears to have involved some conflict, since there are stories about fights between the people of

Khumjung (where the new gembu office was to be located) and the people of Pangboche (where the old, and now superseded, pembuship was located). But there is no indication of further conflict over this office in the course of the nineteenth century, and indeed there is some evidence that it was passed on peacefully from grandfather to father to son until the events to be described here occurred (von Fürer-Haimendorf 1964:121).

Sherap Tsepal was born in the village of Gole; like all the other founders he was a native of the lower region of Solu.[12] Like the others too, he was a trader, and like Karma and Karma's son-in-law Kusang, he sought to get around the trading restrictions, in his case by marrying a Nauje woman and moving to Nauje. And finally, like the brothers Karma and Sangye, he held several government positions, first as pembu, and later as gembu.[13]

The turning point of his story begins in 1895. Sherap Tsepal was living in Nauje, apparently acting as a pembu under the authority of the gembu, a man called Dorje. This Dorje was the grandson and son of previous gembu (hence my comment about the earlier stability of gembu transmission), but apparently he was not doing a very good job. Thus in 1895 "he was dismissed by a touring government official on the grounds of inefficiency and lack of co-operativeness" (von Fürer-Haimendorf 1964:120). And in place of Dorje, Sherap Tsepal was appointed to the gembuship: "In his place Chopal [Tsepal] of Gole clan, a Sherpa from Solu settled in Namche Bazar, was appointed *gembu*" (ibid.).

Tsepal—thereafter always called Gembu Tsepal—held the office for some years. When the idea of founding the first monastery began to develop, he was approached to become one of the sponsors and he agreed. But he was apparently having trouble controlling one of his subordinate pembu. According to von Fürer-Haimendorf:

> In an attempt to curb the high-handedness of one of the pembu . . . and bring him to justice, he aroused the wrath of the latter's supporters, who in turn tried to murder [Tsepal]. The plot was abortive but in the course of the resultant disturbances Dorje, the dismissed *gembu*, was wounded and two other people were killed. (1964:120–21)[14]

In the versions I heard, only one man was killed. Whether Gembu Tsepal did in fact kill the man—in one account a member of the Lama clan—is unclear. In any event, Tsepal fled to Lhasa, although he honored his commitment as sponsor of Tengboche through the agency of his wife and son, who remained in Khumbu and were active in the organization of the construction work.

After Tsepal fled to Tibet, his son seemed to inherit the position. But the son was apparently unable to establish his authority. There was continuing friction and ill-feeling with the Khumbu people, and he moved back to Solu. The official gembu position, with authority over all the pembu, was allowed by the state to slide into disuse. The title continued to be used by the son, but the state began once again to deal directly with the individual pembu (von Fürer-Haimendorf 1964:121).

The Tsepal case illustrates other ways in which the policies of the Nepal state pressed upon Sherpa political relations and exacerbated ongoing contradictions. In particular, state moves to control the pembu destabilized an already fragile legitimacy in various ways, and increased the level, and the seriousness, of big-man conflict. The Tsepal murder story is after all the first known murder in Solu-Khumbu since the killing of Zongnamba and his subjects in the early eighteenth century.

The de-legitimation dynamic works at several different levels. On the one hand, the state created the gembu position in the first place presumably to control, or at least to coordinate, the growing number of pembu. Yet this added another level of (non-seniority-based) hierarchy to a structure that was already intolerant of such hierarchy. Moreover, unlike the pembu position, which once upon a time had an indigenous origin, and was legitimated at least in part through indigenous idioms of kinship and charisma, the gembu position was entirely an exogenous state creation. One may guess then that the gembu had virtually no internal authority at all. As long as he did not seek to exert real power in the execution of his office, he was tolerated by the Sherpas. This seems to have been the case with the ex-gembu (and murder victim) Dorje, who seems to have been rather desultory in the execution of his duties, since he was dismissed by Rana state officials for "inefficiency and lack of co-operativeness" (ibid.). On the other hand, when someone like Tsepal did seek to exert the power the state had bestowed upon him, that is, when he attempted to do what he was there to do—"curb the high-handedness of one of the pembu" (ibid.)—mayhem ensued.

The gembu position in turn undermined legitimacy throughout the political order. By the sheer fact of the gembu's existence, the pembu beneath him were both demoted to second place in the local power structure and placed under a control that was not distant and therefore abstract (like that of the Ranas in Kathmandu), but local and immediate. In the end, the gembu even represented a contradiction with respect to the state's own objectives, since the state did not want local authorities to become too powerful. Thus an alternate reading of the events just recounted might be that Dorje had in fact been gaining significant local power, which was precisely what made him inefficient and uncooperative from the state's point of view. His superiors dismissed him and appointed Tsepal, who seemed more willing to execute their policies, but by that token Tsepal could not gain legitimacy, and eventually things blew up. The Tsepal murder events in turn suggested to the state that the contradictions in the gembu position were insoluble, and the position was allowed to lapse.

The history of Tsepal's gembuship is another instance of the ways in which larger political-economic forces seem to have increased conflict, or the seriousness of conflict, between big people in the late nineteenth and early twentieth centuries. What remains to be considered is the changing relationship between big people and small, as a result of state policies in this era.

Further Political Erosion

I have indicated that the Sherpas probably came under the Nepal state's control in the early eighteenth century, and were probably inherited by the Gorkhas when the latter conquered the state in the late eighteenth century. The Gorkhas in turn were displaced by a minor branch of their own family, later to be known as the Ranas, in 1846. (The Rana coup emerged in part from internal debates in Nepal about the stance Nepal ought to take vis-à-vis the British [see, for example, Oldfield (1855) 1974:chs. 24–27].) Like earlier rulers, the Ranas treated the country as a private estate and a source of personal enrichment. Their main interest was in enhancing revenue collections, and they instituted a variety of measures toward this end. As Regmi put it,

> Under the Rana political system, the Rana family held a monopoly in political power through which it controlled and exploited the nation's resources for its own benefit . . . [I]ndividuals and groups who fulfilled no economic function were able to appropriate the major portion of what the peasant produced, whereas the peasant himself was left permanently stripped of capital. (1978:28–29)

Similarly, Rose and Scholz call the Rana regime "authoritarian . . . and blatantly exploitative" (1980:30; see also English 1985; Höfer 1979).

Despite a variety of tax and corvée exemptions, the Sherpas were apparently squeezed by Rana exactions in the late nineteenth and early twentieth centuries (Regmi says that the regime of Bir Shumshere [Rana], from 1885 to 1901, "became progressively revenue oriented" [1978:26]). The Sherpas were basically freeholders, and it does not appear from the historical records that there had been any widespread tenantry or agrarian indebtedness in earlier eras. Yet by the early twentieth century there are indications that these patterns had appeared. I heard of several cases of debt bondage in living memory during my fieldwork. One young man commented, "In the old days, rich people would lend money at usurious rates and then people would have to sell themselves to them as servants if they could not pay up." Robert Miller also reports the following, from Sherpa informants in Darjeeling in the 1950s who were apparently talking about the 1920s or 1930s:

> There were a few rich families, but most Khumbuwa (the local designation for Sherpa resident in Khumbu) were tenants working the lands of absentee landlords. Many were in debt to the richer families or to the Buddhist monasteries in the region. Added to the local indebtedness, the Nepalese government assessed an annual tax. (R. Miller 1965:245)

Miller's comments must be taken with some caution, as he never visited Solu-Khumbu, and the Solu-Khumbu Sherpas in Darjeeling were not even the objects of his research. Von Fürer-Haimendorf was working in Khumbu itself at the same time that Miller worked in Darjeeling, and did not uncover a vast system of tenantry and debt slavery in Khumbu. Nonetheless, I think there were at least some instances of this sort of impoverishment in Solu-Khumbu under the Ranas, and in any event a local sense that the threat of such things was looming much larger than it had in the past. One indication of this is the growing amount of migration to Darjeeling, which will be discussed in the next chapter.

The big people here played a negative role in two ways. Insofar as the big people were the tax collectors, they represented the unwelcome demands of the alien and illegitimate state. But even if they had no official position, they acted as moneylenders, so that people could obtain cash to pay their taxes. But then if the people could not repay their loans, they could lose their lands and be reduced to either tenantry or debt slavery.

Such economic squeezing would in itself have cost the big people a great deal of social legitimacy in the Sherpa community. In addition, however, it was part of Rana policy to continue the process of transforming tax collectors from independent agents to salaried officials. The Ranas did not entirely succeed, but they still took care to emphasize that the collectors were merely their functionaries, and that the ordinary villagers had what were in effect rights against abuse and ill treatment on the part of the elite, and could complain to the state if such abuses arose. The state thus contributed, quite intentionally, to the continuing weakening of legitimacy of the local elites, including the Sherpa big people.

M. C. Regmi's studies of the political economy of Nepal under the Ranas emphasize the state's competition with other landowners and other elites, and its attempts to establish the primacy of its own rights, both economic and political. Speaking of big landowners he says, "Measures were . . . taken from time to time to bring *rajas*, *birta*-owners, and *jagirdars* [different kinds of landholding elites] under the tighter control of the central government" (1978:47). While the Ranas had to allow them to keep their wealth, they were able to remove some of their authority: "Thanks to these measures, these landlords probably wielded less police and administrative authority over the peasantry by the end of the 19th century than at the time of the commencement of Rana rule" (ibid., pp. 47–48). And while among the Sherpas there were no landowning elites of this sort, since every family was freeholding its own property, there were the traditional "big" people and pembu, who claimed many rights of taxation that the government took as its own. The state thus worked to reduce their authority, as it did in other parts of Nepal. In part it operated through direct edicts and interference. But the sheer fact that the pembu now operated as state agents and functionaries, rather than through their own potency, probably tended in itself to undermine their legitimacy. As Regmi says of other local elites that suffered similar fates in the latter half of the nineteenth century,

> The village elite, even though some of them might have had an ancient origin as the focal point of local leadership under traditional systems of communal authority, thus gradually assumed the role of representatives of the central government through which the landowning elite [of which, in effect, the government was a sector] tightened their economic stranglehold on the peasants. (Ibid., p. 84)

An instance of Rana undermining of local pembu is seen in this 1853 document addressed to the people of Solu-Khumbu by Jang Bahadur (Rana), promulgated in the early years of the Rana regime. The document is a contract between the state and an individual in Zhung for tax collections, for one year only. After a long list of what could and could not be taxed (and there were again many exemptions), and a detailing of how much the collector was expected to pay up, the document concludes with a lengthy exhortation to the collector to be honest, upright, and nonoppressive:

> If you do not pay the installments when they are due, then you must pay a fine. Be fair and do not oppress the folk. Settle people in the country and make it populous. Make the village populous and affluent. Levy no new taxes and do not increase the existing taxes with the exception of those which are indicated in the contract. In the event that crimes occur, listen to the details, speak judiciously, and judge according to the law. Should anyone complain here about the injustices of the person who is Mizar [presumably the addressee of the document], then the agreement is terminated and you shall be held responsible. (Oppitz 1968:67)

As in previous Gorkha documents, then, the state here reiterates that the tax collector does not have the right to be an arbitrary exploiter and power-monger; on the contrary, he is merely a functionary of the state, which will ally itself with the people against such abusive behavior on the part of the local elites.

Jang's decree is very similar in tone and content to earlier Gorkha decrees, stressing that the officials should be fair, and that the state will protect the people against rapacious officials. The difference between the Ranas and their predecessors (and cousins) the Gorkha kings is that the Ranas put more teeth into their constraints, with the institution of the *pajani*, or annual review of local officials (Edwards 1977). And so in 1895 "touring government officials" are recorded in Khumbu dismissing the gembu Dorje, appointing Tsepal to the gembuship, and in general setting in motion some of the events that have been considered in this chapter.

By the early twentieth century, the pembu appear to have had very little legitimacy from a cultural point of view. Although I do not have any direct expressions of Sherpa "class" sentiments from this era, I do have modern expressions of the mutual feelings of big and small people, and these are perhaps indicative of the quality of the relationship in earlier times. In general one finds a sort of mutual dislike and disrespect between the rich and the poor in a Sherpa community (see also Ortner 1978a:ch. 5). Here is an example from the rich side:

> I went to dinner at K's [a middle-status person's] house. KA [the wealthy woman with whom I was staying] was pretty catty about

> the whole business—"We'll cook your dinner here because it probably won't be very good up there." The next day I had a sore throat and mentioned it to KA. [I had forgotten that sore throats are a sign of pollution, often caused by eating food served by a low-status person (see Ortner 1973b).] KA said, "Well, that's what you get when you eat in 'people's' houses."

In another instance, I told another wealthy woman that I was going to stay in an agricultural and dairying village in the west of Khumbu. The woman herself was from Nauje:

> Mrs. A was a big snob about T. village. "What do you want to go there for? It's cold and there's no fuel and the people all have dirty hands from working in the fields. Nauje is much better."

But there were equally negative comments from the lower side:

> I was asking N [a middle-status young man] about native theories of eating and hunger. I asked why people need food at all. He said he didn't know, that it's in a book, but that poor people don't get a chance to look at these books.

> I was asking NH [an upper-middle-status woman] about lama reincarnations, *tulku*. She said that they are born to parents who are not necessarily rich or poor, but who simply have good souls. She then added that rich people generally don't have very good souls.

More generally, there seem to be cultural beliefs that specifically embody the notion that the rich are rich illegitimately, as a result of taking resources that belong to others. Thus:

> KT [a middle-status young man] was discoursing in response to my questions about the difference between the rich and the poor. He said that poor people think rich people get rich by doing sin, e.g., by stealing, or by killing animals and selling the meat, and not because they were good in past lives.

Similarly, there seems to be a notion that the big people reproduce at the expense of the small. One day a son of one of the big families in the village was getting married, and that same day a young man of fifteen died. The wife of one of the village lamas remarked that "every time the ruling family gets married there's a death in the village."

As for the pembu in particular, modern Sherpas remember the system (which was only changed in the 1950s with the overthrow of the Rana dynasty) as hateful and oppressive. One old man in the 1960s recalled with distaste that when the tax collector came around, everyone poured out of their houses with food and firewood and fell all over themselves trying to ingratiate themselves with him. Moreover, pembu were assumed to take bribes, favor the rich, collect "fines" on any pretext, and pocket whatever fines were collected.

> When the *dware* came around, he would announce his arrival by shooting off a gun. The blacksmith would give him a present of a flint, and everyone gave him food and firewood and everything. If there had been no fights, he would collect 2.5 rupees from every house as a matter of principle. If there had been a fight he'd just take the fine. . . . He would settle in favor of the rich party, who would pay him more. If the fight were between two poor people, then he'd collect fifty or a hundred rupees from both sides and tell them to settle it themselves. . . . Everyone [also] had to do five free days of work for the [collector].

Another man said that he never wanted to be a pembu tax collector because the collectors were in effect parasites, getting rich by "eating" other people's money. Indeed the one monastery founder, Kusang, who did not hold a government post said exactly the same thing, and he spat on the floor to emphasize his disgust (see also von Fürer-Haimendorf 1964:121).

The erosion of legitimacy of the big people must be put together with their growing wealth and economic success. The two changes operated partly together and partly separately. Taken by itself, the increasing wealth of the big people would obviously provide much of the material resources for founding the monasteries. It also raised questions for big people about maintaining the unity and value of their estates in the next generation, which in turn had implications for the ways in which they arranged marriages, or considered the monastic option, for their sons and daughters. These issues will be discussed in chapter 9.

But the growing wealth of the big people also interacted with, and exacerbated, the problem of declining legitimacy. Growing wealth meant increased hierarchical differentiation, placing new strains on old contradictions. Growing wealth may have also meant that the big people acted in a more arrogant—ongchermu—manner, producing the kind of irritation on the part of the small people that comes through in the quotations. The support of the small people in turn is critical for the outcome of rivalries between big people. It is in the context of all these shifts in relations—between big men and their rivals, between big people and small, between big people and their children, and even between big people and their consciences—that the foundings of the monasteries must be situated.

CHAPTER

VII

The Big People Found the Monasteries: Legitimation and Self-Worth

I ARRIVE finally at the events that constitute the raison d'être of this whole enterprise, the foundings of the first celibate monasteries in Solu-Khumbu in the early decades of the twentieth century.[1] Having come quite far from chapter 1, it may be well to remind the reader of why the monastery foundings were so significant.

By the early twentieth century, the Sherpas had been in Nepal for almost four centuries. Although they had always (apparently) practiced Tibetan Buddhism, they belonged to the Nyingmapa sect, which probably had no celibate monasteries in the Sherpas' home region of Kham at the time the Sherpas' ancestors emigrated from that region in the sixteenth century (Snellgrove and Richardson 1968). Further, it seems reasonably certain that the early Sherpas in Nepal did not attempt to found celibate monasteries there either. And finally, although there are ethnically Tibetan groups similar to the Sherpas all across the northern border regions of Nepal, and although some of these have certain kinds of celibate arrangements, the Sherpa monastic system was to become the largest and most extensive among them.[2] Thus the founding of celibate monasteries by the Sherpas in the early twentieth century represented a major institutional innovation, both for themselves and for the region.

The question for this book is, why did the monasteries get founded? But one must immediately put this question into the active voice. Why did certain people, at certain moments, find themselves moved to engage in this extraordinary—and it was and is considered extraordinary—activity? Most of the pieces for solving this puzzle are now in hand, but how they fit together remains to be seen.

I began by arguing that there is a fundamental contradiction in

Sherpa society between an egalitarian ethic as seen in diverse manifestations (the equal inheritance rule, the lack of any heritable statuses, the stated equality of all unrelated males, and so forth), and a hierarchical ethic (seen in birth order seniority within the family, public status ranking within the village, and the charismatic authority of certain religious figures). The egalitarianism and the hierarchy constantly destabilize one another, making equality fragile and subject to hierarchical manipulation (as in the way in which, despite the equal inheritance rule, one brother often winds up with more), and making hierarchy weak and subject to challenge. In terms of actors' experiences, this contradiction emerges as a chronic competitiveness in relations between brothers, a chronic competitiveness between political rivals, and a chronic mistrust of most claims of authority.

The general contradiction, and its specific variants within specific relational contexts, are at once reflected in, mediated by, and constituted through meaningful cultural forms. Thus I showed earlier that the Sherpas have stories and rituals that embody a common plot structure, or "schema," in which the hero successfully negotiates one or another of these problematic relations. The contradictions and the schema together constitute a hegemony, a mutually sustaining universe of social experience and symbolic representation through which Sherpa actors would tend to understand themselves, their relationships, and their historical circumstances.

The "outside world" comes up against this complex in two ways. On the one hand it presses on the weak points, on the contradictory relationships that were already giving people trouble. This is the point I have pursued in the last two chapters, particularly with respect to relations among big people, and with respect to relations between big and small people. In particular I have shown that the Nepal state (first the Gorkhas, later the Ranas) tended for its own reasons to undermine the legitimacy of the Sherpa pembu, and that this undermining showed up as one would have expected—in apparently increased conflict between pembu, and in apparently decreased respect and consent on the part of the villagers vis-à-vis the pembu collectors.

The analysis of the two preceding chapters, exploring the impact of external forces on contradictory structures of Sherpa society, sets up a view of the Sherpas as largely passive receptors of, and reactors to, whatever is coming in from the outside. This is partially true, in the sense that they do not have an overview of their total situation and will tend to react to it piecemeal. But it is also partially false, in the sense that the analysis does not reveal how they translate and transform what they experience into something at least meaningful to themselves, and perhaps even valuable and powerful. This is to say that it is still necessary to connect the Sherpas' experience of the Nepal state and the British raj with the foundings of the monasteries and the transformation of Sherpa religion, or rather, to see how they made the connection. This is the task of this and the next two chapters.

The link here is provided by the cultural schema of temple founding: the Sherpas themselves have a logic that links political conflict, and problems of legitimacy, with the foundings of religious institutions. Although in the broadest sense the schema mediates cultural contradictions, provides a recipe for legitimation of the big people, and contributes to the reproduction of the order as constituted, nonetheless it may be read in different ways by actors in different positions. The big people seized upon its legitimation functions, and that point will be explored in the present chapter. On the other hand, the small people appear to have focused on the dimension of the schema in which the hero challenges the established authority; they sought "legitimation" in quite a different sense, as will be discussed in chapter 8. Finally, a new relational weak point in the Sherpa social order began to open up in this era: the relationship between parents and children, especially the children of elites. Elite sons and daughters, whom I call "little-big people," deployed the cultural schema with yet a different set of emphases, and with yet new dimensions to the notion of "legitimation." This process will be explored in chapter 9.

The broadening of the notion of legitimation, central to this final set of chapters, will require some theoretical discussion, but I will defer that discussion until the next chapter. At the moment there is a more immediate need to see that certain issues surrounding the notion of cultural schemas, and particularly of the relationship between cultural schemas and individual action, are clarified.

Actors and Schemas

In this and the coming chapters, I am going to show that the actions of the various participants in the foundings of the monasteries often seem to "follow" the cultural schema. People fight with their rivals, go away, seek protectors, return to "win," and found temples (or in this case monasteries) in "triumph." Losers in these political struggles leave the area in anger and humiliation. The question is, in what sense is it claimed that people "follow" the schema or, in structural terms, in what sense is it claimed that a cultural schema is ordering action, events, history?

Understanding how structures structure is vital to the continuing theoretical health of various forms of cultural and structural analysis. Without such understanding, interpretations that claim to see repeated cultural patterning in social and historical events remain open to the charge that such patterning is imposed by the observer, or alternatively that it is an aesthetic frill. If one wishes to argue on the contrary that such patterning is not only "out there," but that it may have a kind of historical force of its own on a par with the other sorts of forces (individual interest, the inner logic of a social formation, adaptation to environmental conditions, and the like) that are said to shape and drive history, then one must show that there is a comprehensible mechanism by means of which cultural patterning comes to manifest itself in events.

One may envision the positions on this question as a continuum. At one end is what may be called the "soft" or "external" position, concerning the way in which cultural structures operate in social interaction. Here the structures exist as "models" or "symbolic resources" external to actors, on which actors may "draw" in the course of social action. This is essentially the position of the political economists—Wolf (1982) and Fox (1985), among others. The general line here is that people are acting on motives that are commonsensically understandable to the analyst, normally (but not always) some form of rational self-interest. The way in which people enact a particular event thus has nothing much to do with the operation of anything like cultural schemas, such as the one discussed in this book. Insofar as a cultural schema does seem to be operating, this is the result of one or another after-the-fact use of it—to describe what has happened, for example, or to legitimate what has happened.

At the other end of the spectrum there is the "hard," or internal, position. This position holds that cultural schemas may become deeply embedded in actors' identities, as a result of actors growing up within a particular cultural milieu, and as a result of practices (social, ritual, and so on) that repeatedly nourish the schema and its place within the self. In consequence, actors will tend to "do the cultural thing" under most circumstances, and even in some cases under inappropriate circumstances. This is the position that Fox seems to be attacking, or rather, it is the untheorized psychological underpinnings of that position. My own view is that none of the writers who appear to hold it—Bourdieu (1977), Geertz (for example, 1973a, 1973b), Sahlins (1981), Ortner (1973a)—would want to agree that they hold it in this form.[3] Yet in failing to theorize it, that is, in failing to explicate how structures may constrain action and events without "programming" actors, they allow it to stand as an interpretation of their views.

A third position is a combination of several aspects of the other two positions. It begins with the point, as assumed in the external position as well, that people may act for a variety of motives—rational self-interest, genuine spiritual desires, and the like—with no particular intentions (or compulsions) to enact a cultural schema, and no particular tendency to assume that others are doing so either. They may simply be going about their business. Yet even if actors are not themselves enacting a cultural schema, given the fact that the schema is a widely held and pervasively grounded frame of interpretation, *others* will tend to interpret events as if the actors had in fact been following the schema. But—and this is the key point of this middle position—if observers would tend to interpret events in that way, so of course would at least some of the participants. Thus the schema may not begin as part of the events, but insofar as it becomes part of a participant's interpretations, then it enters the event and begins to shape it.

In this view, as in the externalist view, there is a kind of distance between actors' selves and their cultural models, in the sense that not all of a culture's repertoire of symbolic frames will make sense to all actors at all times. Much of the time a cultural story like that of the founding of Zhung temple will seem to any given Sherpa as "just a story," with little relevance for his or her life. Yet there are moments in the course of events when the story seems to make sense of a person's circumstances, and is thus appropriated and internalized. (And as Bourdieu [1977] has emphasized, such moments are not infrequent, since the shape of life in the culture and the shape of cultural stories have at least in part evolved together.) At that point it is no longer "just a story"; it is part of the action, and it takes on structuring force.

In "Patterns of History" (Ortner n.d.a) I emphasized the virtues of the third position. Nonetheless I think the point to stress here is precisely the extreme variability that may exist in the relationship between actors and their cultural universe, at every level—between individuals, across the social spectrum, and across time. People in different social positions will obviously have different relationships to a given cultural form—different interpretations of it, different feelings about it, different senses of its meaningfulness, and so forth. Moreover, these relationships may change over time, evolving into new interpretations, new feelings, new senses of meaningfulness—or meaninglessness. Indeed, talking about culture change really means talking about changes in these *relationships* between actors and culture, as much as, or more than, changes *in* culture.

Thus my claims about how the schema is operating in any given context are flexible. Some actors are manipulating it; some are "driven" by it; some are moved merely by the logic of the moment; and some use the schema to interpret the behavior of others. At one level the variations matter, and I discuss this question at greater length in "Patterns of History" (Ortner n.d.a). But at another level they add up to many modes of "enacting" the schema, the notion of enactment here being a shorthand for the varying ways in which people hold, and are held by, their culture.

The Founding of Tengboche, 1916

KARMA AS HERO

Of the three lay sponsors involved in the founding of Tengboche, the wealthy traders Karma, Kusang, and Gembu Tsepal, Karma is always taken to be the leading figure. He was the oldest, and it was he who was approached first to sponsor the founding. I will thus follow his career first.

Karma was the eldest son of a pembu tax collector from Zhung, in Solu. As eldest son, he inherited the pembu position from his father, as individuals could do if there was no challenge from another person, and if the inheritor was acceptable to the state.

Karma had several younger brothers, one of whom was Sangye, later to found Chiwong monastery. In their youth, Karma and Sangye apparently got along well enough. At some point they went on a pilgrimage together in Tibet and visited the monastery of Tashilhunpo at Shigatse. There was a sizable population of monks there from the Buddhist peoples of Nepal and Ladakh, and Karma and Sangye cosponsored the building of a residence for these monks. There is further evidence of their good relations, or at least of good intentions about the relationship on Karma's part: using his Kathmandu contacts, Karma seems to have got for Sangye the position of steward, or naike, on the government dairy farm established in Solu. Nonetheless, Sangye is believed to have cultivated Karma's Kathmandu contacts behind Karma's back, and (according to most informants) to have had Karma's pembu position transferred to himself.

It was after this, apparently, that Karma left the fine family homestead he had built above Zhung village and moved to a meditation retreat in Khumbu. He was in his early sixties. The meditation retreat had been established on the cliff above Khumjung village by a certain Lama Gulu. Karma and Lama Gulu became good friends. When Lama Gulu was urged by a Tibetan reincarnate lama, the Zatul Rinpoche, to found a celibate monastery in Solu-Khumbu, he turned to the wealthy Karma for financial sponsorship, and Karma agreed. Karma then drew two other Solu natives living in Khumbu at that time into the plan: his son-in-law Kusang, and the head tax collector, Gembu Tsepal. The monastery was started in 1916 and consecrated in 1919.[4]

The story of Karma's life, culminating in the founding of Tengboche, can be cast at least loosely in the mold of the schema of temple founding discussed earlier. *Rivalry*: Karma is the Ego of the story. His younger brother Sangye is the rival, who attempted to displace him through devious means. *Departure of the hero*: Karma then went off, as did the young Dorje Zangbu in the eighteenth-century Zhung temple-founding tale. He moved into the meditation retreat of Lama Gulu in Khumbu and took up religious training. *Acquisition of a protector*: While studying at the retreat, Karma developed a close relationship with Lama Gulu. Through this he acquired by proxy the protection of Lama Gulu's religious teacher, the revered and religiously powerful Zatul Rinpoche. *Defeat of the rival* here identical with *Temple founding*: Under the Zatul Rinpoche's protection, Karma then staged a massive triumph of prestige over his younger brother Sangye, by sponsoring the founding of the first Sherpa monastery. *Departure of the loser*: Sangye then moved out of Zhung village and built himself a house elsewhere, in the manner of a defeated big man who leaves the area.

If Karma was not "following" the schema, his actions nonetheless seem moved at various points by the same pressures and logics that move the hero of the schema. His rivalry with his brother; his departure after an earlier defeat in that rivalry; his cultivation of a relationship with the Zatul Rinpoche, a figure of great charisma (whether to garner his "protection" for further political purposes or not); his founding of Tengboche monastery (which was *taken* as a prestige move by Sangye, whether Karma meant it that way or not)—all of these actions by Karma are part of a cultural logic that was probably experienced piecemeal by the various players, but that appears as a meaningful whole from the perspective of the schema of temple founding.

THE LAMAS AND THE SCHEMA

From the Sherpa point of view the prime movers of the monastery foundings were not the wealthy lay sponsors, but the religious figures involved: the Zatul Rinpoche, and two Sherpa religious specialists from the Khumbu region, Lama Gulu, and the Zamte lama.[5] Since these people have not been introduced in any detail before, it is necessary here to give more background about their lives. I begin with the Zatul Rinpoche, probably the most important figure in Sherpa religious history since Lama Sangwa Dorje. As a matter of fact, he *is* Lama Sangwa Dorje, reincarnated some two hundred years later.

The Zatul Rinpoche (see cover photo) was by all accounts an extraordinarily energetic and enterprising individual.[6] His physical appearance was described by the British climber C. G. Bruce in 1922: "This particular Lama was beyond question a remarkable individual. He was a large, well-made man of about 60, full of dignity, with a most intelligent and wise face and an extraordinarily attractive smile" (1923:45). The lama was born around 1866, in the Tibetan region of D'ing-ri. In 1902, when he was only thirty-six years old, he founded Rumbu (Tib., *rong-phug*) monastery, over the Tibetan border from the Sherpa area, on the north slopes of Mount Everest. Before, the site had been a meditation retreat, and there were a number of small meditation houses clustered there. The lama was one of an estimated 1,700 religious specialists in the region (Aziz 1978:206). When he was a child, he was recognized as a reincarnation, the latest in a long and powerful line that included the Sherpas' own Lama Sangwa Dorje (see von Fürer-Haimendorf 1964:127, 129; Sangye Tenzing 1971:22). He studied in his youth at the major Nyingmapa monastery of Mindroling, near Lhasa, and then returned to his native D'ing-ri region to found Rumbu (most of the above information from Aziz [1978:209ff.]).

The second religious figure to play a major role in these events was the Zamte lama, who appears to have been the dominant lama of Khumbu in that period. The Zamte lama took vows of celibacy at a celibate monastery in Tibet (apparently not at Rumbu), but then returned to Khumbu where he lived as a monk on his own. The son of a wealthy pembu, he also—according to one informant—accrued additional wealth as a result of generous donations from lay people eager to have the service of an ordained *gelung* (a fully ordained monk) for their rituals. In about 1905, close to the time of the founding of Rumbu monastery over the border, the Zamte lama sponsored the founding of a noncelibate temple in Nauje. He planned and oversaw the construction of the building, and provided an endowment for operating expenses as well. He also gradually gathered about himself, in the village of Zamte, a small religious community, including a large number of lay students and four additional fully ordained Sherpa monks. These had taken their vows at the newly burgeoning Rumbu monastery over the Nangpa La.

The final lama involved in the founding of Tengboche was a married lama in the village of Khumjung called Lama Gulu. Born around

1848, he grew to be a man of great piety. As an adult, his family life was quite unhappy. His wife was described as "bad" by a number of informants, and eventually she walked out on him and their children. He also experienced the death of at least one child, his only son (whether before or after the departure of the wife is not clear). He then became embroiled in an extended legal dispute with his in-laws, and had to go to Kathmandu several times to appear in court. Despite all these hardships, however, his spiritual devotion carried him through. He is reported to have said that he did not mind going back and forth to Kathmandu for the legal case—fifteen days of strenuous trekking each way, not to mention endless time waiting for the bureaucratic wheels to turn—because it gave him the opportunity to visit the great Buddhist shrine at Bodnath.

After the departure of his wife, Lama Gulu turned to more intensive pursuit of religion. He went to study in Kham, in eastern Tibet, and spent a number of years there. He returned to Khumbu and moved to a meditation retreat above Khumjung village, where he spent many years, gradually gathering about himself a number of lay students and disciples (including the wealthy Karma). Eventually the ex-wife died, and Lama Gulu then took gelung vows at Rumbu monastery. This would have been some time after the founding of Rumbu in 1902, and Lama Gulu would have been in his early fifties at the youngest.

In taking his vows at Rumbu (and presumably having already spent some time studying there), Lama Gulu established a strong personal relationship with the energetic young head lama, the Zatul Rinpoche. The Zatul Rinpoche evidently saw in Lama Gulu a vehicle for his vision of religious expansion, and Lama Gulu in turn allowed himself to be swept up in the Zatul Rinpoche's nearly boundless zeal and enthusiasm.

It seems that the Zatul Rinpoche was the active party in the relationship. Although some informants said that Lama Gulu had already been thinking of founding a monastic establishment of some sort, most said that it was the Zatul Rinpoche who initiated the idea, and who "ordered" (as it was most frequently put) Lama Gulu to do it. According to one account, Lama Gulu had retired into his meditation retreat, but the Zatul Rinpoche sent him a message not to remain removed from the world, but to go forth and found a monastery. Further, it is said by Lama Gulu's reincarnation (Tengboche Reincarnate Lama n.d.a:5) that when the Zatul Rinpoche ordered Lama Gulu to build the monastery, Lama Gulu immediately thought that he could not do it because he was a poor man. But the Zatul Rinpoche "read his thoughts," and told him to raise the money from wealthy patrons. Still apparently feeling that the task was too difficult,

Statue of Lama Gulu, first head lama of Tengboche monastery.

Lama Gulu proposed a rather modest beginning, with accommodations for perhaps eight monks. But the Zatul Rinpoche told him to think of no such thing, and to plan for a much larger establishment.

The forceful character of the Zatul Rinpoche is also apparent in a rather dramatic move he made to motivate Lama Gulu to overcome his hesitations. He informed Lama Gulu that the two of them had been father and son in a previous existence. Specifically, he said that he, the Zatul Rinpoche, was the reincarnation of the great Sherpa folk hero Lama Sangwa Dorje, and that Lama Gulu was the reincarnation of Lama Sangwa Dorje's *father* (a certain Lama Budi Tsenjen, who was not particularly famous).[7] The Zatul Rinpoche claimed, moreover, that the two, father and son, had been "very close" in their previous shared lifetime. And he said, finally, that there had been a prediction that the (reincarnation of the) father would someday build a monastery. This claim of a prediction is taken by the present Tengboche lama to be the clincher that persuaded Lama Gulu to undertake the founding of Tengboche (Tengboche Reincarnate Lama n.d.a:4).[8]

The monastery was founded and Lama Gulu became its first head. The four celibate monks who had been living with the Zamte lama became the first cohort of Tengboche monks. The Zamte lama eventually left the Khumbu area, claiming ambiguously that there was a vengeful spirit (a *tsen*) around Zamte, or that he himself was afraid of becoming a vengeful tsen after he died.[9] He went off to Sikkim where he is said to have become the personal lama of the king, and never returned to Khumbu.

It is once again a simple matter to strip down and transform the events above into the frame of the schema, with Lama Gulu as the hero, the Zamte lama as the rival, and the Zatul Rinpoche as—of course—the protector. *Rivalry*: The story begins with the Zamte lama as the reigning big (religious) man on the scene, the dominant lama in Khumbu at the time. He had founded the noncelibate village temple in Nauje, he had gone to Tibet and taken monastic vows, and he had begun to organize a small celibate monastic community. He was certainly ahead of Lama Gulu when the story began, both socially (he was from a pembu family) and religiously (he took his monastic vows earlier than Lama Gulu). Lama Gulu, on the other hand, was a modest but highly respected religious individual whose reputation for piety was growing rapidly. Although no direct antagonism is reported between the Zamte lama and Lama Gulu, as the two most senior monks they were in implicit competition for the leadership of the newly emerging monastic community in the region at the time. *Departure of the hero* and *Acquisition of a protector*: Lama Gulu went to Rumbu and took vows. He also acquired a powerful protector—the Zatul Rinpoche—while the Zamte lama did not. Everything then proceeded according to the schema. *Defeat of the rival*: Lama Gulu "defeated" the Zamte lama for the abbotship of the monastery. *Acquisition of the rival's "subjects"*: Lama Gulu then took over the four Zamte disciples, who became the first Tengboche monks. In good structural fashion, *Departure of the loser*: the Zamte lama left the area and never returned. *Temple founding*: Lama Gulu then founded Tengboche.

BUILDING TENGBOCHE: 1916–1919

The site for the new monastery was chosen (by name, sight unseen) by the Zatul Rinpoche. Most accounts by informants include the point that various sites were proposed by various people (accounts differ as to which sites and which people), but that all the other proposed sites were vetoed by the Zatul Rinpoche on the grounds that the site names had negative associations of some sort. For example, the young sponsor Kusang had suggested a place called Tongbo, but it was vetoed because its name sounded too much like a euphemism used to refer to a deceased individual (*tongba*). The present site was chosen by the Zatul Rinpoche as being especially excellent, in large part because Lama Sangwa Dorje had stopped there and left imprints in the rocks while seeking a site for the first Sherpa temple several centuries earlier.

The site in fact is stunning. It is a high flat spur at about 12,500 feet, protruding from a ridge out into the middle of the upper Dudh Khosi valley. From it one has a near 360-degree panorama of Himalayan peaks, including the tip of Mount Everest (29,028 feet) showing out over the top of the ridge running between Nuptse (24,850 feet) and Lhotse (27,890 feet). The monastery, with its red painted temple, black-and-white houses, and gold roof ornaments, sits on the spur in the midst of these white mountain walls and intense blue skies like a perfect jewel, perfectly set. The scene has been photographed so often, and appears on so many postcards and in so many picture books that it is almost a cliché—until one actually sees it with one's own eyes.

Having lined up the main financial sponsors for the building of the central temple, Lama Gulu went around, armed with a letter from the Zatul Rinpoche expressing the latter's spiritual sponsorship, inviting people to volunteer their labor for this highly meritorious venture. The actual building work was begun in 1916.

The operation functioned like any Sherpa construction project. The sponsors paid the wages of skilled workers—the carpenters, and later the painters. They also provided any raw materials that had to be purchased (although the main raw material was stone, which is more than plentiful in Khumbu). And they provided meals for the laborers, buying raw foodstuffs at the weekly market and organizing the cooking and feeding at the site. How much the whole thing cost can probably not be reconstructed. The surviving sponsor Kusang told me in 1979 that he never totaled up his own contribution, since his father-in-law Karma had said to him that if he worried about the cost, he would get no merit. Most of the organizational legwork—purchasing food, organizing daily activities at the construction site, overseeing the preparation of meals—was carried out by Kusang himself.

As for the rest of the people, they voluntarily contributed all the

Tengboche monastery, 1967. Mount Everest (with its usual snow plume) is in the background.

labor, breaking and hauling and fitting stones, and actually constructing the edifice (under the supervision of master craftsmen).[10] They also contributed money, since the sponsors did not finance the interior finishing—wood and woodworking for benches, altar platforms, and cabinets; the making of images and statues; and the purchase of all the religious paraphernalia, such as books and ritual items for the altars.[11] The money for these quite large expenses was raised by Lama Gulu in the form of small donations from "everyone, high and low," as the present head lama put it. Similarly, the sponsors did not provide the endowment for the operating expenses of the monastery. These include, among other things, full lifetime support of the head lama, daily tea for the monks, and the feeding of the monks when they are performing certain rituals. This too was raised by Lama Gulu from among the ordinary villagers, and again, the latter were generous in their donations.

Finally, about three years after the first stones were laid, in the year of the Earth Sheep (*sa luk*), 1919, the external temple structure was completed, and the internal objects essential for the religious life of the temple were installed (the interior painting and woodworking took another year). The Zatul Rinpoche himself came to perform the

Kusang, one of the three lay sponsors of Tengboche monastery, in his early nineties in 1979.

ramne, the consecration of the monastery. Details of his visit are still vividly remembered by older Sherpa informants today. One of the horses in the Zatul Rinpoche's train, carrying all the medicines he had brought to distribute to the local people, fell off the bridge below Tengboche. All the medicines were lost and the horse died. Closer to the monastery, a black snake appeared and frightened the horse on which the Zatul Rinpoche was riding. The snake was actually a *lu*, a locality spirit, which can be quite touchy and unpredictable, and which must be "subdued" before a site becomes fit for human use. The Zatul Rinpoche did some sort of mental feat (*miwa*, "visualization," essentially calling up [the power of] his tutelary deity), and the snake disappeared. After the religious ceremonies, there was dancing and horse racing and general merrymaking, and the day was one of the most joyous in living Sherpa memory.

The Zatul Rinpoche stayed in the area for two months, during which time—as one can imagine from seeing what happens when a very high lama visits the area today—he probably received into his presence and gave blessings to every man, woman, and child in all of Solu-Khumbu. Ever mindful of the importance of tangible symbols, the Zatul Rinpoche also saw to it that the rock on which Lama Sangwa Dorje had slipped when passing through Tengboche several centuries before was brought into the porch area of the main temple. When the Zatul Rinpoche left Khumbu, he was accompanied to the top of the Nangpa La by a large party of Sherpas, including the then-young sponsor Kusang who described some of these events to me.

The founding of Tengboche was a turning point in modern Sherpa history. I have suggested that the process leading up to the founding was, for several of the major figures involved, a de facto reenactment of the cultural drama of political rivalry and triumphant temple founding. The same may be argued of the second monastery, Chiwong.

The Founding of Chiwong, 1923

BUILDING CHIWONG (1923–1929)

Chiwong monastery had a single lay sponsor: Sangye, the younger brother of Karma, the senior sponsor of Tengboche.[12] In contrast with the situation at Tengboche, where religious leaders like the Zatul Rinpoche and Lama Gulu had actually initiated the project, the initiator for Chiwong was a lay person who needed a religious leader. Sangye thus contacted a reincarnate lama called the Kusho Tulku, then a young man in his twenties. The Kusho Tulku was at that time serving as the head of the noncelibate religious community at Thami, in Khumbu. He himself, however, was a celibate monk. Further, although he had been born into a Khumbu family, he had been recognized in childhood as the reincarnation (*tulku*) of a very powerful married lama from the Solu village of Chalsa, near Sangye's residence and the proposed site of Chiwong monastery. Sangye persuaded the Kusho Tulku to leave Thami and become the head of Chiwong precisely on the grounds that the Kusho Tulku was the reincarnation of a Solu lama. Sangye was also able to offer the greater prestige of heading a labtsang, a celibate monastery, as opposed to the noncelibate community at Thami. And of course he was able to offer substantial financial inducements as well.

As in the case of Tengboche, the monastery was launched with a number of adult Sherpa monks who were already living in other parts of the Solu-Khumbu region. The first cohort of monks included a number of young men from Zhung and other Solu villages, as well as a number of monks who had taken their vows in Tibet but had been living at the Thami married religious community. Like the monks surrounding the Zamte lama, who became the nucleus of the first cohort at Tengboche, these Thami monks were also monks without a (celibate) monastery.[13] When the Kusho Tulku went to Chiwong, they went with him. They were not entirely happy at Thami, which was not set up as a celibate monastic establishment. As a result of this situation at Thami, Sangye and the Kusho Tulku were able to, in effect, "raid" it, and to gather a group of relatively experienced monks to launch Chiwong. Among these was an excellent *geken*, or teacher, which many monks feel is as important to the health of a monastery as a good head lama.

In addition, the project needed resources. Thus Sangye, his son Dawa Tenzing (an ex-Tashilhunpo monk), and a married lama (and clansman of Sangye) from the Solu village of Mendopake, went around soliciting donations throughout Solu. The support for the project was widespread, and everyone gave. Members of the Lama clan in Sangye's (and Karma's) home village of Zhung were particularly generous in their donations, and large sums were raised.

Nonetheless, the bulk of the money for the building, and later for the endowment, of the monastery came from Sangye's personal fortune. Of particular note is the endowment for the support of the monks. At Tengboche, the monks were supplied with daily tea, but they were only fed meals out of monastery funds while performing monastery rituals. Ordinary subsistence expenses had to be met by the individual monks. For Chiwong, on the other hand, Sangye pledged full lifetime support for fifty monks in perpetuity. Each monk was to receive a complete set of robes upon entering (the head lama also got fifty rupees annually for clothing thereafter). In addition, each monk would receive nearly four hundred kilos of grain per year, as well as substantial quantities of butter, tea, salt, and chili. This sort of endowment was, and still is, completely unique for any Sherpa religious institution, both in nature and in scale. Although in Tibet the state-run monasteries provided, out of taxes, full support for monks, the non-state-run monasteries generally could not offer such support (see Aziz 1978:ch. 11), nor could Tengboche or any of the later Sherpa monasteries.

Chiwong was begun in 1923 and completed sometime during the period when Bhim Shamsher (Rana) was prime minister of Nepal, or between 1929 and 1932.[14] According to the Kusho Tulku's younger brother, Kusho Mangden, he and the Kusho Tulku did all the organizational work for the building of the monastery.[15] Kusho Mangden was also a celibate monk, living in the Thami religious community where his older brother was the head, and he decided to join Kusho Tulku when the latter left for Chiwong. The two of them then traveled to Tibet to hire carpenters; they also arranged for the transportation, by horse, of the carpenters to Solu. They arranged porters for the construction materials, oversaw the building activities, and saw to the procurement of the Kengyur and Tengyur, the sacred scriptures, for the temple.

The temple finally built was very beautiful. It is large, and finely painted and decorated.[16] From the site one looks out over the broad vista of Solu, rising in the west to the 11,700-foot Lamjura pass behind Zhung, and falling away to the south in row after row of softly rounded ridges, cut through by the Dudh Khosi, the Milk River.

The monastery flourished in its early years. By some accounts it actually reached its capacity of fifty monks, at least for a time. Later it was to fall into difficulties (see Ortner n.d.b), but these must not detract from the original sense of great value and merit in its founding.

SANGYE AS HERO

The founding of Chiwong was dominated by the figure of Sangye. At that point in his career (he was in his middle sixties), he had tremendous wealth. He was also still serving as pembu in the Solu region. As with most of the other key figures in this period, the combination of contradictions in the Sherpa social/cultural order and late-nineteenth-century historical pressures played themselves out in his career. I have already reviewed some of this in the last chapter. Here I concentrate on the way in which these linked up with the founding of Chiwong.

Sangye (see his photo on page 106), was in maturity a physically imposing figure—over six feet tall, muscular, and heavy, though well proportioned. He was also an imposing presence in his interactions with others. He was said to be moody; when in good humor, he could be very liberal, but when in bad humor, even members of his family did not dare to approach him.

To recapitulate the story of Sangye's life briefly: He was the third

Chiwong monastery, 1967. A typical cultivated Solu ridge is in the background.

son (of four) in his family, their father being both a married lama and a tax collector. His older brother Karma was primarily involved in trading, and also inherited the tax collecting position from the father. In his youth his brother Karma arranged his appointment to the position of naike on a government dairy farm in Solu. But Sangye was a middle brother; it is middle brothers who have a problematic inheritance situation and (particularly among the big people) a problematic status in the community. Sangye thus went to Darjeeling with his wife, and worked for about four years doing labor contracting for British road-building projects in the region. While he was away, Karma apparently took over the naike position for himself. Sangye then made independent contact with Karma's Rana connections in Kathmandu, and ultimately not only got the naike position back, but got Karma's pembu position transferred to himself as well. According to most informants, the two brothers fought over this turn of events. Karma then went off to meditate in Khumbu, and eventually founded Tengboche monastery. Sangye subsequently founded Chiwong monastery, in competitive response—according to most informants—to Karma's founding of Tengboche.

Sangye's story can easily be cast into the framework of the cultural schema of temple founding. *Rivalry*: In this reading, Sangye is now in the position of Ego, with Karma as his rival. Karma appears as the reigning big man, "rich and powerful," much like Lama Gombu in the Zhung temple tale. Sangye appears as the rising hero-challenger, much like Dorje Zangbu in the tale. Karma, as the older brother, has the better part of the inheritance (the tax collecting position on top of his normal share of land and herds). *Departure of the hero* and *acquisition of a protector*: Sangye thus goes off to seek his fortune elsewhere. He goes to Darjeeling and becomes independently wealthy. He returns with his wealth and attracts Rana attention. He acquires a Rana general as a protector. *Defeat of the rival*: This in turn allows him to "defeat" Karma and have Karma's offices transferred to himself. *Departure of the loser*: Karma moves up to Lama Gulu's meditation retreat, and here his departure appears as the departure of a losing big man who has been politically bested by the clever and charismatic hero. *Founding of a temple*: Sangye later founds Chiwong monastery, not only as a competitive response to Karma's founding of Tengboche (as it appears when the tale is read from Karma's point of view), but as an expression of his own triumph in besting a formerly powerful figure and establishing himself as the uncontested biggest man in Solu. Karma never returned to live in the Solu area; he died at Tengboche monastery.

The founding of Chiwong is thus a virtual replay of the story of the founding of Zhung noncelibate temple in 1720. There is even some evidence that Sangye was *intentionally* reenacting the life of the hero of that tale, the charismatic Dorje Zangbu. For one thing, in 1914 (just before the founding of Tengboche) Sangye sponsored a major renovation of the Zhung village temple that Dorje Zangbu had built. For another, it may not be accidental that, when Sangye founded "his" celibate monastery a few years later, he chose the Chiwong cliff for his site, which is the cliff where the wicked Lama Gombu had tried to kill the young Dorje Zangbu in the tale of the founding of Zhung temple. Perhaps more than any of the other monastery sponsors, then, Sangye may have seen himself specifically as reenacting, and legitimating himself through appropriating, the powerful cultural schema.

Karma and Sangye, Lama Gulu and the Zamte lama, thus all play out, in one way or another, the cultural schema of rivalry and temple founding. For each this playing out seems to take a somewhat different form. Karma and Lama Gulu seem more passively drawn along by the actions of others, while Sangye and the Zamte lama seem, at least at certain moments, more actively and intensely living the drama. I will not review the unique features of each individual's relationship to the schema here (although I do so in Ortner n.d.a). I only wish to emphasize the point that the notion of "enacting the schema" does not presuppose any cultural programming of actors, and is rather a matter of actors finding a fit (whether pragmatically useful or emotionally meaningful, or both) between personal circumstances and cultural stories at particular historical moments. In such moments, actors forge powerful and productive links between personal agency and cultural forms.

Legitimation from the Big Point of View: Prestige and Merit

Cultural schemas, and their appropriation/enactment by actors, link the "external" political economic pressures to the "internal" events of the foundings of the monasteries. This is perfectly logical since the external pressures exacerbated the contradictions of the Sherpa social/cultural order, while the schema is both an aspect of those contradictions and an apparent way (from the actor's point of view) of resolving them. Specifically with respect to the big people, the pressures coming down in the regional political economy tended to undermine their legitimacy as political leaders, and as figures of status and prestige in the community. Enactment of the cultural schema that culminates in temple founding, in turn, could re-infuse their positions with bigness, insofar as this schema shows the hero to be both powerful and altruistic, capable of protecting others because of his potency, but humble in his desire to serve rather than dominate. This blending of bigness and smallness is, I argued earlier, the essence of "legitimacy" in Sherpa culture.

When I asked the founder Kusang why he cosponsored the founding of Tengboche, he answered entirely in moral terms: to perform an act of virtue (*gyewa*), to make merit (payin). When I asked other informants why the founders did what they did, the informants were rather more pragmatic, saying that the sponsors sought to gain prestige (*ming*, "name"; *namdal*, "reputation"). But even these more pragmatic commentators mentioned the religious motive as well.[17] The desire for prestige fits the arguments concerning the erosion of legitimacy of the big people in the late nineteenth and early twentieth centuries. But what is the relationship between these issues of prestige and legitimacy on the one hand, and the stated desire for religious virtue or merit on the other?

I would suggest that the sense of needing to build merit is another aspect of the need for "legitimacy," here defined not merely as recognized and socially accepted political authority, but as an internal sense of personal worth and value.[18] The big people may not have recognized that their legitimacy vis-à-vis the small people had eroded. In fact, with their increasing wealth, they may have been feeling bigger than ever. Yet they seem to have had a sense that their moral position was not good. *All* of the monastery founders thus show a consistent and noncynical concern for merit-making, even when this could have had no political value, and a discussion of monastery foundings in terms of "legitimation" must include this aspect as well.

I begin with the Tengboche sponsors, and first of all with Gembu Tsepal. His career was covered largely in the last chapter, since his alleged murder of the ex-gembu was the strongest available example of intensification of political conflict in this period. But he could have been included in the present chapter as well, since the events of his life play out the old schema: conflict with a rival (when he moves up to Nauje as a pembu and starts being "big"); acquisition of a powerful protector (the state); defeat of the rival (deposition of the other gembu and ascent to the gembuship, which by definition entails acquiring the other's subjects); and the founding of a monastery (pledging to sponsor Tengboche). The one violation of the schema is that the defeated gembu Dorje did not leave the area, either to gain additional protection or to relocate elsewhere. This was a costly violation, since he was subsequently killed.

Tsepal then moved or fled to Lhasa. He was at this point beyond legitimation, in the sense of seeking rightness in the eyes of those over whom he had power or authority, since he could no longer or ever again be gembu, and indeed he could no longer or ever again live in Khumbu. Yet—perhaps expectably—his need for a sense of self-worth, his sense of needing merit, and his worry about the fate of his soul are strongly manifest in subsequent events. For one thing, he fulfilled in absentia his pledge of sponsorship of Tengboche. Subsequently, in 1925, he was to help in the founding of Devuche nunnery (see chapter 9). And in 1935, after the death of Lama Gulu, he played a major role in the discovery of Lama Gulu's reincarnation (Ortner n.d.b). These acts may have had some political value for Tsepal—for example, in shoring up his son's position as the new gembu. (If this was his objective, it did not work very well—see the next chapter.) In general, however, the primary "audience" for these activities seems to have been himself—both his moral conscience and his own sense of social value to others.

Karma, the senior Tengboche sponsor, shows a similar pattern. Having been politically deposed by Sangye, and having moved up to Khumbu, he never showed any political ambitions again. The founding of Tengboche was, as is universally agreed, a triumph of prestige over his brother, but he did not seek to convert it back into real power and authority. Rather he, like Gembu Tsepal, appears to have translated his legitimation needs at this point largely into questions of self-worth, within the cultural idiom of merit. Thus after the founding of Tengboche, Karma built himself a house at the monastery. Although he never took vows, he adopted the clothing of a gelung, a fully ordained monk. He kept a herd of dairy animals at the monastery and supplied the monks' butter endowment from the herd. Like Gembu Tsepal, he was involved in the founding of Devuche nunnery later, and one of his daughters became a Devuche nun. He died at Tengboche in 1931.

And finally there is Sangye. Unlike his brother Karma, who never went back into politics after the founding of Tengboche, Sangye continued his powerful political career after the founding of Chiwong. Thus one may assume that the legitimation he sought and achieved from founding Chiwong was in part conventional, designed to strengthen his position as a big man and his power as a tax collector and state agent. Yet for Sangye as for the others, the moral considerations are visible as well. Indeed, Sangye's level of religious activism, throughout his life, is almost as impressive as his economic and political career. It also manifests certain complexities of the self-esteem question, particularly with reference to his identity as a Buddhist and a Sherpa. It is worth looking into in some detail here.

First, Sangye cosponsored with Karma the founding of a dormitory for Himalayan monks at Tashilhunpo monastery in Tibet. As it turns out, the impetus for this activity probably came largely from Sangye's side. One of his own sons, Dawa Tenzing, spent eleven years as a monk at Tashilhunpo, and evidently it was he who brought the need for such a dormitory to Sangye's attention.[19] This son was eventually recalled by Sangye from the monastery and married off to the widow of an older son who died. But according to one informant, it was he who influenced Sangye to build Chiwong monastery as well. When the decision to build the monastery was taken, the son also played a major role in the fund raising.[20]

It was also noted that Sangye sponsored the renovation of Zhung temple in 1914, shortly before Karma sponsored the founding of Tengboche monastery. Sangye went about collecting donations and organizing labor for the project, as well as contributing generously from his own wealth. One incident connected with the reconstruction project provides some insight into his style: The temple structure was not properly built, and collapsed suddenly a few days after the work was completed. People were very upset, but Sangye came along and said, "Why are you weeping? This just means that we will build a better temple!"[21]

Next, despite the fact that he was on the outs with his older brother Karma, and felt competitive about the prestige Karma gained from the founding of Tengboche, Sangye contributed most of the cost of a complete set of sacred books (the Kengyur and Tengyur) to Tengboche monastery (Sangye Tenzing 1971).[22]

Another of his projects (whether before or after the founding of Chiwong is not clear) involved helping Kyerok temple, a noncelibate religious community on the Thami side of Khumbu, acquire a set of Kengyur and Tengyur. The Kyerok lamas had raised money themselves to buy a set, and had bought the paper and ink. Sangye offered to take the materials to a Tibetan monastery for printing, which he did. He did not, however, deliver that particular set to Kyerok, and herein lies another glimpse into his modus operandi. He told the Kyerok people that there was a woman in a village in Pharak (the middle Sherpa region, between Solu and Khumbu) who owed him money, and who owned a set of the sacred books. He said the Kyerok people could go and collect that set, telling the woman that it was in repayment of her debt to Sangye. The woman was most unhappy about the whole episode, and blocked the door to her house, whereupon the men removed the books through her window.[23]

After the founding of Chiwong, and for the rest of his life, Sangye personally saw to the provisioning of the Chiwong monks on a year-to-year basis. He arranged for the delivery of rice and maize from his low-altitude lands, butter from his herds, tea and salt on contract from Tibet, and so on.

Most of these activities could be interpreted in terms of normal legitimation dynamics. Most of them show Sangye operating as a big political figure, even as he sponsored some important religious contributions. The renovation of Zhung temple may have been, as suggested earlier, a conscious appropriation of the Dorje Zangbu tale, and of the legitimation dynamics embedded in that tale. The story of the books for Kyerok gompa shows Sangye collecting a debt (itself a sin) and throwing his weight around. Even the founding of Chiwong is not above suspicion. Not only did Sangye continue as pembu after the founding; he used the monastery as an excuse to convert large sectors of his landholdings into *guthi* land, tax-exempt land devoted to the support of a religious establishment. (Although the whole of a guthi holding is nontaxable, there is no rule as to how much of its produce must go to the religious establishment in question. The proportion of its total output used for these purposes may be quite small [see Regmi 1968].)[24]

Yet I think it would be a real mistake to view Sangye's religious activities as political and economic schemes dressed up in meritorious garb. For one thing, as discussed earlier, the distinction between politics and religion is not really appropriate to Sherpa culture in this era. But for another, there are important indications that Sangye's concerns were as much with his own moral worth as with his power. One of the indications is the size of his endowment for Chiwong; while he may have gained some economic benefits from Chiwong (and even this is not clear), he was prepared to spend a great deal of his wealth in return. In addition, his continuing active interest in the monastery, his personal concern with the provisioning, and so forth, betoken more than an instrumental view of its political value to himself.

But his most interesting religious activity along these lines is one that could have had no political value within the Sherpa community at all. In his later years, Sangye became interested in Hindu yogis. He built a rest house for them, and fed them when they came begging. He also provided them with hashish, which he bought from nomadic shepherds.[25] Exactly what the yogis meant to Sangye is not clear. One's first guess might be that Sangye was attempting to Hinduize, as happened to so many local elites in this period of Rana domination (see, for example, Iijima 1963; Messerschmidt and Gurung 1974). Thus one might think that this was a move (whether self-conscious or not) to align himself religiously with his Rana friends in Kathmandu, and to be recognized as one of them. Yet a moment's reflection shows this to be highly unlikely. The whole point of Sangye's religious career was to underscore the Buddhist identity of the Sherpa people, and his own identity as a Sherpa and a Buddhist in the larger Nepal context in which he operated. According to one of his descendants, he always made a point of wearing Sherpa dress when he carried his tax collections to Kathmandu (this despite the fact that such garb is much too hot for the Kathmandu climate), and he always stayed at the Buddhist shrine of Bodnath when he was there. While there might be other reasons for these actions, his descendant believed that they were largely assertions of Sangye's cultural identity in the face of aggressive Rana Hinduism.

Given all this, it seems unlikely that Sangye was attracted to the yogis because of their Hindu affiliations. If anything he may have been interested in their *rejection* of Hinduism, and in the way in which they represented a critique of the Hindu system from within. In addition, however, he seems to have been taken by their strict otherworldliness, and by an asceticism that went even beyond monasticism. By the time he was an old man, Chiwong had experienced serious internal conflict. Sangye may have felt that the wandering yogis were an even more potent source of merit for himself as he approached death.

Like his older brother Karma some years earlier, Sangye died at the monastery he had founded. He died around 1939, in his early eighties.

In sum: I argued in the last chapter that the legitimacy of the Sherpa big people was being systematically undermined by the state, even as the big people were building great wealth and becoming "bigger." But the question of "legitimacy" can only be experienced within a particular framework of social relations and a particular framework of cultural understandings. For the Sherpa big people it appears to have been experienced in two ways: in increased challenges from rivals within the big stratum, and in a gradually intensifying self-doubt about personal moral worth and personal social value. It was experienced, in other words, through the idiom (and practice) of rivalry, and through the idiom (and practice) of merit.

Leaving aside merit for the moment, it is the transformation of the problem of legitimacy (of the big people vis-à-vis the small) into problems of rivalry (between big people) that links the preceding chapter to the present one. The Rana pressures on the big people as a whole made every individual vulnerable to challenges from rivals, and these were pervasive among the people involved in the monastery foundings. But rivalrous challenges in turn generated standard cultural responses, and so placed the individuals in question once again on the classic terrain of the schema. Thus in this chapter I have shown that most of the big monastery founders played out the schema of triumph and legitimation in their lives, with the monastery foundings standing at once as instruments for defeating rivals, expressions of triumph, and conduits of legitimation. The founders' experience of their situation and their mode of responding to it were profoundly structured by the relational shape of their society and the representational shape of their culture.

At the same time I have argued that "legitimation" for the big people had at least a double aspect: a conventional political sense, and a moral/religious sense. Thus in the second part of the chapter I sought to show that the founders were as much concerned with building merit as with justifying and consolidating their political authority. The discussions here may be related back to the arguments posed at a more abstract level in chapter 3. There I argued from a symbolic interpretation of the schema that merit and prestige, religion and politics, could not be disaggregated in Sherpa culture. The twentieth-century monastery founders' lives show that this was the case in practice as well.

In the final analysis, however, it must be emphasized that legitimation is not solely the property of big people. Insofar as it concerns the sense of self-worth, and of one's value to significant others, it is an issue for people at all levels of society. Thus I will argue in the following chapters that the small people, and the ambiguously positioned children of the elites, also play out the schema with themselves as heroes. In these instances the schema appears not as a tool for the legitimation of those in high positions, but as an instrument of self-empowerment and social assertion.

CHAPTER

VIII

The Small People

FROM the viewpoint of Sherpa folklore and memory, religious institution founding happens from the top down—from the machinations of the big people and the high lamas. I have, thus far, largely followed this cultural perspective, partly because it does contain a large kernel of truth, and partly because, as in so much of historical investigation, the bulk of the available information tends to relate to the activities of the big people. Yet the foundings of the monasteries can also be looked at from the bottom up, as it were. The small people as well as the big people financially supported the foundings, with both material contributions and labor. Their material contributions were individually smaller than those of the big people, to be sure, but they added up to a significant sum, as the lamas who tell of the foundings always emphasize. Their labor contributions, however, were enormous, and it is a simple statement of fact that without their labor—generously and voluntarily donated—the monasteries would not have been built. An understanding of the foundings of the monasteries must thus include an explanation of this fact.

But the small people immediately pose a problem. I have argued that the big people participated in the foundings within the framework of a cultural schema that mediates the contradictions of the social order, and thus essentially "legitimated" the big people's dominance. But if this is correct, then it would appear contradictory for the small people to participate willingly in this enterprise. It would seem particularly contradictory to find them acting more or less within the patterns of the same legitimating schema, as in fact I will suggest that they did.

The solution to this puzzle involves two points. First, one of the major shifts in contemporary anthropological thinking about culture has involved a sense that culture is more ambiguous with respect to the established order, and subject to more diverse political interpretations and uses, than had been assumed in earlier perspectives.

Many anthropologists now operate with Foucault's "rule of the tactical polyvalence of discourses," according to which "discourses are not once and for all subservient to power or raised up against it, any more than silences are. We must make allowance for the complex and unstable process whereby discourse can be both an instrument and an effect of power, but also a hindrance, a stumbling-block, a point of resistance and a starting point for an opposing strategy" (1980:101).

There is also an exciting body of substantive studies coming out that show quite persuasively the ways in which subordinate groups deploy, transform, and reinterpret established cultural forms to make their own counterstatements about the world and their place within it. James Scott's *Weapons of the Weak* (1985); the Hall and Jefferson collection, *Resistance through Rituals* (1975); Jean Comaroff's *Body of Power, Spirit of Resistance* (1985), Nicholas Dirks's "Ritual and Resistance: Subversion as a Social Fact" (n.d.), are excellent examples, each presenting a slightly different take on this point. Scott emphasizes the relative nonpenetration of supposedly hegemonic culture, and the capacity of subordinate groups to resist its claims in thousands of tiny practical ways. Clarke et al., in the introduction to *Resistance through Rituals*, discuss the partial encompassment, and partial autonomy, of "class cultures" and "subcultures" vis-à-vis the dominant cultural order. Comaroff comes closest to Foucault's position in arguing that the deployment of symbolic forms rooted in the dominant culture—in the South African case she is discussing, a series of Christian-derived rituals—may nonetheless carry a subversive meaning. Dirks develops similar arguments, in the context of considering assorted breakdowns, fights, and other miscarriages of rituals he studied in south India.

The arguments that I will make about the small people's participation in the monastery foundings are situated within this general line of thinking. I will argue that the wage-labor and petty-enterprise opportunities that opened up in Darjeeling in the late nineteenth and early twentieth centuries gave many small people a sense of empowerment, and that their participation in the monastery foundings expressed this sense. One could say in effect that their participation was a counterclaim, a denial that having fewer material resources defined them as "small," and of no social consequence.

This argument in turn connects with the second theoretical point to be made here, which involves further expansion of the concept of "legitimation." The legitimation problematic is extremely important and deserves far more space than I can give it here. A few brief points will have to suffice.

The legitimation literature may be divided into two broad sets. The first deals with legitimation in the classic sense, which is to say with questions of rendering arbitrary power arrangements nonarbitrary and possibly even desirable. The discussions here go back particularly to Weber (1978), who formulated the typological question of how different forms of "domination" were legitimated, and who also articulated the important related distinction between power and authority. Some sociologists—for example, Giddens (1979) and Therborne (1980)—have remained interested in this question in its classic form. Scott's (1985) arguments to the effect that there is much less successful legitimation than social scientists assume, are also relevant here.

Another body of literature, partly overlapping with the first, subsumes the legitimation problematic within a broader set of questions about the stabilization and naturalization of the general symbolic order. Berger and Luckmann's (1967) discussions of "universe maintenance"; Bourdieu's (1977) discussions of the inscription of the cultural habitus on the body and on personal identity, as well as his discussions of the "doxic" naturalization of arbitrary cultural assumptions; and Foucault's (1980) arguments about the many ways in which the self is historically "disciplined" are all concerned with "legitimation," in the extended sense of being about the ways in which the arbitrary universe constructed by each culture is made to seem natural, nonarbitrary, necessary, and desirable.

I am interested in both sets of issues, and this book is concerned with both. Some of the discussions in earlier chapters—the labeling in chapter 4 of the contradictions-and-schema combination as a hegemony; the discussion in the preceding chapter of "distance" between actor and culture—were implicitly directed to the second set of questions, and I will return to them in chapter 10. For the moment, however, I wish to pursue the notion of legitimation in the more strictly social and political sense. Specifically, I wish to argue that everyone seeks legitimation, not simply big actors or actors in positions of power. That is, if one takes seriously the Foucaultian notions (1980:ch. 2ff.) that power is not strictly a property of those in formally dominant positions, that "the political" is not a separate realm from the rest of social life, and that everyone in some sense is operating with respect to a matrix of power, then one must also accept the idea that everyone is similarly engaged in, or positioned with respect to, "legitimation."

In the last chapter I began the process of broadening the legitimation concept by arguing that the big monastery founders sought legitimacy not only at a political but at a moral level as well. While the founders claimed only moral intentions (in the idiom of the desire to make merit), the small people were more realistic in recognizing that the big people sought prestige (or in the present language, legitimation) as well. But even the small people did not deny that the big founders *also* had moral intentions, and I am inclined to accept this claim.[1] With smaller actors, this moral level becomes even more prominent, although the political level never disappears entirely. Thus I will argue in this chapter that the small people in the Darjeeling labor context gained not only money (which in turn gave them material power), but also—for specific reasons—significant self-respect. Their participation in the monastery foundings, in turn, expressed both the real power of being able to earn resources on one's own, *and* the sense of self-respect they had developed. Their participation was thus a claim of "legitimation," in the sense of a claim to be recognized as significant players in the social process.

In order to incorporate a sense of these kinds of claims within the legitimation concept, I propose using "valorization" as an umbrella term covering all the claims of legitimacy, authenticity, social value, "qualification" (Therborne's term), and so forth, made by actors at any level of society. "Legitimation" is one kind of (claim of) valorization, the kind sought or made by dominant actors for classic reasons of maintenance of power, as well as for reasons (however self-deceiving) of morality. But other types, by other actors, are also possible, and this and the next chapter will be concerned with some of these other types.

The discussion in this chapter will follow, in condensed form, the methodological contours of the book as a whole. That is, I will first review the long-standing structural problems of Sherpa social organization that generate "smallness." I will then consider the historical situation of the small people in the late nineteenth and early twentieth centuries. The critical new circumstances for the small people in this period were, on the one hand, the Rana tax squeeze and, on the other, the introduction of the potato and the expanding labor opportunities in British India. I will then suggest that the many small people who participated in the monastery foundings were like the returning heroes of the schema, newly empowered and expressing or claiming "bigness."

Who Are the Small People?

THE SHERPAS IN THE LARGER ECONOMIC CONTEXT OF NEPAL

Before examining the genesis and nature of "smallness" in Sherpa society, it should be noted first that, overall, the Sherpas appear to have had a relatively high standard of living compared with many other (non-high-caste) groups in Nepal. This is certainly the case in modern times, and seems to have been true in the past as well. By this I mean that every Sherpa family owns its own land, everyone survives at least at the subsistence level, and the vast majority do better than that. In modern times it is unheard of for Sherpas to serve as tenants or sharecroppers for other Sherpas, and it is very rare for Sherpas to do wage work for other Sherpas. I have indicated that there was probably a period in the late nineteenth century in which there was more tenantry, but even then it appears that the situation was not nearly as bad as in some other parts of Nepal (see Regmi 1978:ch. 8).

Some of the community's high standard of living may be illusory, since the poorest people tend to emigrate. Thus one of the reasons one sees so little poverty in Solu-Khumbu may be that it has gone elsewhere. Nonetheless, the well-being of the rest of the community is real enough, and there are also real reasons for it. The first is the distance from the seat of the Nepal state. Compared with groups in the Kathmandu region, who were pressed into all sorts of corvée labor at the whim of the rulers, the Sherpas were simply too far away for this to be done with any regularity. Further, the state was apparently concerned with keeping the Sherpas happy and maintaining their loyalties. Since the Sherpas were ethnically oriented toward Tibet, since Solu-Khumbu was hard to police militarily, and since the state had an interest in maintaining control of the trans-Himalayan trade routes, Kathmandu apparently sought to stay in the Sherpas' good graces. The Sherpas were exempted from unpaid portering for state officials, and several of the tax documents list specific taxes and levies from which they were also exempted. The upshot was that, compared with many other groups in Nepal who were impoverished by state demands, the Sherpas gave up very little of their collective product to the state (see Regmi 1968; Oppitz 1968:52; compare the Tamangs [von Fürer-Haimendorf 1956]).

The other major factor in the Sherpas' comparatively good economic situation in Nepal is that they were never dominated economically by any other ethnic group, as happened, for example, to the Limbu of eastern Nepal. Caplan (1970) and Jones (1976) describe a situation in which Limbu villagers were deeply in debt to Brahman landlords, many of whom did not even live in the local communities. Either the Sherpas effectively kept out foreign groups, or foreign groups were simply not interested in the high, cold, steep lands of Solu-Khumbu. Either way, however, the Sherpas again escaped a situation that would have forced them to give up a good part of their collective product to outsiders.

The result of all this is that even the so-called small people are probably rather better off than the "smallest" groups in many other Nepal communities. They should thus not be construed as a deeply impoverished class, but rather as a set of smallholding peasants who must be careful with their resources, and who have opportunities to move both up and down the economic and social ladder. These points should be kept in mind as the changing fortunes of this group are examined.

THE GENESIS OF SMALLNESS

The big people largely make their money from trade. Rents from tenants, interest on loans, and taxes and fines appear to have been largely used to cushion trade risks and were not, with a few exceptions, sources of major wealth in themselves. This is consistent with the egalitarian ethic in Sherpa culture, and with the fact that Sherpa society cannot really be characterized as a class system. Although there is extraction of resources on the part of the big people, it is not the *primary* source of wealth and thus of social differentiation.

A similar point may now be made with respect to smallness.

Smallness, or the specter thereof, is created largely by the equal inheritance rule for agricultural land, compounded by the fact that the tax extraction process deprived people of the seed capital for engaging in large-scale trade, and thus compensating for land shrinkage. Over the long run, in an expanding population, the equal inheritance rule will tend toward what European historians call parcellization, wherein everyone's share is too small to support a normal family unit. A shortage of land could in theory be compensated for by trade, but this is where the tax extractions made themselves felt, since they took away what few liquid assets a middling family might have had, and made it impossible for the family to capitalize trade at any level large enough to have a compensatory effect. Since these extractions were not the dominant cause of poverty or smallness (the inheritance rule was), they did not challenge the cultural construction of the system as ideally egalitarian. But they were the difference that made a difference.

There are no figures available on wealth differentiation in earlier periods of Sherpa history. Even for the ethnographically observed modern era (since the mid-1950s), there is no general survey of variation in landholdings. Nonetheless, von Fürer-Haimendorf did do a cattle count in the Khumbu region in 1957, and this will provide at least one index of the objective differences that may hold between big people and small:

> Among the 596 householders of Khumbu [that is, the whole upper region] there were in 1957 only 254 owners of cattle, and the total number of yak and cows in their possession was 2,894. The greater part of the livestock was in the hands of a few wealthy families. While even families of modest means owned one or two cows, yak were kept only in herds of at least six or seven animals. Thus in [one village] Khumjung, 347 yak were owned by 17 householders, whereas 16 families kept a few cows. Only 17 of the 108 households of Khumjung were engaged in the type of cattle economy which involved seasonal migrations from one high-altitude settlement to another. (von Fürer-Haimendorf 1964:11–12)

These differences in cattle ownership are significant primarily as differences in participation in trade and commerce, since the animals and their products are sold as commodities, and since the animals are also the sole means of transport, at least for the trans-Himalayan leg of the trade. If these figures held in earlier times as well, and it is not unreasonable to assume that they did, then the degree of exclusion of small people from trade, and thus from the ability to get out of a "small," subsistence-level position in Sherpa society, is fairly clear.

MIGRATIONS

Given the tendency toward parcellization in the inheritance system, various cultural strategies were available to get around the problem. One that was available from the original Tibetan cultural repertoire was fraternal polyandry, which both kept the paternal land together and controlled the population growth in the next generation. The Sherpas did some of this—among the early ancestors of the Lama clan were two brothers, Pachen and Puchen, who married one wife, and who had various other adventures as well (see Sangye Tenzing 1971; I also collected some Pachen and Puchen lore in the field). By and large, however, polyandry as a solution to the parcellization problem was not popular among the Sherpas, and their primary mechanism for coping with the land shortage seems to have been migration. Throughout Sherpa history there is a continuing pattern of moves from the main residence areas and the setting up of new communities.

One presumes there was, especially in early times, a certain amount of individual migration—a man and his family moving away and homesteading in a new area, staking out and developing a piece of virgin property that had more economic potential than the share the man would have inherited. If such an individual encouraged some kin and friends to go with him (as when the Sherpas first moved to Nepal), such a move would have political implications as well. The individual might be removing himself from the authority of his old pembu, and setting himself up as a local pembu in his own right.

Whatever the motives, there is evidence of several relatively early moves outside the confines of Solu-Khumbu, that is, into valleys that are parts of different river systems, and that require the crossing of high passes to reach. One of these moves was into a valley called Deorali Bhandar, just west of Solu, over the 11,700-foot Lamjura Pass west of Zhung. This move apparently took place between 1725 and 1750, led by a certain Ralwa Dorje (not the one who twisted the iron rod and founded Thami temple) of the Lama clan (Oppitz 1968).[2]

Another migrant group apparently left Solu about 1825 and settled in the Arun valley to the east of the Solu-Khumbu. This group is called "Nawa" (possibly *ngawa*, meaning "married lama"). The people live in several villages at high altitudes in the Arun valley, with traditions of migration from Solu, with several Sherpa clan names, and speaking a dialect that is mutually intelligible with Solu-Khumbu Sherpa (von Fürer-Haimendorf 1975:117; also Wahlquist, personal communication).

Slightly different evidence for economically caused out-migration comes from the state documents that have already been reviewed in connection with the changing status of the pembu. The 1810 document suggested that people were being squeezed by loan-sharking: the king fixed the interest rate on loans and told lenders they were not to charge more. Shortly thereafter, it appears that people migrated out of the area because they could not pay their loans. Thus in documents issued between 1825 and 1830, the king urged the local officials to encourage the return to the area of people who had emigrated because of indebtedness.

Early in the second half of the nineteenth century, there was one more move in the traditional mold of setting up new subsistence villages: the settlement of Rolwaling valley, over a high pass northwest of Thami, around 1860. According to Sacherer (1981:157), the move was made at least partly in response to an economic squeeze: "These were the poorest members of other communities, who ran away to escape bad debts, criminal problems, etc." (see also Sacherer 1975, 1977).

The settling of Rolwaling in about 1860 seems to have been the last of this sort of migration within the environs of the Sherpa region. Just about this time, the Ranas took over in Kathmandu and gradually turned up their economic demands. But it was also about this time that the British in India opened up an entirely new set of economic options in the region, thus allowing the Sherpas to respond to state demands in effective ways. The effects of the British presence on the big people have already been described—the opening up of large-scale entrepreneurial opportunities used to advantage by people like Sangye, and the enhancement of the profitability of trade affecting people like the Tengboche sponsors Karma, Kusang, and Tsepal. But there were other such economic innovations: the introduction of the potato, and the opening up of wage-labor opportunities. Both of these developments generated major benefits for the Sherpa small people.

The Introduction of the Potato

It is conceivable that the Sherpas received the potato as early as 1774–75, since "a young writer of the Honourable East India Company," George Bogle, on instructions from the governor-general of Bengal, Warren Hastings, was planting potatoes then in various parts of the Himalayas explicitly with the intention of introducing potato cultivation in the region (Sandberg 1904:103). Nonetheless, the best guess seems to be that the Sherpas only received the potato in the mid–nineteenth century, somewhere between 1840 and 1860 (von Fürer-Haimendorf 1964:9).[3] According to the local folklore, the first seed potatoes in Khumbu came from the British resident's garden in Sikkim.

The potato revolutionized Sherpa agriculture, quickly overtaking the established food crops—barley and wheat—in popularity. One hundred years later, at the time of the early visits of Westerners to Solu-Khumbu (Hillary 1955; Hardie 1957; von Fürer-Haimendorf 1964), it had become the staple crop, grown in every Sherpa village at every altitude of the region.

Not much is known about the specific effects the introduction may have had at the time. For example, von Fürer-Haimendorf has suggested that one of its results was a significant expansion of the Sherpa population. In support of this claim, he cites household counts: "In 1836 there were in the whole of Khumbu only 169 households, compared with the 596 households in 1957" (1964:10). But according to Oppitz (1968), using data to which von Fürer-Haimendorf did not have access, the Sherpa population was increasing anyway, doubling every forty-nine years or so since the Sherpas' arrival in Nepal. If each household were a person (it is not, but the average number of persons per household seems to be unknown), the rate of increase of households cited by von Fürer-Haimendorf would actually be below what would be predicted on the basis of Oppitz's figures. Thus the impact of the potato on Sherpa population growth must remain an open question.

I would suggest that the main social effects of potato cultivation were as follows: In the first place, since it came in at about the same time as the Rana coup, and expanded during the period of what might be called the Rana squeeze, it would have given the Sherpas some defense against the heavy tax demands of that era. It is probable that this prevented more widespread impoverishment in the region.

The other main effect of the potato would have been in conjunction with the Darjeeling wage-work opportunities. Given the Rana squeeze, the potato in itself could not have generated much disposable wealth for the small people, and specifically the resources that went into the foundings of the monasteries. However, it would have allowed more of the wages earned in Darjeeling to be used as surplus rather than for subsistence. Thus a family could probably support itself agriculturally with fewer workers, and the disadvantaged younger brothers could then go off to Darjeeling without having to send every penny back for family survival. What they earned in Darjeeling could thus have been used more as discretionary income, and would have fed into the sense of empowerment that, I will argue below, emerged from the Darjeeling wage-work situation.

Wage Labor and the Empowerment of the Small People

In the second half of the nineteenth century, the combination of the standard cultural inheritance rule and the increased Rana exactions would have put new pressure on "small" Sherpas. Throughout Sherpa history, the problem of inadequate land and other resources had usually been solved by migration and the settlement of new communities. This worked well enough, as long as enough land was available and as long as no alternatives presented themselves. The point to note, however, is that such moves simply reproduced the system as it was previously constituted. The new community was started on the same basis as the old, with the same inheritance rules and the same mechanisms of tax and labor extraction, and with no novel solutions to the parcellization problem that would simply reappear within a few generations.

Enter the British in Darjeeling, with the many opportunities, great and small, they created for making money. One can instantly see the appeal, in light of the property structure and its shrinking tendencies, of those opportunities. Cash would seem to halt the downward slide to "smallness," and to allow one at least to stay even, if not to beat the system. A man could pay his taxes, perhaps capitalize a trading venture, and especially, acquire more land and livestock and expand his original holdings without having to move away and start life over again. In effect, it allowed him to restore his status as a major social player in the community. It restored both security and spice to life.

Going to Darjeeling to earn cash would not necessarily have appeared to be a very radical move. In the first place, the Sherpas were quite used to geographic mobility. Between patterns of transhumance, long-distance trade, and migration, major geographic mobility was very much part of the culture. Further, a seasonal migration pattern to Darjeeling would have fit easily into the agricultural cycle, since construction work (the main thing small Sherpas seem to have taken up besides mountaineering) stopped during the summer monsoons, and the Sherpas could come back to Solu-Khumbu and tend to their harvests. And finally, it is clear that until fairly recently, the cash earned in Darjeeling (or similar places) was, for that majority of Sherpas who returned to Solu-Khumbu, meant to be used for quite traditional ends—acquiring a solid, if not massive, economic base; a respectable, if not awe-inspiring, status in the community; and a chance to win out in some of the rivalries that were generated by the structure in the first place. In *The Monks' Campaign* I will argue that the experience begun in Darjeeling in the late nineteenth century had profoundly transforming effects, but this aspect does not seem to have been visible to, or intended by, those involved at the time.

Mason (1955:157) says that the Sherpas first came east to the Darjeeling district in "about 1902," but there were 3,450 Sherpas counted in the first Darjeeling district census of 1901 (Dash 1947:72).[4] In order to have reached such numbers by this time, the Sherpas must have been going down to the area for several decades before this, at least since the 1860s or 1870s when the British started building the roads and railroads. (It does not appear that the Sherpas ever were much directly involved in tea-plantation labor.) It is possible to reconstruct from various sources some of the things they may have been doing down there.

It would seem that most men (and some women) did construction labor on the crews organized by contractors like Sangye. (Mason [1955:157] notes that they did "coolie work.") But it would also seem that at least some of them quickly moved out of those jobs, in two rather different directions. On the one hand, some (apparently a small number) joined the Gurkha regiments (Dash 1947:72) and the police (Bishop 1978:68).[5] On the other hand, a fair number of ("small") Sherpas went into various forms of petty enterprise. Mason (1955:157) says that some of them became rickshaw drivers. One of my informants ran an arak (distilled spirits) shop near the tea plantations. Indeed, there is a suggestion that the Sherpas in the police jobs used their positions to protect other Sherpas' enterprises:

> After 10 months they [some people from the Helambu region of Nepal] left [Gangtok] and went to Assam because the police jobs in Sikkim were held by Khumbu Sherpas who wouldn't give Helambu families permits to set up restaurants and tea shops (Bishop 1978:68).

It was perhaps in 1907 that a major turning point was reached in the Sherpas' and Darjeeling's economic use of one another. It appears that the first mountaineering expedition to take Sherpa porters, or at least the first to notice them, took place at that time. According to Mason's history of Himalayan mountaineering (1955), the first expeditions to take Sherpas were those led by the Scot Dr. A. M. Kellas (whose first of many expeditions took place in 1907) and the Norwegians Rubenson and Monrad Aas. The latter pair returned from a failed 1907 climb of a peak in the Darjeeling district "high in their praise for the Sherpa porters who accompanied them" (Mason 1955:127). As Rubenson wrote,

> The important thing is to have good and willing coolies, as we had. Properly fitted out and with kind treatment they will achieve the impossible! We could not persuade them to be roped when loaded, but by making good steps, fixing in pegs and ropes, and helping them over difficult places there seems to be no limit to what they will surmount. Our experience is that the coolies, especially the Nepalese Sherpas, are excellent men when treated properly. What success we achieved was due to the willingness and bravery of these people. (Quoted in Cameron 1984:154)

Kellas wrote in that same period:

> Their behaviour was excellent. By the end of the trip we were all working together most harmoniously. Really they are the most splendid fellows. Of the different types of coolie, the writer has found the Nepalese Sherpas superior to all others. They are strong, good natured if fairly treated, and since they are Buddhists there is no difficulty about special food for them—a point

> strongly in their favour at high altitudes. (Quoted in Cameron 1984:161)

Mason summarizes the Sherpas' virtues in this period as follows: they were "adventurous, light-hearted, courageous, and splendid material for the making of first-class mountaineers" (1955:157). It soon became the practice for expeditions to take only Solu-Khumbu Sherpas with them as porters, and indeed the Sherpas soon distinguished themselves so much that they eventually moved into (or in some cases created for themselves) higher positions on the expeditions—as guides and as sirdars (essentially foremen).[6]

Himalayan mountaineering was to become a major industry. Initially it was tied largely to exploring and surveying, a matter of "passes rather than of peaks," as Mason put it (ibid., p. 95). Even in the period in which the Sherpas first became involved, most of the expeditions were for "technical reconnaissance," although the number of such expeditions evidently increased in that period (1885–1918) because of the building of roads up into the Sikkim corridor. It was not until after World War I that the notion of climbing primarily for sport took hold in earnest, particularly with respect to climbing Everest, simply because it was "there." And when the opportunity came, with the very first (1921) Everest expedition, the Sherpas were in position to take it. The expedition "engaged about 40 Sherpas and Bhotias at Darjeeling" (ibid., p. 157). By the following year (note that this is six years after the founding of Tengboche and one year before the founding of Chiwong), there were fifty Sherpas, all of whom were distinguished from the "Bhotias" or Tibetans, and all of whom were established as specialists in the more skilled high-altitude portering (ibid., p. 167). Once again the Sherpas distinguished themselves: "Above all, the best of the Sherpas had shown themselves devoted, disciplined, and reliable at great heights, and capable of carrying loads to 25,500 feet" (ibid., p. 171).[7]

The Sherpas' role in mountaineering will be explored more fully in another context (Ortner n.d.b). The point here is that, early in the twentieth century, the Sherpas who went to Darjeeling to make money began to have very dramatic success. Previously a big man like Sangye had been able to make a lot of money. More ordinary Sherpas could evidently do reasonably well in that earlier period too; they were able to capitalize some petty enterprises, and had enough success to attract the more than three thousand people who were living in Darjeeling before the first of the Sherpas' mountaineering expeditions in 1907. But the success in mountaineering was different. For one thing, although I cannot find any actual figures, it is probable that the wages were higher than for any other form of unskilled labor, or rather that mountain portering quickly became distinguished from ordinary coolie work precisely as a form of skilled labor—which indeed it was. Equally important, however, were the nonmaterial benefits of the Sherpas' successes in mountaineering. In the close quarters, and the life-risking environment of the expeditions, they developed warm personal relationships with the Western mountaineers (whom the Sherpas seem to have cast as "protectors"), who in turn were deeply grateful for the kind of support the Sherpas provided. And they developed a "name," a special kind of reputation relative to the many other ethnic groups in the Darjeeling district of the time, standing out from among the several kinds of "Bhotias" with whom they had been jumbled before the turn of the century. The fact that they had been distinguished from other Bhotias in the 1901 census, before their first noteworthy expedition performance, suggests that their ethnic identity was not entirely created by their mountaineering success. But it certainly received an enormous boost through their expedition work, setting them on the road to the explosion of international fame that would come after the Hillary-Tenzing conquest of Everest in 1953.

Founding the Monasteries: Feeling "Big"

In discussing the role of the big people in founding the monasteries, I argued among other things that they sought to establish themselves as simultaneously altruistic and powerful, "small" as well as "big." This combination is both "legitimating" in the political sense, in that it shows the big man to have the interests of others at heart, and "meritorious" in the religious sense, in that it mitigates the egotism of bigness, and recasts bigness as the kind of egoless power that the gods use in their protection of all sentient beings. I will now try to show that the reciprocal argument is possible for the small people, who were being socially and economically depressed in this historical time, but who also were able to respond to their situations effectively and make themselves, if not objectively big, then at least subjectively somewhat efficacious and powerful.

There is very little to go on in trying to interpret the small people's intentions in the foundings of the monasteries. Neither big people nor small are very verbally expressive of motives, but at least for the big people, various anecdotes about their lives and their actions are available. These constitute behavioral "texts" that can be interpreted in attempting to establish intention. For the small people, only the most fragmentary sorts of indications are available. The following must thus be taken as very tentative.

Reports of the level of participation in the building constitute the main form of evidence. These suggest that the monastery foundings generated a great deal of solidarity among Sherpas of all levels, since everyone, "high and low" as it is always put, participated actively and enthusiastically. The small people do not appear to have seen the foundings as big-man projects, but rather as generative of merit for all. The impression that emerges is that virtually everyone thought the founding of the monasteries was an excellent enterprise that needed little explanation or justification. If one asks modern Sherpas at all levels of society why they thought monastery foundings were such good things, or why people thought so at the time, they simply say things like, "It makes our Sherpa religion higher," "It makes our religious work go better," "It is meritorious work," "It brings merit for all." One also gets a whiff of some of this unqualified and unreserved positive response in accounts of the ramne, the consecration, of Tengboche in 1919. After the religious ceremonies for the consecration, there was singing and dancing, drinking and horse races, and general merrymaking far into the night. Many older Sherpas interviewed in 1979 were there as children, and still remember it all very vividly.

But I have been arguing that the period preceding the rise of the monasteries was a period in which two major social developments were taking place: the division between big and small people was becoming more sharply and more negatively demarcated, and the small people were gaining access to material resources and identity reinforcement that allowed them to hold their own against the big. I would suggest then that the solidarity of big and small in the monastery foundings is based on inverse motives for the two sectors: the big were making statements of smallness, of (political) concern for the people and (religious) egolessness, while the small were making statements of bigness, of ability to harness the gods (the British, or the mountaineers, or simply money) as protectors, to defeat the demons (the Ranas, the big people, or simply the specter of poverty), and to control their own fates.

And if one asks in turn what generated this very positive and optimistic frame of mind among the ordinary villagers, one can see that indeed they were both doing well and expecting to continue to do well. Agricultural productivity was up, thanks to the potato. Cash income was up, thanks to the many opportunities in Darjeeling, most recently and most spectacularly at that point, in mountaineering. With cash, in turn, many small people could enlarge their field holdings and their herds, and reverse the slide to smallness set in motion by parcellization. And finally, the mountaineering success was in all likelihood producing a great deal of ethnic pride, as the Sherpas were singled out for personal affection and public praise in the very competitive arena of Darjeeling, where members of scores of other groups were also seeking to make a living. The positive valuation of Sherpa-ness takes on additional significance in relation to the increasing intrusion of the Nepal state in Solu-Khumbu, and in relation to the Sherpas' ethnic (construed as "caste") smallness vis-à-vis the Hindu Ranas, that was operating at the time (see Höfer 1979).

The religious activism of the small people, then, derived from an initially disadvantaged situation, but one to which they were finding a solution. In founding the monasteries with great enthusiasm, the small people were expressing a sense not of being ground down and trapped but a sense of being liberated and empowered. Everyone was feeling "big."

There is further support for this interpretation in a set of events that took place shortly after the founding of Tengboche. Robert Miller, who did research in Darjeeling between 1953 and 1955, and who interviewed some Khumbu Sherpas there, paints a picture of a virtual revolution against the political big people in Khumbu, a revolution fueled by the wages earned by young men doing mountaineering work out of Darjeeling. Having argued, perhaps too strongly, that the Sherpas were severely exploited and oppressed in the early part of the twentieth century, he goes on to emphasize that the wages from Darjeeling played a major role in undermining those exploitative relations:

> The young [mountaineering] porters represented a secondary source of income to the families at home, and there was less need to borrow money from the few rich families. Few men remained to work the land of the wealthier landholders, who in consequence lost one of their lines of control over the less favored population. Fewer poor families were forced to mortgage their small holdings to the rich, and the reduction of many families to tenant-status was slowed. In short, tenants and debtors became fewer, and the preeminent economic role of the rich declined. (1965:245–46)

But in addition to economic liberation, Miller indicates that the Darjeeling wages engendered a certain sense of political power in the small people. He describes a situation of political domination by two individuals from "Sola" (Solu) who, among other things, enforced a Rana/Hindu law requiring individuals who had been away working in India for an extended period of time to undergo purification. But then,

> The increased flow of Sherpas to Darjeeling in the 1930's . . . made great inroads on this tight system. The control by the [officials] was broken. As more young Khumbuwa returned from Darjeeling, they refused to pay to reenter their village and scoffed at the idea of impurity. (Ibid.)

This act of defiance may have had long-term consequences. It is probable that the Solu-born officials in Khumbu to whom he is referring include the son of Gembu Tsepal, the son having initially inherited the position of gembu after his father got involved in the alleged murder and fled to Tibet. If this is correct—and I think it must be, because he was the last Solu big man to hold a major position in Khumbu—the defiance of the gembu's directives would be part of the weakening of the legitimacy of the big people in general, and the decline of the gembu office in particular, as discussed in chapter 6. According to von Fürer-Haimendorf, after Tsepal fled to Lhasa,

> his son Pasang Gyalje succeeded him as *gembu* and at first he lived in his house in Namche but the opposition which had driven his father to Tibet continued to smolder, and he ultimately moved to Gole [in Solu], his family's ancestral village. (1964:121)

One speculates here that the "opposition" in question may have included the episode, or more probably the series of episodes, in which the young wage workers refused to comply with the gembu's directives, and in which the gembu's loss of authority and legitimacy became increasingly evident. As von Fürer-Haimendorf continues:

> From that moment he lost touch with Khumbu, and though nominally still *gembu*, could no longer exert any effective influence on local affairs. His son Lhakpa Gelbu retains only the title of *gembu* and is not recognized by the government, which now deals with the *pembu* without any intermediary. As an institution the office of *gembu* has ceased to be part of the Sherpa political system. (Ibid.)

What emerges here is that the undermining of the legitimacy of the big people did not simply come from on high, as appears to be the case when one takes the state's point of view. It also came from the active resistance of the small people, who had found a major source of self-empowerment in the wage and other opportunities in British India. It is worth noting that the dismantling of the gembuship represents a small but nonetheless real structural change, and a change in an egalitarian direction. As has been discussed, the office had been created by the Nepal state in the late eighteenth or early nineteenth century. It evidently represented an attempt to centralize and rationalize the Sherpa political system in a way that had never existed before. This attempt at centralization and rationalization worked for virtually the whole of the nineteenth century, and the gembu had evidently become quite dominant in the region, having linked himself with the Nauje trade monopoly, and having actively represented and enforced state policies (like the purity regulations) beyond simple tax collections and labor exactions. The dismantling of the office of gembu thus pulled the Sherpas back to the political status quo ante, which was not exactly egalitarian but was at least less hierarchically elaborated, thereby giving people a more direct (because more local) hold on their own big people. And while this change was not entirely the result of the small people's actions (the state itself undermined the position, and some big people also challenged it in challenging the Nauje trade monopoly), nonetheless the small people, emboldened in part by Darjeeling economic success, evidently made a significant contribution to the total process.

In sum, one can say that a significant number of Sherpa small people successfully enacted, at least in a metaphoric sense, the cultural schema of political/religious conflict in the late nineteenth and early twentieth centuries, casting themselves as "rivals" to the big people. That is, the small people were being economically squeezed by pembu who had lost much of their legitimacy by this time. Many small people thus went off and took advantage of the opportunities for earning cash opened up by the British in north India. Here they appear in aggregate as the political contender who leaves the area in order to gain greater powers through finding powerful "protection." They found this protection in the form of the British sahibs, and more generally in the form of an economic system that allowed them to earn wealth independently of all social relations. They returned to Solu-Khumbu with their newfound wealth and pride, and successfully stood up to the reigning big man. The loser left the area: the gembu went back to Solu, and the office of gembu disintegrated. The small people founded the monasteries, evidently in a mode of "triumph" and exaltation.

CHAPTER

IX

Monks and Nuns

THERE was another nonbig sector very actively involved in the foundings: the small but highly motivated set of ordained monks and nuns on the scene at the time. Although their activities, like those of the small people, are overshadowed by those of the wealthy sponsors and the great lamas, it is possible to bring them into focus. Indeed it becomes possible to suggest, with some conviction, that the monks and nuns, as much as the big people and high lamas, triggered the whole monastic movement. Looking back at the stories of the foundings of Tengboche and Chiwong, one can see their hands in these events. In the Tengboche story, there was Lama Gulu who took vows at Rumbu, and who began to gather disciples about him at his meditation retreat above Khumjung. There was also the Zamte lama, who went and took vows, and the four young monks who became his disciples. The group at Zamte can be seen in fact as a kind of proto-monastery that took shape through a grass-roots process without benefit of high secular or religious sponsorship. After the Zamte lama left the area, the four monks became the first cohort of Tengboche monks.

At Chiwong, next, the founder Sangye's son was a former Tashilhunpo monk who had come back to Solu and married, but who was still apparently much committed to monastic ideals. In most versions of the story of the founding of Chiwong, Sangye took the lead (out of rivalry with his brother Karma), but even in these versions his son Dawa Tenzing is represented as helping him actively with the fundraising. In at least one version of the story that I heard, however, Dawa Tenzing was a much stronger instigator.

And finally, there were the ten nuns who became the first cohort of Devuche nunnery. I have not introduced the founding of Devuche yet, largely for reasons of simplifying the exposition. Founded in 1925, just two years after Chiwong, it was the last of the set of celibate institutions sponsored largely by the big Lama clan people, and the first of the nunneries in the region.

The founding of Devuche is introduced here because the account of this event, more than any of the others, provides more of a ground-level view of the founding of a religious institution. It is also the only one of the first three celibate institutions to have a member of the founding cohort still alive at the time of the 1979 fieldwork—an eighty-three-year-old former nun by the name of Ngawang Samden (no connection with the monk of the same name at Thami monastery). Ngawang Samden was not only one of the original cohort of Devuche nuns; she was one of the chief instigators of the founding. Her story reveals the very active role played by the nuns in launching the nunnery, despite the fact that, at first glance, this is simply another event staged by big people and big lamas. Indeed it was her story that cued me to look more carefully at the other foundings, and to try to see the activities of the smaller people more clearly.

This final analytic chapter introduces some final theoretical points. For one thing, another transformation of the notion of "legitimation" is introduced. The monks and nuns were largely children of elite families, and their involvement in the foundings of the monasteries seems to have represented a different kind of need for "legitimation"—in the sense of affirmation of social value—than that of either the big people or the small. Not surprisingly, it involved aspects of both modes, as I will discuss later in the chapter.

Second, this chapter provides the first glimpses of a dynamic that will become increasingly important in subsequent Sherpa history: the unintended consequences of the monastery foundings themselves, as these began to interact with the other processes already at work in Sherpa society. Thus far I have treated the monasteries as the end points of the analysis, effects of multiple interacting causes. Yet as soon as the realistic possibility of monasticism entered the Sherpa universe—basically with the founding of Rumbu, in Tibet, in 1902—it began to become as much a part of the causes as of the effects. Specifically, the monasteries (first Rumbu in Tibet, and later the Sherpa monasteries themselves) seem to have joined with the wage-labor opportunities in giving young people a sense of alternatives to existing modes of social adulthood. Thus one can see the emergence of parent-child conflict (over marriage arrangements), which had previously been noticeably absent from the historical record (see the discussion in chapter 2), but which was to become in the twentieth century almost as much of a friction point in the social structure as brother relations had been all along. Although the consequences of the monastery foundings, intended and unintended, will be the primary subject of the sequel to this book (Ortner n.d.b), it must properly begin here.

This chapter will have much the same shape as the last one, that is, the shape of the book as a whole condensed into a single chapter exposition. After describing the founding of Devuche nunnery, I will examine the social situation of the monks and nuns—their origins as "lesser" children (daughters and middle sons) of the elites, or as I have called them elsewhere, "little big people" (Ortner 1983). I will consider the structural problems faced by such children not only in terms of inheritance (stressed throughout this book) but also in terms of marriage, as well as the particular pressures on the marriage system in this historical period. I will then consider the way in which the founding of Rumbu monastery in the adjacent region of Tibet at the turn of the century served for many of these young people as a matrix of new opportunity and empowerment, which in turn was expressed in the foundings of the monasteries on the Sherpa side of the border.

Time Frame

1902	Founding of Rumbu monastery in Tibet
1916	Founding of Tengboche
1923	Founding of Chiwong
1925	Founding of Devuche nunnery, near Tengboche
1952	Transformation of Thami noncelibate temple into a celibate monastery

The Founding of Devuche Nunnery

Devuche nunnery was begun in 1925, just two years after Chiwong, and was completed in 1928.[1] Many of the same people who had founded Tengboche were involved in the founding of Devuche: On the secular front, Karma, an affine of Karma's called Phule, Karma's son-in-law Kusang, and even—at long distance from Lhasa where he had fled after the murder case—the former gembu Tsepal.[2] And on the religious front, the Zatul Rinpoche made contributions, although the main religious figure in this case was Lama Gulu at nearby Tengboche, as well as the Tengboche monks themselves. In fact, Devuche was defined from the outset as a branch of Tengboche. The Tengboche head lama was established as the authority over the Devuche nuns, although for most purposes the nuns would handle their own internal affairs and conduct many of their own rituals.

Later in the chapter I will tell the story of how Ngawang Samden came to take her vows in the first place. I pick up the Devuche story here at the point of emergence of the idea of founding a nunnery.

Around the time that Ngawang Samden took her vows, nine other women, who with her were to become the founding cohort of Devuche, took vows in Tibet as well. (One of them was a daughter of the Tengboche sponsor Karma.)[3] All of them eventually migrated back to the Khumbu area, where they pursued their religious studies together, probably under the instruction of one of the Tengboche monks.

The idea of founding the nunnery, according to Ngawang Samden, came entirely from the nuns themselves:

> One night, she and the other nuns were sitting together and drinking tea. They were talking about building a house where they could do religious work together. They did not sleep all night. The next morning they got up and decided to go and put their request to Lama Gulu, the head of Tengboche monastery.

Lama Gulu commended the nuns for coming with this meritorious request, and he gave them the chayik, or charter, to build the temple for the nunnery. Later, he gave them money, as well as certain symbolically important religious objects. At that time, the Tengboche monks also gave the nuns money from their own personal resources. This last act seems quite significant, in indicating a kind of solidarity across the ranks of the newly developing celibate community. Later, when the nunnery was being built, the monks also helped with the physical labor.

Concerning the fund-raising for the nunnery, Lama Gulu told the nuns to go begging for more donations, which they did. Armed with the chayik, the nuns went to virtually every Sherpa village. In each case, they approached a prominent individual, who in turn called the villagers together and explained the nuns' mission. They went as far south as Phaphlu and Zhung in Solu, and Ngawang Samden said that the contributions were enormous. Virtually every individual in Khumbu and Solu gave something.

There were also large contributions from the big monastery sponsors, secular and religious. Yet despite these contributions, the initiative was carried along by the nuns themselves. For example, one of the contributions from the Zatul Rinpoche took the form of two large loads of old woolen clothing.[4] Ngawang Samden personally sold these clothes to raise money for the building.

Ngawang Samden and Karma's daughter Ani Tarchin built their own small houses at the nunnery site even before the temple was begun. The nuns coordinated the entire building process, cooking and serving for the great numbers of volunteer workers who turned out for the project. Ngawang Samden said that so many people turned out to help that there weren't enough plates to feed them on. On at least one occasion, the nuns had to buy a bolt of cloth, lay it out on the ground, and dump people's food portions directly on the cloth—an utterly unheard of (and normally utterly unacceptable) mode of serving food. The nuns also each donated, out of their own resources, one day's food for all the workers building the temple.

After the temple was built and consecrated, it still required more internal furnishing, and once again the nuns went into action.

> After the consecration, Ngawang Samden, Ani Tarchin, and one other nun went to Lhasa, where they contacted Gembu Tsepal [who was permanently resident there] and also Ngawang Samden's two younger brothers. These three men helped the nuns, calling people together, buying them all beer, and raising a lot of donations. With the money the nuns bought carpets and dragon-hangings in Lhasa for furnishing the interior of the temple. You can still see [Ngawang Samden said to the ethnographer] all these things inside the temple today.

The story of the founding of Devuche offers the first glimpse of what might be called monastic activism—the efforts of nuns and monks to create and expand their own institutions. It may be assumed that similar dynamics were in play in the foundings of Tengboche (in the activities of the Zamte monks) and Chiwong (in the activities of Sangye's ex-monk son Dawa Tenzing). And while it may seem obvious that monks and nuns would want to found monasteries, this is not necessarily the case. Individual Sherpas had probably gone off into Tibetan monasteries over the whole of Sherpa history, in effect simply dropping out of Sherpa society. It is known that there was a significant number of Sherpa monks at Tashilhunpo, in central Tibet, in the early twentieth century. Yet by the second decade of the twentieth century, Sherpa monks who took vows in Tibet were returning to Solu-Khumbu, setting up their own little groups (such as the one at Zamte, or Ngawang Samden's group of nuns on the fringes of Tengboche) and lobbying for the foundings of full-scale monasteries and nunneries. Clearly the situation had changed.

Who Are the Monks and Nuns?

THE MONKS AND NUNS AS LITTLE BIG PEOPLE

In the last chapter I examined the structural position and changing historical circumstances of the "small people." The small people, I said, are the products of the sibling/inheritance/taxation system over time—the descendants of middle brothers who got the smallest inheritances, and who could not recoup because of the continuous exaction of goods and labor. For them, the Darjeeling labor and petty capital market provided a solution to both their property and their status problems, and their enthusiastic involvement in monastery building expressed—I argued—their newfound sense of both security and empowerment. Insofar as the religion is primarily elaborated from a "big" point of view, the point here is that everyone seems to have been feeling big.

The monks and nuns can be looked at from a similar perspective. One may view them as the disadvantaged children (daughters and middle sons) of the elites at the point in the developmental cycle before the decline to smallness. The difference between them and the small people is simply time: as unmarried sons and daughters of big people, the (prospective) monks and nuns are still "big," but if they were to make less than ideal marriages, they and their descendants would be on their way to smallness. Let us look a bit more closely at their positions.

On the one hand, the monks and nuns have always come from the wealthier sectors of Sherpa society. This is almost necessarily the case, since the child who became a nun or monk stopped contributing to the family's productive economy, yet continued to require financial support. The family thus had to be able to absorb this double cost. Even in the state-supported Tibetan monasteries, and later among the Sherpas at Chiwong monastery (where the monks' and nuns' subsistence was paid for), an individual needed to pay a variety of other costs (including paying for some of the teaching). If the individual had no personal resources, the only alternative was to work as a servant for another monk or nun.

Yet if the monks and nuns were children of wealthy families, they were precisely the less advantaged children in those families—the middle sons, and the daughters. It will be recalled that, although all sons are supposed to get equal shares of the parents' productive estate, in practice things do not always work out so evenly. At issue are both property and status, in varying combinations. The eldest son has the status, since by birth order he is the highest and most deserving of respect. The eldest also generally gets a full share of the property, including a house, although he may have to wait a relatively long time to get it, since his marriage comes at a relatively early stage in his father's economic career. The youngest does not have the status of birth order, but he has a secure set of property expectations (the parental house, as well as his own share of land), and he is also often the sentimental favorite of his parents. It is the middle sons, then, who fall in between the two stools of secure status and secure property.

As for the daughters, I have argued elsewhere that in many respects they are similar to middle sons (Ortner 1983). Just as the middle son, by virtue of birth order, is second in respect to his elder brother, so a daughter is, by virtue of gender, second in respect to her brothers. And just as a middle son has an unpredictable property situation relative to his brothers, a girl confronts the same type of situation. This is the case because, although all girls are technically entitled only to movable goods—jewelry and household effects—some girls do get a field or two and some animals in their dowries (see March 1979). But the father's sentimental or political urge to enhance the girl's dowry cannot be counted upon with any certainty. The dowry, in turn, has direct implications for the girl's marriage prospects. Thus, just as a middle son might get a poor share of the estate, and so be set on a course toward "smallness," so a daughter with a poor dowry will likely get a poor marriage, and so be set on a similar course. For all girls, then, there is an uncertainty about maintaining status after marriage, for themselves and for their children, similar to the uncertainty that is particularly marked for middle sons.

All daughters and all middle sons do not of course take monastic vows. It is the case however that all nuns are (by definition) daughters, and that a significant majority of monks are middle sons. Although there is no information on the founding cohorts of the celibate institutions, there is good information from the fifties and sixties, and there is no reason to imagine that the early period would have been any different. It should be noted first that the proportion of middle sons in the overall adult male population is probably around 30 percent.[5] In contrast, at Tengboche in 1957, out of ten monks reported on, seven were middle sons, one was an eldest, one a youngest, and one an only son (von Fürer-Haimendorf 1964:140). The Tengboche proportion is thus 70 percent. At three other monasteries (Thami, Takshindo, and Chiwong) surveyed in 1967–68, of twenty-two monks for whom data were available, eleven were middle sons, five were eldest, four were youngest, and two were only sons.[6] Here the proportion is lower (50 percent) but still well above the average in the population as a whole. Further, at least some of the apparent exceptions can probably be disregarded. I know that some of the only sons, for example, are illegitimate children of former nuns.

There is thus strong evidence that the monks and nuns, like the small people, are products (at different levels of society, and at different points in time) of the family/property/inheritance contradictions of Sherpa society. Starting from a high position, however, their problems are somewhat different. In terms of overall family status, they begin as "big" people, yet at the same time they are subordinate (by birth order, or by gender) *within* the family status order. Their alternatives are to accept this permanent second-class status (their genders/birth orders will affect their statuses in the village for the rest of their lives), or (for boys) to compete with their eldest brother for primacy in the local arena. Obviously many men and women do accept one or the other of these alternatives. But monasticism offers a third possibility, not available within the secular status system: a chance to be morally "high," without being "big" on the lay scales of status and power. Monasticism transforms the negative potential of little-big liminality into a positive role that is not only of value to the individuals but to society as a whole. In fact, given the contradictions of the Sherpa social and cultural order, monasticism creates the most perfect—and indeed most culturally valued—form of legitimation. The monk or nun is (theoretically) higher in status than even the biggest lay people, yet at the same time (again theoretically) the monk or nun is "smaller"—materially poorer, spiritually less self-interested—than even the smallest villager. It is symbolically, as well as pragmatically, the perfect solution to the contradictions of the little big people's positions.

THE NINETEENTH-CENTURY MARRIAGE SQUEEZE

By the late nineteenth and early twentieth centuries many fathers had gained in wealth—at the very least because of the introduction of the potato, but in many cases because of profiting from other economic opportunities as well. It is precisely under such conditions, however, that Sherpa (and Tibetan) parents become concerned over the disposition of their estates. One might think that with more resources, the decisions over transmission of property would be easier, and every child could get a satisfactory share. In fact quite the reverse tends to be the case. In Tibet, it was precisely the more propertied families that enforced the indivisible estate norm much more strictly, with much higher rates of polyandry and of sons in monasteries than among the smaller people (see Aziz 1978; Goldstein 1971a).

For the Sherpas, there is some evidence that, as newly wealthy parents sought to keep their property intact in the early twentieth century, they too turned more to the option of arranging polyandrous unions. Thus while the early Sherpa genealogies show virtually no polyandry (see chapter 2), von Fürer-Haimendorf reported that 8 percent of Khumbu marriages were polyandrous in the 1950s, and these were largely among the bigger families (1964:68–70).

Specifically among the big monastery-founding families, there were no instances of polyandrous marriage arrangements for their children. There were, however, several other kinds of politically and economically motivated marriages arranged among this group. Karma, for example, married one of his daughters to Kusang, apparently as part of an end run around the Nauje trade restriction. Sangye was married to a woman seven years older than himself, in what must have been a political or economic arrangment that fortunately worked out well. Gembu Tsepal was married to a Nauje woman; this was presumably connected to his move to Nauje. There were also enough marriages between Lama-clan children from Solu and Nauje big people's children from Khumbu to generate a local aphorism on the matter.[7]

It is not clear whether there was an actual overall increase in more narrowly instrumental marriage arrangements, made with less concern for the children's wishes, than there had been in the past. But there is evidence of increased *resistance* to such arrangements. In the early textual and oral sources, resistance to parental wishes never appears at all. And while negative evidence can never be conclusive, given the reporting of sibling conflict in these sources, it seems reasonable to guess that if parent-child conflict is not mentioned, this is because it was not common.

The appearance of parent-child conflict seems to represent a significant shift in the Sherpa social and cultural order. The earlier emphasis on fraternal conflict seemed to exclude any sense that the parents might be part of the child's problem. In the cultural schema, and apparently in actual social relations as well, an unfair or unequal inheritance distribution was always blamed on a brother, who was thought to have manipulated things to gain the advantage. A son could have blamed the father, or the parents, for favoring his brother, but it does not seem that he normally did so. This is an aspect of the hegemonic force of the cultural schema: it provides one interpretation of a state of affairs, and renders others hard to think.

The increase in parent-child conflict appears to be a function of several different factors. On the one hand, as just suggested, there were reasons why parents might have been manipulating their children's marriages somewhat less considerately than they had in the past. On the other hand, there were also certain alternatives open to young people that did not exist before. The availability of (realistic) alternatives is one critical factor in breaching a hegemony; much of a hegemony's force derives from an absence of such alternatives (although the hegemony itself may make available alternatives appear unrealistic). In any event, from the early twentieth century on, young people began to resist the marriage arrangements being made for them. Since marriage was tied to inheritance, however, the forms of resistance to marriage also had to provide the young person with alternative forms of support. Here, of course, is where—for some young people—Darjeeling came into the picture. In Darjeeling, a man (and in a few cases a woman) could make money on his own and not *need* his inheritance. His wages could become a kind of declaration of independence from the whole property/marriage/status game being played out with his person at this stage of his life.

With respect to this set of issues, one Khumbu man in his forties described to me his early conflict with his father:

> P said that he hasn't lived at home since he was 18 . . . He couldn't tolerate being home much—his father was *kyongbo* (hard) and had a *kha tsende* (hot mouth). He rode him hard about work.

His brother later elaborated with special reference to marriage arrangements, and to the Darjeeling alternative:

> In the past [he said] marriages were arranged by the fathers and this generally worked out badly with much divorce. I said P and his wife seem to have worked out well. N said yes, that now they're ok, but that they had had a bad time. P split for Darjeeling . . . and then to Kathmandu, and he and his wife finally got together [many years later back in Khumbu].

Here is a similar story of unwelcome marriage arrangements and the use of the Darjeeling option:

> C [a man of fifty-seven in 1979] wanted to be a celibate monk but his parents married him off. He stayed in Tengboche [studying] for two and a half years, between the ages of 7 and 9. When he was 9 his parents chose a wife for him. His mother and his wife's parents were very close. He was very angry with his mother and father. When he was 13 he was sent to live in his wife's house. So he ran away to . . . Darjeeling.

Von Fürer-Haimendorf reports similar patterns of resistance, in this case to polyandrous marriage arrangements; he also connects the resistance to Darjeeling, not so much because it provided an economic alternative to inheritance as because it introduced new values:

> [Polyandry] is . . . considered a laudable sign of fraternal solidarity, and I have heard older people complain about the 'selfishness' of present-day young men, who will break up a paternal estate because each wants a wife to himself. If there is in fact a

> decline in the number of polyandrous marriages . . . it must be due to the return to Khumbu of young men who have spent some time in Darjeeling and other places where polyandry is frowned upon. (1964:70)

In sum there is suggestive evidence—in the elevated rate of polyandry, in certain cases of clearly instrumental arrangements, and in stories of children's resistance[8]—for an increase in "political" marriage arranging among big Sherpa parents in this era. The increase would have been related largely to the parents' growth in wealth and enlarged concerns about maintaining status for themselves and their children.

But there is one other strategy (besides strategic marriage arranging) for overcoming some of the contradictions in the property and status system: sending one or more of the sons to become a monk. Although the son or brother in the monastery will have to be supported, this is far cheaper than giving him a full-scale house, and his full set of fields and animals. At the same time it brings merit to him and to his family, and makes him "high" in ways that stand apart from the usual questions of power and prestige. Prior to the turn of the century, this option was rare and difficult to utilize. The nearest monastery, or at least the nearest one that was hospitable to Sherpa monks, was at Tashilhunpo, deep in central Tibet. Some Sherpa monks did go there, but it probably required either very high motivation on the part of the young person, or very determined parental pressure.

All of this changed with the founding of Rumbu monastery in 1902, since the monastery was relatively close to Solu-Khumbu, since the big Sherpa traders normally operated in that region, and since the head lama made Sherpa monks welcome in his newly growing establishment. Rumbu thus became a serious possibility for parents concerned with their children's economic and status prospects, as well as for children reacting to their family's inheritance and marriage manipulations. It was, for some children of the elites, what Darjeeling was for the small people—a place to go that gave one a new start and a new set of resources with which to pursue the Sherpa game of life.

Rumbu Monastery and the Seeds of Monastic Rebellion

THE FOUNDING OF RUMBU

Rumbu was founded in 1902 by the great lama whose life has figured so largely in this book, the Zatul Rinpoche.[9] The lama was only thirty-six at the time of the founding, and he is aptly described as a man of "exceptional energy" (Aziz 1978:210).

The site of the monastery was on the very inhospitable north slope of Mount Everest, where a few nuns' meditation huts were already in use. The Zatul Rinpoche established his own residence among the nuns, and began to draw together both male and female disciples. The lama also began fund-raising, in both the immediate D'ing-ri vicinity and in Khumbu, in order to establish the monastery and to expand the establishment as a whole. He "secured the patronage of wealthy D'ing-ri agriculturalists and traders. He also brought Nepali traders, Sherpa from Khumbu and Newar from Kathmandu under his aegis" (ibid.). The monastery grew quickly and by the time of the first Mount Everest reconnaissance in 1921, there were "20 permanent lamas who always live there, together with the reincarnated Lama . . . [and] three hundred other associated lamas who come in periodically" (quoted in MacDonald 1973).

The growth of Rumbu was precisely in the period in which the Sherpa traders would have reached the peak of their wealth, and would have faced the various questions I have discussed throughout this work—questions of political legitimacy, of personal salvation, and (most relevant to the present discussion) of the material and social well-being of their children in the next generation.

With Rumbu now a viable possibility, many people began to consider the monastic option for at least some of their children. Although Sangye sent his son Dawa Tenzing to Tashilhunpo, almost all the other monastics who played a role in the foundings of the first Sherpa celibate institutions took their vows at Rumbu: Lama Gulu; some or all of the Zamte lama's disciples; the Kusho Tulku and most of the early Chiwong monks; Karma's daughter Ani Tarchin and most of the founding Devuche nuns. At least some of these people were probably sent by their parents, although others were clearly runaways from unappealing marriage arrangements.

Unlike the situation with respect to strategic marriage arrangements, there are no indications that children resented being sent to monasteries by their parents; quite the contrary. Although many monks and nuns ultimately broke their vows (the rate has been a more or less constant 50 percent), this does not appear to represent discontentment with having been sent into the monastery in the first place. In general most young people were apparently pleased to have been sent, and did not feel that this was an unappealing life choice. From both the parent's and the child's point of view, problems of property and status were solved by taking monastic vows. In addition, the child entered an attractive and comfortable situation in which—

as the Sherpas themselves emphasize—he or she did not have to do physical work, had no family responsibilities, and had an interesting and culturally respected life career (see Paul 1970:ch. 6; Aziz 1976a; Ortner 1983).

There is thus no evidence of conflict between parents and children over parents' sending children into the monasteries. Indeed it would be very unlikely that parents would send an unwilling child (although they might send a merely passive one), since such a child would in all likelihood break the vows, or cause trouble in the monastery, or otherwise embarrass or bring religious demerit to the parents. The monastic choice was (and is) thus generally a very successful and positive solution to both the parents' and the childrens' problems of property, status, and identity.

But the increasing use of the monastic choice on the part of the parents appears to have had a certain unforeseen effect on the marriage system, and here is where the unintended consequences come in—the point at which the effect becomes part of the cause. Children began to resist the marriage arrangements being made for them, demanding instead that their parents send them to be monks or nuns. For all the reasons that monasticism was such a good solution to family contradictions in the first place (as well as for other reasons intrinsic to the attractiveness of the monastic career), many children apparently sought it, even when—as was the case for the majority of people—the parents had other plans.

Such resistance was buttressed by the ideology of monasticism itself, then emanating strongly from Rumbu. The Zatul Rinpoche and the Rumbu monks were eager to propagate monastic values, stressing the renunciation of sex, marriage, and family, and extolling the spiritual life. Not much is known about the specific programs the Rinpoche put into effect at his own monastery, but it seems a safe guess that the program of observances he instituted later at Tengboche was also the program he had established earlier at Rumbu. The program is complex and cannot be reviewed here. But one observance in particular is relevant for the present discussion: a ritual called Nyungne, specifically designed to give the lay people a taste of monastic practice (Ortner 1978a:ch. 3). Nyungne is founded on a myth of a great female monastic who resisted her parents' attempts to marry her off to wealthy kings and princes, and instead gained salvation and transcendental bliss. I will look briefly at the myth, and then return to the Sherpa monks and nuns who, I will argue, were not only being sent to monasteries by their parents but were also choosing the monastic option even when their parents—like those in the myth—were opposed to it.

GELUNGMA PALMA AND MONASTICISM BY CHOICE

Gelungma (that is, "female-fully-ordained-monastic")[10] Palma began as the daughter of a king and queen in India. At the age of three, she observed butchers slaughtering royal sheep for a feast. She was repelled by the scene and announced that she would not be a lay person when she grew up, but rather would—as it is always put—go to religion, *cho*. When she was seven, she asked her parents for permission to go to cho, but they refused on the grounds that girls could not do (effective) religion.

When Gelungma Palma was eleven years old, four kings came to ask for her hand. Her father asked her which one she wanted, but she said that she would not be anyone's wife. She tried to persuade her father to let her go to cho, but he promised her to one of the kings. She then approached the god (who is also the patron god of the Nyungne ritual) Pawa Cherenzi and asked him to make her ugly with leprosy, so that no man would want to marry her.

Once again she asked her mother, then her father, for permission to go to cho, but in this case they told her she must get permission from her brother. She tricked the brother by telling him that the parents had agreed, so he agreed too and sent her off, with an elephant and two loads of gold.[11]

It was at this point that Gelungma Palma's religious career really began, and the story goes on at great length, through many trials and many moments of triumph and elation. She became a brilliant religious practitioner, winning religious debates against high monks, and eventually being asked to head a (male) monastery. But then the leprosy struck her. She retired to an inner chamber of the monastery saying that she was going into meditation retreat, but her blood dripped down through the ceiling. The monks thought she was having a baby and she was forced to leave the monastery. She wandered for years with her servant and finally achieved nirvana. She joined Pawa Cherenzi in heaven, but returned to the monastery that she had been forced to leave and brought the monks the Nyungne texts for their own salvation.[12]

One would not wish to claim that the Gelungma Palma tale in itself motivated young people to avoid marriage and take vows. The tale and its associated ritual, however, constitute one element of a multidimensional symbolic assault on marriage, family, and secular life in general that emanated from the monasteries. This can be documented very substantially for the Sherpa monasteries (Ortner n.d.b), and there is every reason to assume that this was true for Rumbu as well. Indeed, the foundings of the Sherpa monastic institutions are themselves evidence of the spread of Rumbu's ideology.

This larger religious campaign against marriage and for monasticism almost certainly influenced some of the Sherpa young people to resist their parents' arrangements, providing a sense of positive life alternatives and a way out of the bind created by the fact that marriage was the only cultural route to property and full social adulthood. Many examples of young people seeking to avoid marriage and take vows can be cited. I have already described the case of C, the young man who spent two and a half years studying at Tengboche but was married off against his will by his parents. Here is a similar case:

> H [a married lama of about fifty in 1967] started studying religion at age 10 or 11. It was all his own idea. His father was against it, so he had to run away to study with the Pumboche lama. H wanted to be a celibate monk, but his father really got mad at that, and made him take a wife at age 11 or so, with the result that there was lots of fighting/trouble among H, his wife, and his parents.

I am inclined to think that at least some of these cases, in which the parents resisted the monastic choice, represented problems of marriage manipulation at the smaller levels of society. Manipulations were probably intensive at this level too, not for reasons of inheritance and status as among the big people, but because of the Rana tax squeeze on the small people. Marriage manipulations among the small people were largely for purposes of gaining the labor of the child-in-law, as is made clear in these further cases:

> When G. [a man of about sixty in 1967] was young, 12 or so, his father arranged a marriage for him with a girl who was much older. The motive was so that the father would have another working hand or servant around the house. G resented this and did not like the wife, so he sent her back. Once again his father married him off against his will, and once again it broke up.[13]

> She [a fifty-two-year-old woman in 1967] was born in Takto of middle wealth parents, and had many brothers and sisters . . . [When her father died?] she went to Sete, where she "helped" (was a servant) in the big house there. From there she was married off to a Changma man who already had one wife. She hated the marriage, fought all the time with the first wife, and finally ran away back to Sete. [This woman did not say that she had wished to become a nun when she was younger, but by the time

of the interview she was a *genchu*, an old person who takes a limited set of monastic vows and styles her- (or him-) self as a monastic.]

When he was young he [a man in his thirties in 1967] didn't want to take marriage, he wanted to be a monk. . . . When he was 14 there was an epidemic, and within 12 days both of his parents and a brother died. His uncle took over care of the family. . . . At the age of 14 his uncle married him off, because there weren't enough people in the house to do all the work.[14]

Even at this smaller level of Sherpa society, it is evident that monastic ideology was extremely appealing to young people, and was felt to be a positive alternative to the problems of marriage. But at this social level the parents simply could not afford to let the child go. Among the big people, however, at least some of the children won out. Here are two examples:

When he [the head lama of a new Sherpa monastery] was young [in the 1930s] he studied Nepali school subjects for a couple of years. Then he decided he wanted to do religion. His father was against this: it's the Sherpa custom to give the clever boys fields and wives, and send the dull ones to the monastery. Since he was smart, his father wanted him to do secular work and, to prove his point, married him off twice, at ages 10 and 11. He sent both wives back. He wanted to be a monk. So at 13 he went [to study religion, apparently with his father's blessing].

He [a senior monk at a major monastery] was the son of wealthy parents. He was also the youngest son. His parents wanted him to stay home and marry, but he wanted to do religion. [Apparently his parents acquiesced and sent him to become a monk.]

And two of the people in the monastery founding stories also succeeded in taking monastic vows, contrary to what their parents had in mind for them in the first place. The first was Lama Gulu who accepted his arranged marriage as a young man, but was very unhappy and went off and took monastic vows as soon as his (ex-) wife died.[15] The other person was the nun Ngawang Samden, whose activities in the founding of Devuche nunnery were related at the beginning of this chapter, and whose personal history may be told briefly here.

Ngawang Samden was born into a family of some substance. Her father may have been a pembu. One of her brothers was a pembu, and he and another brother were both apparently powerful men in

Ngawang Samden, one of the founding nuns of Devuche nunnery, in her eighties in 1979.

their time.[16] One of these brothers in turn was the father of a man serving as a government official (the *pradhan panch*) at the time of my fieldwork. And one of her sisters married another pembu, whose son in turn has become one of the most prominent, respected, and influential men currently active in the area.

As can be seen from the fact that Ngawang Samden's sister was married to a pembu, this was precisely the sort of family in which the disposition of the children in appropriate marriages was carefully considered. Thus when Ngawang Samden was twenty-four (around 1920), her father betrothed her to a wealthy older man who already had one wife. Polygyny is relatively rare in Sherpa society.[17] It is almost entirely confined to wealthy and high-status men, and one must assume that the prospective husband was chosen largely for political and economic reasons. But this arrangement triggered Ngawang Samden's rebellion: she did not want to get married, and so she ran away from home to become a nun. She fled to Rumbu monastery, where she took vows from the Zatul Rinpoche. Later she returned to Khumbu, where her parents acquiesced in her decision.

The departure for Darjeeling on the part of a dissatisfied middle brother in a "small" family had only the legitimacy of pragmatic effectiveness. But the flight to a monastery on the part of an unhappy child from a high-status family had enormous cultural, as well as pragmatic, value. Every such child was in effect Gelungma Palma, set on a course of accruing vast amounts of merit and ultimate salvation. Some parents—mostly, I think, the poorer ones who could not afford the economic costs—resisted the child's decision and arranged a marriage anyway; others—those, I think, who could afford it, like Ngawang Samden's—acquiesced with good grace in a fait accompli.

FOUNDING THE MONASTERIES

I have suggested that parental marriage manipulations were probably up (or were perceived as up) in the early twentieth century. This would have been true at the small level because of the tax squeeze, and at the big level for reasons of maintaining the wealth and status of the family into the next generation. In the same period, a strong dose of monastic ideology was emanating from Rumbu monastery. The monastic option was appealing to young people at all levels, but only the big families could afford it. Here the parents both sent some of their children to take vows, and found that other children chose the monastic option on their own, even when their parents did not want them to. All of which accounts for the growing number of celibate Sherpa monks and nuns who become visible in the historical record at about this time. What remains to be accounted for, however, is why these monks and nuns did not stay, as they apparently used to do, in the Tibetan monasteries—in Tashilhunpo or Rumbu—but rather came back to Solu-Khumbu and formed what might be called a monastic lobby.

Part of the explanation probably lies with the Zatul Rinpoche, who was interested in expanding monastic Buddhism in general, and his own sphere of religious influence in particular. It is known that he urged Lama Gulu to found Tengboche, and it is likely that he urged many of the other young Sherpas who came to take vows at Rumbu to return and involve themselves in upgrading Sherpa religious life.

But there may be another level of motivation operating here, one that by now will be familiar to the reader. Although a young person sent (or gone by choice) to a Tibetan monastery or nunnery may feel that this is the best possible solution to the various contradictions of family life and personal status discussed earlier, yet nonetheless it is clear that going to a monastery far away in Tibet is more or less the end of one's role within one's natal social world. It is the analogue of leaving the area after losing a political struggle, or migrating and setting up house elsewhere after getting the short end of the stick in an inheritance situation. It is the end of the social game, and it leaves the arena to the winners. One may assume that, after entering a monastery and becoming committed to high religious ideals, the individual no longer cares about such things. But for new monks and nuns, whose motivations are unlikely, except in rare cases, to be highly spiritual, I should think this would still matter very much.

Thus just as the small people could come back from Darjeeling and reestablish themselves with respect and self-respect in the community, so the monks and nuns, in involving themselves actively in the foundings of the monasteries and nunneries, were reentering the Solu-Khumbu scene with a new status and a new sense of self. Where Darjeeling gave the small people cash, the vows gave these young people an autonomous role in the world; they were independent of kin and family and in control of their own moral fates. (Although they were still for the most part dependent on their parents for material support, such support was no longer defined by parent-child relations, but rather by monk-lay relations in which the receiver is superior to the giver.) In both cases, I suggest, the individuals felt "legitimated," although in somewhat different ways.

A good example of this dynamic may be seen in the life of the Kusho Tulku, the lama who became the first head of Chiwong monastery. The Kusho Tulku was an extremely imposing figure, most comparable perhaps to Sangye in the intensity of his character and in the drama of his life history. His career illustrates well the way in which Rumbu monastery could be used by a middle son of a big family in that era. The Kusho Tulku was a middle son of the (married) head lama of Thami temple, one of the original three noncelibate lama temples in Khumbu. His older brother was destined to become the head lama in turn. In the past, the Kusho Tulku might simply have become a "smaller" married lama, but these were the enthusiastic early years of Rumbu monastery. The Kusho Tulku thus went off to Rumbu to take vows. When he returned, he was invited by the Thami lamas to become head lama at Thami, thus displacing his older brother. He was then invited by Sangye to join in the founding of Chiwong celibate monastery and to become its first head. For the Kusho Tulku the Rumbu option was thus very clearly the analogue of Darjeeling, to which the disadvantaged brother could go off, build up a stake of social resources (money, status, religious power), and return to compete successfully with his more advantaged siblings.

I argued earlier that the Darjeeling wages gave the small people a sense of empowerment, of being able to maintain themselves as social players and significant members of the community. I argued that it was this sense of being "big" and having some control over their lives that was expressed in their active participation in founding the monasteries. I would now argue much the same thing about the "little big people," and the meaning of their participation in the foundings. Their subjective sense of having achieved a satisfactory redefinition of their place in the Sherpa world was expressed partly (as it was for the small people) in the exuberance with which they threw themselves into the work of building the monasteries, or in the best-documented case, the nunnery. The young nuns' enthusiasm as they planned what was to become Devuche nunnery is obvious. They did not sleep all night before going to see Lama Gulu to ask for his authorization for the project. They went around fund-raising in distant Sherpa villages and in Tibet. Ngawang Samden and her friend built their houses on the site before construction on the nunnery even started. They organized the construction themselves, cooking the food and serving the volunteer builders. They contributed their own wealth to the building project. They raised more funds through various methods, including the sale of old clothing received from the Zatul Rinpoche. They bought the interior furnishings and furnished the temple themselves. This kind of energy can only come from a sense of the tremendous meaningfulness of the project—not just from finding a practical solution to a material problem, but from finding a whole new way to construct one's self and one's life in society. For them, this was "legitimation."

Further, just as the small people expressed their empowerment not only in the foundings, but later in the secular realm as well (with the resistance to the gembu's directives), so the monks and nuns were similarly rebellious later, within the religious context in which they were operating. There were many aspects to the monks' and nuns' subsequent religious activism, but these cannot be dealt with here. For now I will focus on one rather dramatic event: the attempted expulsion of the married lamas from Thami temple, and the conversion of the temple to celibacy.

Revolution at Thami Temple

It will be recalled that the temple at Thami is one of the three original noncelibate temples of Khumbu, probably founded in the late seventeenth century. Around the time of the founding of Tengboche monastery in 1916, there were apparently some moves to convert Thami to celibacy. There were a number of celibate monks already living in the temple community. It was they who influenced the decision to invite the celibate Kusho Tulku to head up the temple, despite the fact that Thami was a noncelibate religious community and all its previous head lamas had been married, and despite the fact that the Kusho Tulku's older brother, a perfectly respectable married lama, was actually the appropriate successor. Further, the Zatul Rinpoche apparently encouraged the temple to begin to perform the Mani Rimdu festival—a festival normally associated only with celibate monasteries—and gave some resources toward that end. The temple was actually moved and rebuilt around 1920, apparently in order to provide a larger and better-situated courtyard for the Mani Rimdu dancing (see also von Fürer-Haimendorf 1964:134).[18]

But then the Kusho Tulku left Thami in 1923, and this whole move toward celibacy collapsed. On the one hand he was said to have been having trouble with some of the Thami supporters. On the other hand, he was lured by Sangye to take over the headship of the newly planned Chiwong monastery in Solu. When the Kusho Tulku left Thami, most of the celibate monks went with him to Chiwong, and he is said to have taken the Mani Rimdu costumes as well. When he left, the Thami leadership was taken over after all by his older brother, the married Lama Tundup, who presided over the community until his death in 1958.

After only about five years as head of Chiwong, however, the Kusho Tulku "fell" with a nun. He left that monastery, and many of the celibate monks from the Thami area began to drift back to (still noncelibate) Thami temple. And so the process of upgrading Thami began again, culminating in the conversion of the temple to a labtsang in the early 1950s. The conversion of Thami as a result of the active efforts of the celibate monks can be fairly described as a revolution, in the sense that the attempted changes were both symptoms and instruments of a transformation of the whole purpose of the institution.

Moves toward converting Thami to celibacy may be seen once again in restarting the Mani Rimdu rituals, which had not been performed since the Kusho Tulku left. According to informants, the festival was begun again in the early 1940s (see also Jerstad 1969; von

Fürer-Haimendorf 1964:211), although it consisted only of the long-life ritual (*tse-ong*), and did not include the masked dancing that gives it the dramatic character it has today.

By most accounts, by around 1950 there were more celibate monks living in the Thami community than there were married lamas. According to the regent Ngawang Samden, there were twenty-three celibate monks and only twelve married lamas at the time of the conversion; according to another monk, the numbers were respectively eighteen and nine.[19] All but two of the monks had taken vows at Rumbu monastery.[20] It was the celibate monks who began to make the moves toward conversion. They approached Lama Tundup, head of the temple, about converting, and he said he thought it would be a good thing to do. Although it might have appeared anomalous to have a celibate monastery with a married lama at its head, Lama Tundup recalled that there was at least one such monastery in Tibet, and that there was some sort of ritual way in which the anomaly could be handled.

But there was actually a more difficult, and more practical, problem to be resolved: what to do about the existing married lamas in the community. They owned their own houses and fields in the area immediately surrounding the temple, and could not be evicted. Further, they had contributed much, socially and religiously, to the development of the temple, and they had legitimate claims to a certain kind of seniority in its communal and ritual life. Some monks simply wanted to ask the married lamas to leave, but it was clear that this would not work, if only because the married lamas owned property there. It was then proposed to buy the lamas out, but this plan never materialized. Some of the monks then suggested building a brand-new monastery, down on the valley floor across the stream from Thami village. A few even began breaking rocks, to begin building their houses in that area. According to one account, Lama Tundup seemed amenable to this plan to build a new gompa, although he said that the monks in the new one would have to continue to help the old one with religious rituals. In another account, however, Lama Tundup questioned the division on the grounds that the proposed site of the new monastery was too close to the secular village.

The problem was resolved, and the actual formal conversion completed, when the Tushi Rinpoche, who had become de facto head of the Rumbu monks after the death of the Zatul Rinpoche in 1940, left Tibet with the Rumbu monks in 1950, at the time of the first Chinese invasion. The whole group stayed for at least a year in the Thami area. The problem of how to convert Thami to a labtsang in the face of the religious legitimacy and material entrenchment of the married lamas was put to the Tushi Rinpoche, who was then about twenty-four years old. He said the married lamas should not be evicted or bought out, nor should a separate monastery be built. He said the lamas should simply be allowed to stay on in the status of *korwa* ("peripheral ones," a status available in all monasteries), with their own segregated row of seats in the temple. He also said that the married lamas would, over time, just disappear naturally—some would leave, and some would die—and this is in fact what happened.

The actual date of the conversion is hard to pin down. Ngawang Samden, the regent, said "Maybe *shing duk* [Wood Dragon] year," which would have been 1952. It does not seem that there was a formal ceremony, just an agreement that henceforth no noncelibate candidates would be accepted. But there were a number of internal changes. The summer *yerne* retreat, for monks only, was instituted. During that time there could be no women within the precincts of the gompa without permission, and those who were there with permission would have to leave at night. The married lamas could not participate in the yerne retreat, which is dedicated to the spiritual purification and renewal of the monks. In addition, the masked dancing was added to the Mani Rimdu festival, bringing the festival up to the level of impressive drama it manifests today.

But the married Lama Tundup continued to head the monastery until his death in 1958, and apparently there was some notion that the headship, which had always passed through biological descent, would continue to do so. Thus, according to von Fürer-Haimendorf, who saw Lama Tundup preside over Mani Rimdu in 1957 (the Lama died during Mani Rimdu the following year), the lama's second son "was the chosen successor" (1964:147). In fact, however, after Lama Tundup died, the monks seemed to have assumed without question that the Lama would reincarnate, and that the monastery would be headed henceforth, like any self-respecting monastery, by a reincarnate lama. The reincarnation was found in the family of a married lama of the high Rolwaling valley, northwest of Thami, and that tulku has headed Thami monastery ever since.

One may still ask what happened to the Thami married lamas. The monks insisted that the married lamas were pleased when the married temple community was turned into a labtsang—"everybody likes a labtsang"—and that in effect the married lamas got a good deal. They could remain if they wanted to, and participate in most of the important rituals, and yet they were not subject to the monastery rules. For example, they would not be fined as the monks were if they failed to show up for a ritual, or if they refused to take one of the managerial posts, or if they left the monastery without permission.

There were three of them still living at the gompa and participating in its rituals in 1979, and a few of them then living down in the surrounding villages. I interviewed one up at the gompa, and one down in a village, about themselves and others. I confess I expected to hear tales of resentment at their loss of status, and at having been marginalized within the institution to which they had contributed so much. Instead I heard a relatively consistent tale in which was evident the power of monastic ideology and monastic values to revolutionize not only the institution, but even those who were displaced by the change. Both of those interviewed insisted that they harbored no resentment, although the one now living in the village displayed some ambivalence in his comments. In response to my questions he said:

> The conversion was good for the temple. The married lamas said if it were converted to a celibate monastery, they would leave, no problem. It makes the temple more *tsachermu* [potent], makes it more *sangye temba tarup* [holy, sacred], and so the married lamas were happy.
>
> [SBO. Then why did you move out?]
>
> He has a wife, he drinks beer, he had a little trouble with the monks. [Here he implies that the problem was his own fault.] There weren't many married lamas at the time, they couldn't say anything. [Here he suggests that they would have resisted the changeover if they had not been in a minority.] But anyway the change was good, it was important.

Despite the hint of ambivalence in this man's statement, however, his insistence on his positive attitude toward the changeover is borne out by developments in his own family: his son became a monk.

Nor is this an isolated case among the former married lamas of Thami. A lay informant provided what appears to be a nearly complete list of the married lamas at Thami at the time of the conversion, and of the religious statuses of their children. Of the eleven individuals listed, seven had children who grew to adulthood, with the possibility of taking monastic vows. Five of these seven (71 percent) had at least one child who took vows, and in some cases more than one child within such a family took vows. One of the former married lamas himself became a monk. Only one of the eleven former married lamas had a son who became a married lama as a primary career choice (rather than as a secondary choice after breaking monastic vows).

I would suggest that the revolution at Thami is analogous, within the Sherpa religious system, to the overthrow of the gembu in Sherpa politics. In both cases a disadvantaged sector of Sherpa society found a novel solution to old structural problems. For the small people it was wage labor in Darjeeling; for the "little big people," it was monastic vows at Rumbu. In both cases the novel solution gave the actors a sense of legitimacy, of moral rightness and social efficacy. Their subsequent participation(s) in founding the monasteries was in this spirit of moral and social legitimacy.

But the situation is also slightly different for the two groups, in the sense that the monks and nuns really did gain higher status by their move, while the small people only gained a subjective sense of empowerment and "bigness." Yet this difference is perhaps more apparent than real. For one thing, the small people gained money, and over the long run this could be—and was—parlayed into real status change. For another, I would argue that the subjectivity of bigness is at least as important as the actual changes. It is this subjectivity that allowed and provoked these people, both small and little-big, to push not only for personal advancement, but for institutional changes with potentially far-reaching effects for the social order as a whole—the founding of the monasteries, the overthrow of the gembu, the revolution at Thami temple, as well as other changes and reforms in popular religion.

The extensive religious changes wrought over the following decades by the monks and nuns will be the subject of another book. For now, it is time to reflect on what has been learned in this one.

CHAPTER

X

Conclusions: Sherpa History and a Theory of Practice

THE question for this book has been: Why did the Sherpas found their monasteries? I translated this question into a question of practice: How did various structural and historical forces come together in the actions of particular people at a particular historical moment? How were the abstract dynamics of "structure" and "history" converted into intentional human activity with long-term consequences for "structure" and for "history"? The answer has encompassed much of Sherpa history, economic organization, family structure, political organization, folklore, cultural beliefs, religious ideology, and more.

A theory of practice is a theory of history. It is a theory of how social beings, with their diverse motives and their diverse intentions, make and transform the world in which they live. It is a theory for answering the simplest-seeming, and yet largest, questions that social science seeks to answer: Why does a given society have a particular form at a particular moment—that form and not some other? And how do people whose very selves are part of that social form nonetheless sometimes transform themselves and their society? It is a theory that allows social and cultural analysts to put all their various methodological tools to work—ethnographic and historical research; structural, interpretive, and "objectivist" analytic approaches—in ways that enhance and enrich the effectiveness of each.

In chapter 1 I organized a preliminary discussion of practice theory through a discussion of four key terms: practice, structure, actor, and history. I will do this again here, reviewing some of the main theoretical points clustered around each term, and the ways in which those points have been illustrated in this book.

Practice. I said in chapter 1 that practice is any form of human activity considered in terms of its "political" implications and considered in the context of "structure." The term "practice" is thus already loaded with two other major terms, which cannot be separated from it. Activity considered from a perspective in which it is not linked with these phenomena is not "practice" in the same sense. Thus one must begin by bringing in one's baggage about "the political" and about "structure."

"The political" is taken in a broad Foucaultian (and perhaps ultimately Nietzschean) sense of that aspect of all relations in which the relative power, authority, agency, legimacy, and so forth of actors is negotiated and defined. It may be individual or collective; it may involve constituting equality, parity, sharing, and the like as well as dominance, asymmetry, and so on. But the point is that such issues are at stake not just in formal institutions defined as "political" or "public," but in most forms of relationship, and in most contexts of interaction. A good example of this point in this book has been the way in which relations between brothers in Sherpa society had essentially the same "politics" as the relations between actors in the explicit realm of politics.

Concerning "structure," there will be a fuller discussion below. Here I will simply repeat that *every usage* of the term "practice" presupposes a question of the relationship between practice and structure. At least three usages can be isolated in the preceding discussion. A first involves routine or repetitive or ordinary or everyday practice. In Marx this is often called "activity," and in contemporary discussions it is often pluralized: "practice*s*." The structural questions here normally concern the "internalization" (if one takes an actor-centered perspective) or "reproduction" (if one takes a system-centered perspective) of structure through practice. That is, one looks at routine activity and interaction for the ways in which it lays down certain structures of thought and feeling in actors' selves, or for the ways in which such activity/interaction would predispose actors to reenact and reproduce certain publicly encoded structures. The discussions in chapter 4 concerning the "grounding in practice" of the cultural schema of temple founding are an example of such a usage. Here I was concerned to show how the schema both emerged from and fed back into the repetitive, structurally constituted practices of fraternal, political, and ritual/cosmological relations.

A second usage of "practice" involves something like "intentional action." Here actors enact their interests, desires, and intentions; pursue their goals, plans, and projects. The structural question concerns the ways in which such interests, intentions, projects—those subjective frames which give form and purpose to practice—have been structurally constituted in the first place. The whole book has been an illustration of how one would go about answering this question. In asking why the monasteries were founded, I was asking why particular people formed the intention, or "interest," to found the monasteries. I answered the question by showing how structural forces of various kinds—social contradictions, cultural frameworks, political pressures, historical opportunities—connected with people's lives, straining their social relations, or appearing as new solutions to old problems, or presenting alternative modes of constructing social identities, and so forth. I showed how people were pushed by these forces, or actively appropriated them, or both, to transform their historical situations at that point in time. And finally, I showed how, given the cultural meanings attached to the foundings of religious institutions in Sherpa culture, for different sets of people (and in some cases for different individuals) the act of monastery founding would have meaningfully articulated with their transformed historical situation(s). In sum, I showed how people's lives were changed, actively or passively, in that era, giving them new "interests," and making monastery founding at that time a materially feasible, or politically practical, or morally powerful, or personally exciting—or all of these at once—thing to do.

A third usage of "practice" is close to the Marxist notion of praxis: sustained engagement in activity built on an alternative logic, different from the routines of everyday life, and different too from intentional action, which, though nonroutine, shares the logic of everyday life. In "praxis" the actor's consciousness is reshaped, although the mechanisms involved are much the same as those involved in routine practice. What is different, and what produces different results, is the shift of context. The structural questions here concern the relationship between these novel contexts of practice and the existing social order: What are the intended and unintended structural consequences of alternative praxis? These questions were broached in the final chapters of the book, as I looked at the ways in which the wage-labor experience in Darjeeling, and the monastic experience itself, seemed to have opened up a sense of alternatives for some Sherpa actors, particularly young people.

Structure. If considerations of practice must always take place with reference to structure, then the reverse must be true as well. That is, an analyst can no longer look at structures purely in terms of themselves—their inner logic, their architecture, their laws of motion, their modes of reproduction, and so forth—apart from the ways in which these things emerge from and have implications for practice. If this point is fully accepted, however, then one will find, as I said in the first chapter, that the image of structure itself will change. I pointed to Bourdieu's notion of habitus, which is, as its name implies, a lived-in and in-lived structure, and to Foucault's "discourse," a symbolic order in play—controlling yet manipulable—in a world of power relations. A similar term is Raymond Williams's "hegemony," which he defines as "a 'culture' . . . which has . . . to be seen as the *lived* dominance and subordination of particular classes" (1977:110, emphasis added).

All three of these terms are terms for structures—one can talk of *a* habitus, *a* discourse, *a* hegemony, and about its internal order. All three are meant to encompass the totality of social and cultural relations—they are not about "culture" as something distinct from "society"; they refuse a base/superstructure distinction and treat culture/society as a totality informed by common principles (often contradictory ones) of one sort or another. All three share a sense of the diffusely political quality of social life. And finally, all three emphasize that structure is practiced, it is lived, it is enacted, but it is also challenged, defended, renewed, changed.

In the present work I used two interrelated concepts of structure, both of which share these qualities. The first was a notion of structure (with no special label) that emphasized its internal contradictions, and the ways in which these contradictions press upon actors. The point here is that the structure does not just sit there, constraining actors by its formal characteristics, but recurrently poses problems to actors, to which they must respond. The second notion of structure was the notion of "cultural schemas," standardized plot structures that reappear in stories and rituals. These schemas portray actors pressed by the contradictions of the structure, but finding ways to resolve them that generate both personal satisfaction and social respect. Here structure is dramatized, *shown culturally as practice*, pushing actors, being responded to, being transformed by actors from part of the problem to part of the solution.

The social and cultural order with its inbuilt contradictions, and the explicit cultural schemas in which the contradictions are visibly represented and enacted, stand in complex relationships with one another. From the actor's point of view, the schemas appear as solutions to the structural problems. But from an analytic point of view, the schemas and the contradictions are two manifestations of a single set of problems. The two sides are mutually constituting, forming a totalizing entity that I called, in the spirit of Williams and Gramsci, a hegemony.

These notions of structure—contradictory structural orders, dramatized cultural schemas—are thus more active, both in the sense of being more actor-oriented, and in the sense of being more internally dynamic. But there are limits to the theoretical injection of dynamism into structures. That is, while I think one can and should recognize, in one's definition of structure, its origins in practice, its consequences for practice, and indeed its own *recognition* of itself (in stories, tales, dramas, rituals) as practice, nonetheless one must immediately back off from the potential for reification here, and turn to the third term:

Actor. "The problem of the actor" has two very broad aspects: a substantive one, which takes the general form of asking, What do actors want? and a structural one: How should one conceptualize the relationship between actors and structure (or culture)? I will discuss each question in turn.

What do actors want? On the substantive question, first, I have tried to show the ways in which the contradictions of Sherpa society tended to generate for actors a chronic "need" or "desire," which they recognize culturally as a desire to make or protect one's "name" or "reputation," and which I have glossed as the desire for "legitimation." For people in different social positions this desire took slightly different forms. For the big people it was for "legitimation" in the classic political sense—repairing and shoring up positions of power—as well as in an extended moral sense (speaking to their own consciences in an idiom of merit). For the small people and the little-big people, on the other hand, the desire was (or came to be) for the right to participate fully in the Sherpa social game. This is legitimation in the sense of "valorization," of being recognized by others as a person of social consequence and social value.

The arguments about legitimation connect to the discussions of "the political" presented earlier. If politics are diffused through most social relations, then so too are issues of authority, legitimacy, and social value. At some level, then, everyone is seeking legitimation, and this must be recognized as involving more than the shoring up of formal power. Big people seek religious merit and assurances of their moral worth; small people seek a sense of social efficacy and social recognition, and all of these are modes of seeking "legitimation."

The discussions of legitimation may also be connected to the discussions of structural contradictions. While a desire for "legitimation" in the broad sense in which I have defined it here may well be existentially constituted for all human beings, it is clearly constituted in its particular form, intensity, and pervasiveness for Sherpas out of the contradictions of the Sherpa cultural order. More specifically one may say that, just as there is one core contradiction in the Sherpa hegemony—between egalitarian and hierarchical discourses—with several variants and transformations, so there is one core "desire," with several variants and transformations. Moreover, the desire is virtually inherent in the contradiction, which is to say that the chronic need for "valorization" at all levels of Sherpa society is in effect the flip side of a contradictory, egalitarian/hierarchical, system, in which bigness is always fragile, smallness is always unfair, and equality must always be competitively maintained.

The relationship between actors and culture. Cultural anthropology has always made certain claims, either explicitly or implicitly, about the relationship between culture and the consciousness of actors. In general the line has been that actors are cultural products, deeply shaped through socialization and through ongoing practice in adult life. The position goes back at least to Margaret Mead and Ruth Benedict, but recent theorists like Williams and Foucault have also emphasized the degree to which actors' selves are ordered by and rendered homologous with cultural structures. The culturalist position has been articulated against one or another universalist conception of actors, usually a rationalist one: actors are rational beings, acting on universal motives of self-interest that we can all commonsensically understand. At most, actors "use" their culture, but they are not in any important way shaped by it.

I have myself been a culturalist, but the cultural position in pure form causes a number of theoretical problems. The assumption that actors simply internalize and enact their culture leaves little room for understanding how either actors or cultures can change. It also gets bogged down in debates about false consciousness and the like, as one asks how people can subscribe—as they often seem to do—to cultural views that apparently denigrate or subordinate them.

It seems important to articulate a position that recognizes the ways in which actors are indeed cultural products, and yet that does not conflate actors' intentions and cultural forms. Correspondingly, it seems important to articulate a position in which there is some distance between actor and culture, and yet which does not postulate a culturally unconstrained actor rationally manipulating cultural imagery and options. My solution to this problem is to propose an actor who is "loosely structured," who is prepared—but no more than that—to find most of his or her culture intelligible and meaningful, but who does not necessarily find all parts of it equally meaningful in all times and places. The distance between culture and actor is there, but so too is the capacity to find meaning, in more than a manipulative way, in one's own cultural repertoire.

It is easy to envision this point if one thinks about the normal process of growing up. Different parts of the culture seem important to one, illuminating, compelling, or whatever, at different stages of one's life. Things that one thought of as deeply meaningful when one was a child no longer seem so, even though one can still understand what they mean in an abstract sense. Things that seemed boring to one as a child in turn become significant and emotionally powerful later, as one's circumstances change. Both the child and the adult are cultural actors, yet one can clearly speak of their having different relationships to the shared culture. The same may obviously be said about people in different social positions: even when they appear to share the same symbols, and even though they are all equally socialized as cultural actors, they may have different relationships to their culture.

Most important, for present purposes, the same may be said about people's several and collective relationships to their culture over time. As their circumstances and their experiences undergo change, different individuals, different social types, different groups, will change their relationship to their cultural repertoire. This is not a matter of picking and choosing different bits of it opportunistically, although some of that may of course go on. It is a matter of finding meaning where one did not find it before (or indeed changing or losing meaning as well). This is the dynamic I have tried to articulate for Sherpas across the social spectrum in the early twentieth century. For different reasons, and in different ways, everyone's needs for or expectations of "valorization" were intensified by the historical changes of the era. For everyone, for different reasons, the schema of political empowerment and monastery building became personally meaningful and emotionally compelling. People "connected" with the schema, and in this context the distance in question was momentarily closed. The whole point of the book has been to show how people got to that momentary point of closure, in which abstract cultural schemas became part of people's personal intentions, or, at the very least, to show the ways in which people worked out for themselves in practice the same solutions that the heroes found in the schemas.

But such closure between personal intention and cultural form can always be reopened. The world changes. People change. Things move out of old alignments and into new ones. In the last analysis it is these changing relationships that constitute what anthropologists think of as "culture change," as much as, or more than, any substantive changes in symbolic structures. This brings me to the final term:

History. If a theory of practice is a theory of history, then the discussion of "history" must close the circle and return to "practice." Both Eric Wolf (1982) and Richard Fox (1985) pose a false dichotomy (within the field of anthropology) between historical studies on the one hand, and ethnographic or cultural studies on the other. They equate "history" with the investigation of a group's "external" relations—with the state, the regional economy, the world capitalist system—and "ethnography" or "cultural studies" with the investigation of a group's internal structure, unconditioned by larger forces. The dichotomy is false because, while some of the practitioners of the political economy approach (Wolf himself, and also Mintz [1985]) have indeed virtually excluded ethnography from their methods, most ethnographic historians (Bloch 1986; Comaroff 1985; Dirks 1987; Sahlins 1981; and others) *include* the study of a group's "external" interactions in their analyses.

A theory of practice, as I said early in this work, is a theory of the conversion, or translation, between internal dynamics and external forces.[1] One dimension of this concerns how people react to, cope with, or actively appropriate external phenomena, on the basis of the social and cultural dynamics that both constrain and enable their responses. Put in other terms, one dimension of the theory concerns the ways in which a given social and cultural order mediates the impact of external events by shaping the ways in which actors experience and respond to those events. The mediation of outside forces, through the social and cultural shaping of actors' responses, has been illustrated many times over throughout this book. The analysis has shown how the Sherpa cultural pattern of calling in a "protector" to resolve a political struggle may have contributed to the political takeover of the Sherpas by the Nepal state. It has shown how the culturally constituted dynamics of fraternal and political rivalry have for centuries pushed some people to leave and seek their fortunes elsewhere, paving the way for the ease and effectiveness with which Sherpas at all levels of society took advantage of novel "external" economic opportunities in the late nineteenth and early twentieth centuries. And it has shown how the weakening of the legitimacy of the Sherpa big people, as a result of various externally generated pressures (the Nepal state's agenda, the ability of "small" people to earn wages in Darjeeling, and so forth) was internally mediated by structural contradictions and cultural schemas in ways that eventuated in the foundings of the monasteries. In every case, it would have been virtually impossible to understand the impact or influence of external forces on Sherpa history without a prior understanding of the internal social and cultural dynamics of their society.

If one side of practice theory concerns the ways in which culture constitutes practice, and thus the ways in which people react to the world, the other side concerns the ways in which such culturally constituted practice in turn reproduces or changes the world, and thus makes or remakes history. The theoretical issue here is largely the issue of "hegemony" and of the possibilities of alternative perspectives. Reproduction takes place either because people cannot see alternatives, or do not have the power to institutionalize the alternatives that they see. Change takes place because alternatives become visible, or because actors have or gain the power to bring them into being.

Over the course of much of Sherpa history, it appears that people could see no alternatives to the given order. They used standard cultural patterns to solve standard cultural problems. Moreover, they applied the standard patterns in ways that did not embody novel forms of practice that might generate alternative perspectives—for example, they established new communities on much the same basis as the old ones. The Sherpas of the late nineteenth and early twentieth centuries also used standard cultural patterns to solve their problems, and indeed the same patterns. The patterns encouraged them to go away and start over again, as in the past. The difference was that there were new places, literally and metaphorically, to go—Darjeeling and the wage-labor experience, Rumbu and the monastic experience. These new places and new practices embodied alternative perspectives and so embodied the possibility of challenging the frameworks from which people started. Wage labor, particularly in the form of mountaineering, embodied the notion of gaining material resources without dependence on familial relations, and also the notion that this kind of economic activity could generate social respect. The effect was to give the small people both material resources and a sense of agency, and so to transform their stance vis-à-vis the rest of the community. The effects of this transformation are still going on (see von Fürer-Haimendorf 1984) and will be discussed in future works.

Monasticism had much the same capacity. Becoming a monk or a nun involves, like wage labor, novel modes of gaining subsistence, a restructuring of relations of dependence on the family, and a transformation of social status within the larger community. Monasticism too could thus rupture the hegemony, providing not only alternative perspectives but the material ability and the social prestige to bring about the changes that people could begin to imagine.

But monasticism as a novel practice has one additional dimension, which is lacking in the practice of wage labor: it embodies both a license and a charge to critique the existing order. Unlike wage labor, monasticism actually has an organized critical ideology, and the monks and nuns of the early Sherpa monasteries were quick to pick up on its potential. One strand of activism for change that was generated among the monks and nuns was seen in the discussion of the revolution at Thami temple. And while the critical discourse of monasticism was largely confined to the religious sphere, it could not fail to have implications for the social changes that were going on in that same period. It is the interaction between the changes that emerged from the novel practices of mountaineering labor, and those that emerged from the novel practices of monasticism, that will be the subject of the sequel to this book.

APPENDIX

I

Two Zombie Stories of Early Khumbu

THE first of these stories was told to me by a Thami monk, in response to my request for "old stories." It is about a Mo'ung lama, possibly Lama Budi Tsenjen, father of Lama Sangwa Dorje:

> The Mo'ung lama was very powerful. He had a marvelous yak. A man killed and ate his yak and the lama cursed him. The man who killed the yak [later] saw a man with a very long chin, down to his chest. The man with the long chin chased the yak-killing man, but the latter climbed up on a chorten. Because of his long chin, the strange figure could not raise his head to see the man on the chorten, and so he went away. Then the yak-killing man went home, and he and his household all died but became zombies, who appeared to come back to life but were really dead. Zombies walk around but they can't bend; if they go into other people's houses then those people become zombies too, which is why Khumbu people make small doors and windows—the zombie people can't bend over and come in. Then eventually the lama's curse brought an avalanche and wiped out all the zombies, and now there are no more. But people say that Kunde [a village in Khumbu] people still have short bodies and short lives because of the curse.

The second version was told to me when I asked a prominent villager of Khumjung about whether Pangboche, the first temple, was originally a celibate monastery. The answer was basically yes, but all the celibate monks were wiped out in a fire that was set to wipe out the zombies. The first part of the story was omitted by the informant, and filled in later by my assistant, Nyima Chotar, who was helping me translate the tape.

[Nyima Chotar's section:] There was a man who stayed all the time at his yak pasture, at Tang Ngak, behind Gokyo. One day, he saw—what? A *yeti* [abominable snowman]? A *hrendi* [ghost]? A man with a long chin. The man ran all the way back from Tang Ngak to here, with the strange creature very close behind him, and he climbed up the chorten. The creature couldn't find him, because he couldn't pick up his head. The creature went back. The man came down to the ground and went home. He told his family the story. Then his heart became very black, and he died. He was very rich.

[The informant's part of the story:] The family called 100 monks and 1 [head] lama for the funeral. In the middle of the night, when everyone was sleeping, there was one monk by the kitchen not sleeping, and watching everything. The dead man got up, took the lama's beads, broke them, put one bead on each monk's head, and the large bead on the head lama's head. The zombie laid down and the monk woke up the head lama. He told him what had happened. The lama asked, did he touch me too? And the monk said, yes, he put the large bead [on you]. And the lama said, you go out immediately, forget me and the monks, lock the door and burn the whole house. So he did. He called the Kunde people for help and burned the whole house. Afterwards it was called the *shakang*, the flesh house. It was between Khumjung and Kunde, where the line of mani walls stands.

APPENDIX

II

Addendum to the Tengboche *Chayik*

THE present head lama of Tengboche asked me to publish the following document, an addendum to the chayik, or rules laid down for the monastery at its founding. It was composed by the leading lay sponsors and supporters of the monastery at the time of the consecration. In it are described the lands given to the monastery by the Sherpa residents of the region. These lands were understood to become the legal property of the monastery. (The lama would not let me copy, or even handle or look at, this document, presumably out of fear of female pollution. He read it into a tape recorder, and I transcribed and translated it with the help of Nyima Chotar. The spellings of proper names are thus all phonetic.)

> Dated the 8th day of the 10th month of the Earth Sheep year [1919]
>
> Great Laws of King and Lama
>
> In Solu-Khumbu, we adhere to the Buddhist religion. From the time of Lama Sangwa Dorje, Nyingmapa religion has been well established [here]. Lama Sangwa Dorje built Pangboche Pa-riwu temple, and he made the rules for the monks and nuns. This is the same thing [that is, this document is in the same tradition]. If there are any disputes within the monastery precincts, the lama has full power to settle them. It is the custom established by Lama Sangwa Dorje that the lama has full powers to make and enforce all the rules within the monastery. The Dza-rumbu lama [the Zatul Rinpoche] said that if a monastery were built at Tengboche, everything would go well for the King and his kingdom. Khumbu people agreed, and Lama Chatang Chotar [Lama Gulu], Shorung Lama Karma [Karma], Gembu Tsepal, and Takto Kusang Tsering [Kusang] were the main sponsors. The monastery was built in the Fire Dragon year [1916]. Now three years later the Rumbu lama has come here and named this mon-

astery Dongak Terchok Choling. He has performed the *ramne* [the consecration], and has given the chayik [entitled] *Shar Khumbu Rolwa Lingi Dabdil Dongak Terchok Cholingi Chayik Kunsal Melong*, and has explained what more the monastery needs.

At this time, we Khumbu people think we should add to the chayik the monastery area, to wit, from Pungitenga and Pubichungyu to Devuche. Within this area no one may cut grass or trees without the permission of the monastery. No animals of any kind may be killed within the area. Within the area the monastery makes its own rules [consistent with the laws of the kingdom]. This document may not be contradicted.

[Signed by:]

Norbu Gyaldzen (Golile) [Gembu Tsepal's son]
Murmin Yula Phutar
Murmin Yula Tarkye
Murmin Gyale
Gordze Tenzing Tarkye
Murmin Tarkye
Murmin Dorje
Kartanga Temba (Kunde)
Murmin Yula Namgyal (Nauje)
Norwu Phutar (Nauje)
Ang Dorje
Kunde Yula Tarkye
Khumjung Sumdokba Sungi
Takto Chamba [Takto Kusang's younger brother]
Purbi Dawa Hlundup
Phortse Yungdung Tempa
Dawa Sumba
Purba Yishi
Kishong
Pemba Drolma
Panche Nami (Pangboche)
Kebi (Kapa) Pasang (Pangboche)
Dawa Phinzok

Notes

Chapter I

1. For a view much like von Fürer-Haimendorf's, see Thompson 1982; for a view much like mine, see March 1979.

2. There were various reasons for this. If monasteries had written records, they denied this, or refused to let me see them. Some local tax collectors had some old tax lists, which I photographed, but one would have needed a bigger set of them for any individual one to be of much use. Material in the Nepal state archives is very difficult to use (see Edwards 1977:preface), especially since I do not read Nepali.

3. Some Sherpas have also read at least some of the major Western-language ethnographies, and often comment that they contain mistakes. When I gave a copy of my own monograph (1978a) to the Thami reincarnate lama, he flipped through it and spotted the diagram of the *gyepshi* altar on page 97. He immediately said that the Buddha's hand in the diagram was facing the wrong way (once I looked at it in light of his comment I realized it was the wrong [left] hand altogether), and that there were only seven petals to the lotus when there should have been eight. Interestingly enough, mistakes in Western ethnographies are often not blamed on the ethnographer but on his or her Sherpa translator or field assistant.

4. I began a discussion of the issues of practice theory in a 1984 paper, "Theory in Anthropology since the Sixties." Several pieces have since been written in response to that paper: Yengoyan 1986, Appadurai 1986, and Hannerz 1986 (published as a set in *Comparative Studies in Society and History* 28[2]), as well as essays by Bloch, Bourdieu, Collier and Yanagisako, Gibson, and Stephens (all presented at a panel of the 1987 meetings of the American Anthropological Association). In response to all these, and with the present book very much in mind, I presented a rejoinder at the same panel. The following discussion is adapted from that rejoinder. A copy of the rejoinder, entitled "Theory in Anthropology Three Years Later," is available as a Working Paper from the Program in the Comparative Study of Social Transformations, 4010 LSA Building, University of Michigan, Ann Arbor, MI 48109.

Chapter II

1. No doubt there are more such accounts of visits to Solu-Khumbu by Nepal state agents, but they have not yet been unearthed. All scholars owe a great intellectual debt to the economic historian Mahesh Chandra Regmi, who has devoted a large portion of his scholarly energies to retrieving and analyzing materials from the poorly preserved and poorly organized government archives.

2. "Gorkha" is a region in west-central Nepal whence came the ethnic group that conquered the capital of Nepal in the eighteenth century and has ruled the country ever since. This ethnic group is a Hindu caste society now called (after the name of the valley of the capital) "Nepali." The British Gurkha regiments were originally drawn largely from the Gorkha region, and included not only caste Nepalis but "tribal" Gurungs and Magars as well. The regiments now also include men from many other regions and groups of Nepal.

3. The British had to send an Indian, under false pretenses, as they were themselves not normally allowed to travel in the outer areas of Nepal. Hari Ram evidently did a

great deal of service for them, in Nepal and in Tibet. See also Survey of India 1915a; Sandberg 1904.

4. Hari Ram also writes that there had been a smallpox epidemic "brought over from the east" some thirty years before his visit, which "carried off a large number of the inhabitants of Khumbu" (Survey of India 1915a). This epidemic does not show up anywhere in Sherpa folklore or oral history. It probably played some role in the events discussed in this book, but I could see no way to draw any implications from it, and it does not enter the discussions that follow.

5. Sherpa words are given in normal English spelling, meant to reproduce for the reader the pronunciations as I heard them. Tibetan spellings, if available, are given in the Glossary.

6. For translated examples of chayik from Tibetan monasteries, see Michael (1982:177–88). Von Fürer-Haimendorf (1964:196–97) gives a summary of the chayik of a noncelibate Sherpa temple.

7. Apparently the ancestors of the Sikkim royal house left Kham at about the same time, for the same reason (Oppitz 1968:76).

8. Von Fürer-Haimendorf says that "most Khumbu Sherpas" believe that the migrants came over the Rongshar Chu route west of the Nangpa La, settling first in Solu and later moving up to Khumbu. But he also notes the other tradition given here (1964:143). Oppitz does record one later group of migrants who found the Nangpa La blocked with snow, and so entered Nepal over a pass further west (1968:48).

9. Apparently meaning *yemba*, descendants of freed "slaves" (Oppitz 1968:98). The origin of these slaves is not clear, but presumably they were debtors who lost their freedom for a limited period of time, having to work for their creditors for several years in order to pay off their debts. Debt slavery was widespread in Nepal until it was outlawed by Chandra Shamsher Rana in 1926 (Regmi 1978; Oppitz 1968).

10. The remainder of the Sherpa population now lives in Kathmandu (no population figure available) and Darjeeling (7,000 in 1965 [Oppitz 1968:109]).

11. Oppitz thinks, however, that at least some of the clan names predate the Sherpas' arrival in Solu-Khumbu (e.g., 1974:177).

12. See March 1977b on the continuing greater herd-orientation of Khumbu.

13. In the story the eldest brother got the house, while in modern times the youngest son normally gets it. It is not clear whether this is a significant point, in terms of the fraternal rivalry, or whether perhaps the norm for house inheritance was simply less fixed in earlier times.

14. The egalitarianism basically refers to relations between men. Women are "naturally" a little "lower." But Sherpa society is not heavily gender-asymmetrical either. See Ortner 1983.

15. Thomas Fricke, an anthropologist who works among the Tamang, has calculated that, given Sherpa fertility and mortality rates, the average Sherpa couple will have two sons who survive until maturity (personal communication). The majority of families will thus be forced to split land between sons.

16. Von Fürer-Haimendorf (1975) provides extensive information on Sherpa trade in the 1950s. After the Chinese invasion of Tibet in 1959, much of this trade ceased.

17. There were undoubtedly certain ecological imperatives for trading, such as the absence of salt in Solu-Khumbu. But it is not at all clear that ecological conditions created the primary impetus for trade—for example, that the short growing season generated a grain deficit. Fisher has recently shown that a group in northwestern Nepal, living under much the same ecological constraints as the Sherpas, actually produced a grain surplus (Fisher 1986). Comparable data for the Sherpas are not available, but a grain deficit should not be, as Fisher says, "casually assumed" (p. 71).

18. Among contemporary Helambu people (who are sometimes also called Sherpas), lamas seem to play active political roles (Clarke 1980). But among the modern Sherpas of Solu-Khumbu, no lamas hold pembu positions.

19. Shamanism presumably existed among the Sherpas in the early period, since it is found over the entire Tibetan culture area and indeed predates Buddhism. But it is never mentioned in any of the texts or folklore that form the basis of the present study, and plays no role in the discussions of the present book. It will, however, be important in the sequel to this book (Ortner n.d.b), since the monks in the newly founded monasteries will disparage it and cause it to go into decline in the first half of the twentieth century. A preliminary discussion of the decline of Sherpa shamanism was sketched out in Ortner n.d.c.

20. Before the pembu position was abolished entirely, von Fürer-Haimendorf was able to observe a number of paternalistic aspects of the pembu role (1964:124).

21. The Sherpas use *gonda* and *gompa* interchangeably for any religious temple.

22. Stories of gods directly responding to the intense faith of common people form a certain body of folklore among Sherpas and Tibetans. Sherpas tell the story of the pious old woman who every day worshiped a dog's bone (or tooth) with great intensity, thinking it was a holy relic. She was rewarded with salvation. They also tell the story of the simple man who believed that the statue of Jowo Rinpoche in the Jokhang at Lhasa was really the god, and asked it to come to dinner; his landlady laughed at him but the god came to his house.

Chapter III

1. This figure is arrived at by combining Oppitz's estimate for the maximum size of the original migrant group (fifty persons) and Oppitz's deduction that the Sherpa population has doubled every forty-nine years. Thus if in 1533 there were fifty Sherpas, there would have been one hundred forty-nine years later in 1582, two hundred in 1631, and four hundred in 1680 (see Oppitz 1968:103). Thomas Fricke has worked out on retrospective demographic grounds that the doubling time for the Sherpa population "is roughly 60 years" (personal communication). The difference between Fricke's and Oppitz's numbers should not undermine any of the arguments of this book.

2. Although Pangboche is the name of the location of the temple, everyone also calls the temple by that name. Its religious name is Palriwu gompa (Tib., *dpal-ri-bo dgon-pa*).

3. The Tengboche lama (n.d.b [ca. 1985]:12) says that Thami was founded "370 years ago." This would place the founding in 1615. Again, all the dating must be taken as very tentative, but I consider the late-seventeenth-century dates to have more plausibility on demographic and economic grounds.

4. One informant placed the foundings "at the time of King Miwong of Shagar [i.e., Shelkar, near D'ing-ri] and Kungsang Ngawa of Lhasa." Perhaps a scholar of Tibetan history could place these individuals in Tibetan chronology.

5. If Pangboche was never a celibate establishment, but if this piece of etymology is correct, it could refer to the era before the ancestors of the Sherpas settled in Khumbu, when the Pangboche region was a meditation retreat for Tibetan hermits.

6. There were however no potatoes at that time.

7. They may perhaps be likened to the *serkim gompa* of married hereditary lamas that Aziz describes for D'ing-ri (1978:ch. 4).

8. Others say, however, that according to certain books, he was born in Kham, the home of the Sherpas' ancestors. His *namdar*, or religious biography, is said to be in Kham and hence unavailable in Solu-Khumbu.

9. Those who claim the authority of the texts, however, say that Lama Sangwa Dorje was not Budi Tsenjen's son. If Lama Budi Tsenjen *was* a member of the first party of settlers, and if Lama Sangwa Dorje was his son, this would change the dating of the founding of Pangboche, putting it into the mid to late sixteenth century as von Fürer-Haimendorf has suggested (1964:127). (Lama Budi Tsenjen is also the central actor in an oft-repeated tale about why there is no salt in Solu-Khumbu. See Ortner 1983). I prefer the later dating for the demographic and economic reasons given earlier.

10. According to von Fürer-Haimendorf, Lama Rena Lingba was a disciple of Guru Rinpoche, Padma Sambhava (1964:191). (The Guru Rinpoche founded Buddhism in Tibet in the eighth century.) According to Sangye Tenzing (1971:22), Rena Lingba (*ratna gling-pa*) was a *reincarnation* of Padma Sambhava. According to Oppitz, it was Rena Lingba (*Terton Ratna Lingba*) who had established Pangboche as a meditation retreat before the Sherpas migrated into Solu-Khumbu, and it was one of his grandsons who guided one of the migrants over the pass and into the area (Oppitz 1968:36–43). According to another piece of folklore, Lama Sangwa Dorje's daughter married Lama Rena Lingba's son. The confusions in the chronology here are presumably resolvable by assuming that various reincarnations of Lama Rena Lingba are being referred to, rather than a single individual.

11. The nangden of a temple includes all its idols, books, and other sacred contents. The Pangboche nangden also includes Lama Sangwa Dorje's sitting stone. Both quantity and quality of nangden are important. It was said, for example, that the reason Tengboche was destroyed in the 1933 earthquake, while Pangboche was unharmed, was because Pangboche was old and had many nangden. Similarly, it was strongly suggested that the reason Rimijung gompa has fallen into decline is that its nangden were not very powerful. Nangden are the subjects of endless conflict, and also theft and countertheft. (See, for example, the story of Lama Sangwa Dorje's reliquary, below.)

12. See Snellgrove (1967:12) for the cultural expectation that any good lama will have effective magical powers.

13. *Chu* means water, which is a very auspicious symbol in Sherpa culture; its flow (in dreams, or in poetry) symbolically implies the coming of wealth.

14. He said that these three qualities—fear, shame, and pity—make a good person. If one has these one never lies, kills, or steals. On the other hand he added that "if one has too much fear, one [is paralyzed and] never does anything; if one has too much shame, one never eats [i.e., one never accepts hospitality]; and if one has too much pity, one never works [out of pity for the worms in the soil] or eats meat [out of pity for the animals]."

15. The third brother, Kemba Dorje, was apparently neither ongchermu nor sufficiently tsachermu, and as a result he (or anyway the temple that he built) lost his clients. Thus Rimijung temple has fallen on hard times, now having only one lama and few financial sponsors. In the absence of enough attached clients/sponsors, the remaining ones are said to have to go begging around the village each year in order to raise money for the Dumje festival. The decline of the gompa was unanimously related to the fact that the seven grains of barley and the idol have fallen down, and the barley has become moldy, in turn a sign that Lama Kemba Dorje was not all that tsachermu in the first place.

16. In some versions, Lama Sangwa Dorje was pembu of the Pangboche area, and Zongnamba of the Thami area, each collecting taxes on his own side.

17. See also Sangye Tenzing 1971:18–23; von Fürer-Haimendorf 1964:128.

18. This is also where, in the other tale, he meditated and was visited by his tutelary god, Gombu, in the form of an idol.

19. Because Lama Sangwa Dorje left no patriline, the head position of Pangboche

temple has been filled by unrelated lamas. I do not know by what principle they were chosen. A document at the gompa, written by a Western visitor, claims that the post is rotated every year, but the present head lama found this a rather amusing notion. The head lama claimed that the headship is for life, and is filled on the basis of superior religious skills. But this last may be a postmonastic view.

20. Von Fürer-Haimendorf says three days, but "poor people who are anxious to gain the pembu's favour may do even more" (1964:122).

21. While it was possible to borrow capital for trade, and some people certainly did this, borrowing reduced profitability (because of the interest on the loan) and heightened risk—if the venture failed, the borrower was seriously indebted.

22. Von Fürer-Haimendorf tells two stories from the 1950s about pembu being displaced by their own clients, who complained to the authorities that the current pembu was not doing a good job, and who bribed other clients to support their complaints (1964:122).

Chapter IV

1. Large parts of this chapter appear in Ortner n.d.a.

2. See also Fernandez's discussion of rituals as "scenarios" for the enactment and realization of metaphoric predication (1974:125ff.).

3. See also MacDonald 1980a; Sangye Tenzing 1971.

4. There is a potential problem in using Oppitz's twenty-five-year generation span for the early years of Sherpa residence in Nepal, since people apparently married at younger ages in that period. But earlier marriages would not necessarily have immediately produced children. Sherpa women experience relatively late menarche (ca. age 17 [Weitz et al., 1978]) and may not immediately become fertile even after that. Again, however, the absolute dating of the temple foundings is not crucial to the present argument.

5. This resembles a certain technical maneuver in modern mountain climbing, and is appreciated as such by modern Sherpa climbers.

6. The tales could probably be read in terms of political *succession*, and not simply "rivalry" as I read them here. The succession gloss would bring to the fore certain Oedipal readings of the tales. See Paul 1982 for a brilliant discussion of Tibetan and Sherpa politics along these lines.

7. There are several different terms that I am glossing as "protector." A lay person functioning as a protector would normally be called a *zhindak* (sponsor, patron). A lama would be called a *tsawi lama* (root lama). A personal deity would be called a *yidam* (tutelary deity), and the patron god of a gompa would be called a *sungma* (protector).

8. It often seems that twentieth-century Sherpas cast Westerners in the role of "the protector." Much of Sherpa loyalty to "their" sahibs may be understandable in these terms.

9. The statue is kept in an inner room and is especially honored at Dumje, when the temple's gods are maximally mobilized against the forces of evil.

10. The ancientness of rituals can no longer be facilely assumed. It is now recognized that some supposedly timeless rituals were only recently invented (see Hobsbawn and Ranger 1983). On the other hand, historical research is also beginning to demonstrate the extraordinary durability of at least some rituals (see, e.g., Bloch 1986).

11. Sometimes they are converted to the true religion and become minor deities, part of the retinue of major ones. This transformation would be the equivalent of the political victor acquiring the political loser's followers and clients.

12. Samye is famous for its perfect mandala shape. See Tucci 1969 on the significance of mandalas in Tibetan Buddhism.

13. For a discussion of merit as having both a spiritual and a political dimension among the people of Helambu, who also call themselves "Sherpa," see Clarke 1980. The relationship between merit and power has received substantial attention in the literature on Theravada Buddhism. See for example Tambiah's *World Conqueror and World Renouncer* (1976), and Obeyesekere et al.'s *The Two Wheels of Dhamma* (1972).

14. The same point is made linguistically; a person who sponsors a religious ritual may either be called the *zhindak*—lord or master—of the ritual, or the *lawa*—the servant of the congregation. The term *lawa* was losing favor in Solu when I did my first fieldwork there. I got the term from von Fürer-Haimendorf (1964:185) and people understood what I meant by it, but someone made a point of telling me it wasn't the "nice" way to refer to a ritual sponsor. The term most used was *chiwa* (offering-one ?).

Chapter V

1. There is a long line of Sen kings called "Makanda" or "Mukunda" Sen, beginning with Mukunda Sen I, who reigned between 1518 and 1533 (Stiller 1973:36), and continuing (at least) through a Mukunda Sen (no number given) who was the Raja of Palpa in 1779 (Hamilton 1819:142). The capitol of the Sen kingdom was a city called "Makwanpur," and Sher could easily be a Sherpa transformation of Sen (probably pronounced "shen" even in Nepali).

2. In another version, the lama told Zongnamba's people that they could kill him by wrapping a widow's underpants around his head, thereby polluting him and causing him to lose his invulnerability. "Then they grabbed him by his *ralwa* hair and dashed him against the ground and killed him." This version echoes both the end of the story of the founding of Zhung gompa (see chapter 3), in which a lama's powers were undone through female pollutants, and the component of the Lama Sangwa Dorje tale in which Taki and Ziki smashed Zongnamba's agents against the rocks.

3. Landon recounts a story collected in Walangchung, to the east of Solu-Khumbu, that is reminiscent of this one: "Kangpa-chan was once a far larger center. But as punishment for the murder of an oppressive mayor chief, nearly the whole population was exterminated. His widow revenged herself by inviting the Sherpas, who had been guilty of the crime, to the funeral feast, and there poisoned nearly a thousand of them" (Landon 1928:45).

4. The Tibet trade was of interest to earlier Nepal kings as well. But none of the earlier Nepal kingdoms covered as much territory, or had as much military power, as the Gorkhas. See Stiller 1973:100.

5. The equivalence of the terms *gembu* and *amali* is given in von Fürer-Haimendorf (1975:61). See von Fürer-Haimendorf (1964:117–125) for a description of the way the tax system worked in Khumbu. See also Regmi's *Land Tenure and Taxation in Nepal* (1963–68) for an overview of the entire system. And compare with Carrasco 1959 and Goldstein 1971b for Tibet.

6. Nauje people would later (1905) break away from Khumjung temple and found a temple in Nauje for much the same reasons.

7. The line resumed again only two generations ago in the twentieth century. Information on Pangboche was partly collected from the current head lama, a Tibetan émigré scholar with the religious title of *geshe*, roughly equivalent to a Ph.D. The date of the end of the first list of Pangboche lamas is calculated from the fact that five generations of head lamas are recorded, starting with Lama Sangwa Dorje. Again allowing twenty-five years per generation, the last recorded Pangboche lama before the twentieth century would have died in 1792.

8. Since the people are hereditary clients of the temple, obligated to provide for its

support, they must formally get permission to secede. In addition, no new religious institutions can be founded without formal authorization—a chayik—from some higher religious figure.

9. In an 1825 document, the Sherpas were exempted from presumably Hindu-inspired adultery laws (Oppitz 1968:66). In both cases the state showed a certain cultural leniency, paralleling its material leniency, toward the Sherpas. See Burghart (1984) on the state's tolerance of customary law in different regions.

Chapter VI

1. In 1846 Jang Bahadur (Rana) first took office as prime minister. He did not formally arrogate all power to himself until 1856.

2. In these sources, the authors say the temples were "founded" at those times, but this almost certainly means that the temples were rebuilt or renovated, unless all the other evidence for the earlier founding dates is wrong.

3. The land was neither "sold" nor "exchanged" by the Chogyal, but explicitly presented "out of friendship" (Kotturan 1983:61). Nonetheless the Sikkimese clearly expected something in return, and were not at all satisfied with "a gift parcel" consisting of "one double barreled gun, one rifle, one 20 yards of red-broad cloth, [and] two pairs of shawls, one of superior variety and the other of inferior variety" (ibid., p. 62). The British thus eventually, and grudgingly, set up an annuity payment to the Chogyal (ibid., p. 62).

4. Birth dates are from Oppitz (1968:insert, "Lama Serwa Genealogy"). Dates are approximate, although it is safe to say that Sangye was born somewhere between 1850 and 1860.

5. Labor contracting involved delivering labor crews to the British for a given project, or even for a given day, at a given price. The contractor made a profit on the difference between what the British paid him (per man per day) and what he paid the men. If he could not round up the necessary men at a wage below what the British were offering, he would have to take the loss. The financial mechanism was nearly identical to that for tax collecting.

6. While in general the economic conditions of the Tarai improved significantly in the second half of the nineteenth century, there was also a famine in 1865–66. The state inaugurated relief measures but many people died (Regmi 1979:46–53).

7. The moves by Solu traders to get around the restriction may not have gone uncontested by the Khumbu traders. In 1885, there was a case brought before the authorities in which some men, specified as Khumbu men, complained about violations of the trading rule by six other men, implicitly Solu men. The Rana commander in chief, General Jitsang Bahadur Rana, found in favor of the Khumbu plaintiffs (von Fürer-Haimendorf 1975:61). Regmi also notes a complaint dated 1892 described as "Complaints of Sherpa Kipat-owners of Solu-Khumbu" (Nepali date Aswin Sudi 3, 1949; Regmi Research Collections, 1891) that may pertain to the same incident, but I have not been able to track this document down.

8. "*Birta* were given to individuals in appreciation of their services to the state, as ritual gifts, or as a mark of patronage . . . [Of all forms of land grant] *birta* alone was a form of private property which usually could be subdivided, inherited, sold, mortgaged or bequeathed" (Regmi 1978:35–36).

9. There are other Solu families that came to be absentee owners of non-Sherpa lands in the middle hills of eastern Nepal, probably in this same period (Håkan Wahlquist, personal communication). The more land-based wealth of Solu contrasts in general with the more herd- and trade-based wealth in Khumbu. Unfortunately detailed data are not available on these differences.

10. When Sangye became dware, he gave up the naikeship, to which he appointed one of his cousins. But the farm was closed shortly thereafter.

11. One Lama clan descendant insisted that there was no falling out between Karma and Sangye, and that rivalry only developed later between their descendants. Another Lama clan descendant similarly refused to acknowledge conflict between Karma and Sangye. However, every other Sherpa with whom I talked on this matter, including one very reliable informant who had been a Lama clan affine while Sangye was still alive, but who did not seem to have any particular vested interest in one or another version of the story, said that the brothers were intensely competitive, and that Sangye had "taken" these posts from Karma. I discuss the problem of handling these conflicting interpretations in Ortner n.d.a.

12. I cannot establish a date for his birth.

13. Only the son-in-law Kusang never held a government post.

14. Von Fürer-Haimendorf does not connect the Tsepal of this tale with the founder of Tengboche, perhaps out of respect for Tengboche monastery, or perhaps because he was unaware of the connection. I myself had heard about the murder during my first fieldwork, but nobody told me that the protagonist was also one of the Tengboche founders. The cat was let out of the bag for me by Kusang, the son-in-law of the senior sponsor Karma, who was still alive at the time of the fieldwork in 1979. This was one of those mystery-solving moments of the fieldwork referred to in chapter 1. Parenthetically, I might note that I have increasingly come to appreciate, for purposes of writing Sherpa history, von Fürer-Haimendorf's practice of naming names in his ethnography. In my ethnography (1978a) I followed the standard practice of disguising the names of the village and the individuals mentioned, in order to protect people from embarrassment or worse as a result of the publication of my account. Yet this strategy does not allow for historical reconstruction (or for discussions of the relationship between individual actions and larger structures) the way von Fürer-Haimendorf's does. Given current interests in historical reconstruction, and in practice approaches that (in at least some forms) involve attending to specific individuals, the choice of one or the other strategy must perhaps be more carefully considered by anthropologists than it has been in the past.

Chapter VII

1. Parts of this chapter appear in Ortner n.d.a.

2. Peissel (1967) describes a form of celibate religious commitment in Mustang in which the monks live at their parents' homes rather than at a monastery. The Thakali (Parker 1985) and the Tamang (Holmberg 1980) have recently begun moves toward celibacy, but the initiatives are on a relatively small scale, and they come at any rate at least fifty years after the beginning of the Sherpa movement.

3. Lévi-Strauss is the only one who has explicitly taken a position close to this one, as in this famous passage from *The Raw and the Cooked*: "I therefore claim to show, not how men think in myths, but how myths operate in men's minds without their being aware of the fact . . . [I]t would perhaps be better to go still further and, disregarding the thinking subject entirely, proceed as if the thinking process were taking place in the myths, in their reflection upon themselves, and their interrelation" (1969:12).

4. Von Fürer-Haimendorf (1964:130) and Jerstad (1969:44) give 1923 for the founding date. Snellgrove (1957:214) may be interpreted as giving dates of 1915–16. The Tengboche Reincarnate Lama (n.d.a:5) gives the Tibetan year *me duk*, or Fire Dragon. The latter spans 1916–17, but mostly falls in 1916. The Tibetan New Year

comes around the end of February. The English date of 1915 on that page is probably my mistake as translator.

5. When someone is called "Lama X," X is usually his name. When he is called "the X lama," X is a place name—the lama's village or religious institution. To confuse matters further, there is a Sherpa clan called "Lama," and the monastery founders Karma and Sangye were members of this clan. In ordinary Sherpa speech, Karma and Sangye were thus often called Lama Karma and Lama Sangye, even though they were not lamas in the sense of being religious specialists. I have cleaned these usages out of quotations in order to keep the exposition as clear as possible.

6. His religious name was Ngawang Tenzing Norbu. He is also sometimes called the Rimbi Sangye, the Bodhisattva of Rumbu. Since he died and has been reincarnated in other bodies, the historical individual Ngawang Tenzing Norbu is also sometimes simply called the *ku kongma*, the "former body" (of the present incarnation).

7. One informant explained that Lama Gulu had no memory of this previous incarnation because he had been polluted by having eaten some "dirty food" earlier in life. This is one of the standard explanations for how some reincarnate lamas may lose touch with the reincarnating entity within themselves.

8. In one account, however, the Zatul Rinpoche did not realize that Lama Gulu was a reincarnation of Lama Budi Tsenjen until he came to Khumbu for the *ramne*, the consecration of Tengboche, after the monastery was already built.

9. The Zamte lama in the Pangboche tale said he would return to Zamte as a tsen. See chapter 5.

10. One informant said that if people didn't "volunteer" their labor, the monks would refuse to perform religious services for them later. This informant tended in my view to be rather cynical, and no other informant even hinted at such coercion.

11. Sangye Tenzing lists 431 block printed volumes of books, seventy-one statues of gold, copper, and silver, four clay statues over nine feet tall, four stupas of gold and copper, and "countless religious objects and instruments such as ritual daggers, bells and thunderbolts and cymbals, etc." (Sangye Tenzing 1971:62).

12. For an account of the founding of Chiwong, as well as some details concerning Sangye and his parents, see Sangye Tenzing (1971:31–33). Sangye Tenzing also provides a list of some of the many religious objects the monastery contains.

13. They could, of course, have gone to Tengboche, closer to their own home area. But there is a tradition of relative separateness between the west side of Khumbu, where Thami is located, and the east side, where Tengboche is located. People felt they should socialize, marry and religiously congregate largely in their own *golak*, or local subregion.

14. For the date of the founding of Chiwong, Snellgrove implies 1915–17 (1957:217). Sangye Tenzing gives 1917 or the Tibetan year *me dul*, Fire Snake (1971:31); he was also quite emphatic about this date in personal conversation. There is said to be a document at the monastery that reports 1917 as the founding year. Despite all this authority, however, I have decided that the monastery was actually begun in 1923 (also suggested by March [1977a, 1979]). Several of my informants spontaneously and convincingly said it was built around 1923 or even later. One ex-Chiwong monk said he was ten years old when it was built, that he was sixty-four at the time of the interview (1979), and that therefore the monastery was started around 1925. Another man, a member of the Lama clan familiar with the Western calendar, said it was built the year he was born—1923. The 1923 date also fits much better with the biography of the Kusho Tulku, the first head lama of Chiwong. The Kusho Tulku spent three years as a Tengboche monk, and since Tengboche was not begun until 1916, he could have been there no earlier than 1916–19. He then spent several years

at Thami. He thus could not have got involved in the building of Chiwong (as he did) much before 1923. Finally, according to another Lama clan informant, the ramne, or consecration, of the monastery did not take place until 1929 at the earliest. If this is correct (unfortunately I did not double-check it), and if the monastery was started in 1917, then it would have taken twelve years to complete—an inordinately long time about which one would certainly have heard comment. But I never heard any comments on this point.

15. Kusho Mangden was old but well in 1979, when I was able to interview him.

16. The iconography of Chiwong temple has been the subject of detailed study by March (1977a) and Snellgrove (1957). Snellgrove also describes some of the monastery's ritual practices.

17. As a general rule, Sherpas are not very informative in response to questions of motive. If one asks why somebody did something, one often gets a shrug and a one-word answer ("merit," "prestige," "money," etc.), or even a hostile response: "How should I know, we can't see into other people's heads." The apparent lack of interest in, or more active refusal to consider, motive in the Western sense is an interesting cultural fact in itself, but it cannot be explored here.

18. The increasing hegemony of the discourse of "merit," viewed as a discourse of the self as an individual moral unit, was probably itself part and parcel of the rise of monastic values. This issue will be taken up in Ortner n.d.b.

19. Dawa Tenzing was his youngest son. The decision to send or allow him to become a monk was quite unusual.

20. Dawa Tenzing and another Solu man also cosponsored the building of a (noncelibate) temple in Mendopake. Whether this was before or after the founding of Chiwong is not clear.

21. The renovation of Zhung temple, like the founding of Nauje village temple by the Zamte lama in 1905, may be taken as part of the early stirrings of religious activism in the first part of the twentieth century that culminated in the foundings of the celibate monasteries. It even appears to be the case that the renovations represented an upgrading toward "higher" Buddhist orthodoxy, which the celibate monasteries would later represent in much stronger form. Thus the trio of statues at the front of the reconstructed Zhung temple—with the Buddha at the center, the compassionate Bodhisattva Cherenzi on the Buddha's right, and the culture hero Guru Rinpoche on the Buddha's left—is more often found in celibate monasteries, and in temples and chapels built or renovated after the foundings of the monasteries. Premonastic temples tend to have the Guru Rinpoche, who was a married lama, at the center. (See Ortner n.d.b on postmonastic iconographic changes.)

22. According to one modern informant, Sangye did not give as much as Sangye Tenzing gives him credit for.

23. The woman never gave the end flaps for the books, on which are written the titles of the individual volumes. Eventually a Sherpa benefactor in Darjeeling contributed these to Kyerok.

24. Thanks to Kathryn March for calling the guthi factor at Chiwong to my attention. According to some accounts, Sangye had *intended* to make the permanent guthi endowment, but had delayed doing so because of troubles at the monastery. In this version, it was his descendants who carried out the guthi conversion.

25. In contrast with some other groups in Nepal, Sherpas themselves do not use drugs as part of culturally accepted practice. Members of the older generation will not even smoke cigarettes, the smell of which is said to be offensive to people and to gods.

Chapter VIII

1. Whatever this may reveal about my own worldview.

2. One is tempted to think that this move is identical with that of Lama Gombu and his retinue, after the lama's humiliation by Dorje Zangbu in Zhung, as recorded in the oral folklore. The dating, at about the time of the founding of Zhung temple, and the location (Bhandar is called Changma in Sherpa) fit this supposition perfectly. Unfortunately the names do not fit.

3. Von Fürer-Haimendorf cites two separate elderly informants who recalled in the 1950s that people of their parents' generation were the first to plant potatoes in their respective parts of Khumbu. Oppitz also collected information that supports this claim (1968:51f.).

4. The following population figures are available for the Sherpas in Darjeeling: 1901, 3,450 (Dash 1947:72); 1931, 5,295 (ibid.); 1941, 6,929 (ibid.); 1951, 7,539 (B. Miller 1958: 302).

5. The number of Sherpas who joined Gurkha regiments must have been fairly small, since I know of no Sherpas in Solu-Khumbu who were getting Gurkha army pensions, unlike the situation in some of the Magar communities, where these are a major part of the economy (Hitchcock 1966:17). Axelson, however, mentions three individuals receiving pensions in Yalung, a mixed Sherpa-Nepali area west of Solu (1977). As for the police jobs, according to my only source on this subject, Khumbu Sherpas seem to have monopolized certain police jobs in the town of Gangtok, north of Darjeeling (Bishop 1978:68).

6. In modern times they have demanded and received statuses as "members" of the expeditions, theoretically giving them full equality with foreign members.

7. Seven Sherpas died on the expedition.

Chapter IX

1. The story of the founding of Devuche is told in full, and analyzed with reference to its gender implications, in Ortner 1983.

2. Sangye's wife seems to have played a major role too, although my notes are not clear on this point.

3. The ten founding nuns were Ama Digi, Ngawang Samden, Ani Zhinba (the elder), Ani Zepa, Ngawang Konjok, and Ngawang Diki, all from Khumjung village; Ngawang Ongmu and Ngawang Chokar, both from Nauje; Ani Tarchin, Karma's daughter, from Zhung; and Ani Ngawang Zangmu, from a village in Pharak.

4. After a person dies, it is traditional for the family to bring his or her clothes to a monastery for the head lama to distribute as he sees fit.

5. Thanks again to Tom Fricke for the demographic calculations. Fricke based his estimate on information given in Weitz 1984, in conjunction with analogies from his own Tamang data.

6. Monastery census data are from R. Paul's field notes; Paul has also called attention to the significance of birth order in monastic choice [1970:ch. 6]. In point of fact, it is a culturally explicit notion, both among the Sherpas and in Tibet, that it is the middle sons who should become monks.

7. "Eight Phaphlu [where Sangye built his house] daughters; eight Nauje pembu sons" (*Phaphlu pum gye; Nauje pembu puzhung gye*).

8. Some of the examples cited postdate the monastery foundings, but they all derive from the period prior to the modern influx of tourism, that is, from the period in

which economic conditions were similar to those that prevailed in the early decades of the century.

9. The name of the region in which the monastery is located is Dza-rong-buk. This is normally shortened to Rong-buk, pronounced Rumbu by the Sherpas. The "Za" in Zatul is actually the "Dza" from Dza-rong-buk. The "tul" is short for *tulku*, or reincarnation. Rinpoche means "precious" and is the term of both address and reference for a reincarnation. The lama's personal (religious) name was Ngawang Tenzing Norbu.

10. Sherpa nuns cannot be ordained up to this level, but only to *rabchung*, the next level down.

11. It is interesting that it is Gelungma Palma's brother who assists her in becoming a nun, after her parents opposed her. The point might be interpreted as reflecting the shift from sibling conflict to parent-child conflict very tentatively suggested earlier.

12. Condensed from a version told me by Au Chokdu, the most senior monk at Tengboche monastery. Any mistakes are of course my own. I hope to publish the full version of this tale, and a more complete analysis, in Ortner n.d.b. Kathryn March (1979:277–78) gives another version of the story.

13. In another interview this man told the story slightly differently, although the point that the marriages were arranged for purposes of gaining a servant was still made: "His mother, at some early age of his, arranged for him to marry two women from Ringmo, in the hopes of gaining two free servants for herself. These women were much older than he and kept inviting him to sleep with them. They made him sweet cakes and caressed him to entice him to their sides. He was frightened and went to the [pembu] to effect a separation." (See Paul n.d. for an analysis of this man's life history.)

14. All three of these people became shamans. All three also manifested strong religious leanings. I would tentatively suggest that the shamanic and religious callings are essentially transformations of one another, at two different economic levels of Sherpa society. See Ortner n.d.c. See also Paul 1976b; Aziz 1976b.

15. His daughter later took vows as well, after a love affair that produced a child who tragically died young.

16. They were described to me in another context as ongchermu, "bully-powerful." The man telling me about them said, "They took everyone's money."

17. The prevalence is around 2 percent (Lang and Lang 1971:3; von Fürer-Haimendorf 1964:68; Oppitz 1968:122). It is possible that all these sources are simply quoting each other, but the figure sounds right to me. Sherpas find polygyny much more amusing—and exotic—than polyandry.

18. The temple in this line has itself been relocated and changed several times. In addition to a relocation that is said to have taken place following a fire shortly after the founding, the temple was apparently rebuilt just above its present location by one Ngawang Tile Hlundup, the grandfather of the former body of the present reincarnate lama. Ngawang Tile Hlundup's tenure as head lama of Thami must have been from about 1865 to 1895, which jibes with a date of 1870 given by one source for the "founding" of Thami temple (Sestini and Somigli 1978; see also Fantin 1971). It was said that the lama had another location in mind, but then a rainbow, or a ray of light from the sacred peak Khumbila, pointed to this particular site and so it was built there. Ngawang Tile Hlundup is said to have been an enormously powerful (tsachermu) lama, under whom many lamas, including Lama Gulu, came to study. He is also said to have "started" Dumje at Thami, that is, to have taught the particular set of texts currently in use. The launching of Dumje festivals is closely tied up with the founding (or in this case the rebuilding) of noncelibate temples. (See also Sangye Tenzing 1971:59.)

19. Ngawang Samden gave the names of five monks whom he considered to be the original group that initiated the conversion: himself, the son of a married lama;

Ngawang Tsendu and Ngawang Taye, brothers, and sons of a married lama; and Ngawang Leshe and Gönden Gyatso, sons of lay families.

20. Thami monastery, like Tengboche, was defined from the outset as a branch of Rumbu. This means that the Rumbu head lama has authority over the Thami head lama. For a sense of how these relationships between monasteries work, see B. Miller 1961.

Chapter X

1. I have not had time to be more careful about notions of "internal" and "external," which are themselves problematic terms. I cover myself here by noting that the Sherpas themselves conceptualize their relations with other groups in terms of an inside/outside idiom—for example, they speak of "our inside religion" (*ore nangbi cho*). See also Paul 1970:70–71.

Glossary

Tibetan spellings for Sherpa words are provided where likely equivalents could be found (the transliteration system is from Melvyn C. Goldstein and Ngawang Thondup Narkyid, eds., *English-Tibetan Dictionary of Modern Tibetan*, Berkeley and Los Angeles: University of California Press, 1984). But the definitions refer to *Sherpa* usage and may not match the normal meanings for the words as spelled in Tibetan. Nepali terms are transliterated according to the system given by R. L. Turner (*A Comparative and Etymological Dictionary of the Nepali Language*, London: Routledge and Kegan Paul, 1931). The definitions again correspond to Sherpa usage.

amali	(Nep.) see *gembu*
amji	(Tib., *aem-chi*) doctor
arak	(Tib., *a-rag*) distilled spirits
ashang	(Tib., *a-zhang*) mother's brother
balabenzin	(from Nep., *balaabal*?) playful competition
birta	(Nep., *birtaa*) land grant from the state
chang	(Tib., *chang*) beer
chayik	(Tib., *chad-yig*) the founding charters (and rules) of a temple or monastery
chhetri	(Nep.) a high-caste Hindu Nepali
chiwa	(Tib., ?) sponsor of a ritual
cho	(Tib., *chos*) religion
chorten	(Tib., *mchod-rten*; Skt., *stupa*) Buddhist monument, often containing sacred relics
chu	(Tib., *chu*) water
chu chermu	(Tib., *chu chen-po*) having a knack for making things flourish—a "green thumb" or a "Midas touch"
dikpa	(Tib., *sdig-pa*) sin or demerit
dongbi	(Tib., ?) tribal
dorje	(Tib., *rdo-rje*) ritual thunderbolt
dukta	(Tib., *sgrub-thabs*) magically/spiritually effective
dware	(Nep., *dwaare*) see *pembu*
dzo	(Tib., *mdzo*) cow-yak crossbreed
geken	(Tib., *dge-rgan*) teacher
gelung	(Tib., *dge-slong*) a fully ordained monk

gelungma	(Tib., *dge-slong-ma*) fully ordained female monastic
gembu	(Tib., *rgan-po*; Nep., *amali*) head tax collector, in authority over the *pembu* tax collectors
genchu	(Tib., *rgan-chos*) an old person who takes a limited set of monastic vows
geshe	(Tib., *dge-bshes*) a monk with advanced training, roughly equivalent to a Ph.D.
golak	(Tib., ?) subregion
gompa	(Tib., *dgon-pa*) temple or monastery; also a wilderness
gonda	(Tib., *dgon-sde*) temple or monastery
gongdzo	(Tib., *dgongs-tshogs*) memorial rituals
gonpa	(See *gompa*)
guthi	(Nep.) tax-exempt land devoted to the support of a religious establishment
gyelwu	(Tib., *rgyal-po*) king
gyepshi	(Tib., *brgya-bzhi*) an exorcism ritual
gyewa	(Tib., *dge-ba*) act of virtue
gyo sgyu	(Tib.) clever
gyudpi lama	(Tib., *brgyud-pa'i bla-ma*) lineage or descent lama, contrasted with reincarnate lama
hamba chermu	(Tib., *ham-pa chen-po*) ruthless
hulak	(Tib., *'u-lag*) corvée labor
jagirdar	(Nep., *jaagirdaar*) one kind of landholding elite
kami	(Nep., *kaami*) blacksmith
kha tsende	(Tib., *kha tsha-po*) temper, literally "hot mouth"
khamu	(Tib., *mkhas-pa*) expert, skilled
korwa	(Tib., *skor-ba*? or *'khor-ba*?) a peripheral status in a monastery, available to married individuals
ku kongma	(Tib., *sku gong-ma*) the former body of a reincarnate lama
khukuri	(Nep.) curved knife
kurim	(Tib., *sku-rim*) offering ritual
kurpa	(Nep., *khurpo*) sickle
kyongbo	(Tib., *kyong-po*) hard
la	(Tib.) mountain pass
labtsang	(Tib., *bslab-tshang*) a celibate monastery
lama	(Tib., *bla-ma*) a religious specialist; the term is applied to both married "priests" and heads of celibate monasteries
lokpar	(from Tib., *log-pa*?) an exorcism ritual

lu	(Tib., *klu*) a locality spirit
Me Duk	(Tib., *me 'brug*) Fire Dragon Year
Me Dul	(Tib., *me sbrul*) Fire Snake Year
merap	(Tib., *mes [po'i] rab*) clan genealogy
ming	(Tib.) name
mingen	(Tib., *mi ngan [-pa]*), wicked man
misir	(Tib., *mi-ser*) subjects
miwa	(Tib., *dmigs-pa*) visualization, the mental feat of calling up religiously significant images
molom	(Tib., *smon-lam*) blessing
molom lokta	(Tib., *smon-lam log-lta*) a curse (literally, a backward blessing)
naike	(Nep., *naaike*) steward
namdal	(Tib., ?) reputation
namdar	(Tib., *rnam-thar*) biography of a religious figure
nangden	(Tib., *nang-rten*) sacred treasure
ngargyal	(Tib., *nga-rgyal*) competitive, aggressive
ngawa	(Tib., *sngags-pa*) a term for married lama, with an implication of particular powerfulness
norwu	(Tib., *nor-bu*) wealth-producing gem
nosu shetu	(Tib., ?) triumph
ong	(Tib., *dbang*) empowerment, initiation
ongchermu	(Tib., *dbang chen-po*) powerful in the sense of domineering
pajani	(Nep.) annual renewal of appointments of government officials
pak	(Tib., *spags*) a dough figurine
pangup	(Tib., *spang-ba*) to renounce
payin	(Skt., *punya*) religious merit
pembu	(Tib., *dpon-po*) tax collector; more generally, a political chief or regional headman
pradhan panch	(Nep., *pradhaan panch*) elected head of the *panchayat*, the local administrative unit in contemporary Nepali politics
purwa	(Tib., *phur-pa*) a magical dagger
rabchung	(Tib., *rab-byung*) novice monk
ralwa lama	(Tib., *ral-pa bla-ma*) one who follows a particular line of teaching that requires not cutting the hair and nails
ramne	(Tib., *rab [-tu] gnas [-pa]*) consecration of a religious edifice
Rinpoche	(Tib., *rin-po-che*) "precious," term of both address and reference for a reincarnate lama

roblang gyaup mi (Tib., *ro-langs rgyab mi*) zombie, the walking dead

rongba (Tib., *rong-pa*) lowlander, ethnic Nepali

Ruyi (Tib., *rus-yig*, contraction of *rus-rigs-kyi-yi-ge*) "The account of the clans," a Sherpa text

Sa Luk (Tib., *sa lug*) Earth Sheep Year

Sangye temba tarup (Tib., *sangs-rgyas bstan-pa mtho-ru*[*-gtong*]) to make Buddhism "higher"

sem (Tib., *sems*) soul/mind

serkim gompa (Tib., *ser-khyim dgon-pa*) married lama community

sheka-shek (from Nep., *sekhi*?) competition

Shing Duk (Tib., *shing 'brug*) Wood Dragon Year

sirdar (Nep.) foreman of a mountaineering expedition

sungjen (Tib., *gsung-sbyin? or gsung chen*[*-po*]*?*) respect term for voice or speech

tak (Tib., *stag*) tiger

tangbo (Tib., *dang-po*) long ago

tatok (Tib., *phrag-'dog*) competition, jealousy

teka (from Nep., *thekaadaar*) contractor

temba nuwup (Tib., *mtho-ba gnon-pa*) to lower what is high, to humble

temba taru (Tib., *mtho-ba mtho-ru* [*-gtong*]) to raise in status

tolden (Tib., *rtogs ldan*) yogi, hermit

tongba (Tib., *stong-pa* [*-nyid*]) empty, void, a euphemism for a deceased individual

torma (Tib., *gtor-ma*) offering cake

towu (Tib., *grogs-po*) ritual friend

tsachermu (Tib., *rtsa chen-po*) magically potent

tsen (Tib., *btsan*) a vengeful spirit, often of deceased lamas

tulku (Tib., *sprul-sku*) reincarnate lama

tutang nuwa (Tib., *mthu dang nus-pa*) magical powers to transform things

yemba (Tib., *ya-ba*?) low "caste" Sherpas

yenden chermu (Tib., *yon-tan chen-po*) having a talent for learning; mental quickness

yerne (Tib., *dbyar-gnas*) summer retreat of monks

yidam (Tib., *yi-dam*) tutelary deity

zhindak (Tib., *sbyin-bdag*) master, sponsor, patron

zik (Tib., *gzig*) leopard

References

Appadurai, A.

1986 "Theory in Anthropology: Center and Periphery." *Comparative Studies in Society and History* 28(2):356–61.

Axelson, H. G.

1977 "The Sherpas in the Solu District." *Det Kongelige Danske Videnskabernes Selskab Historisk-filosofiske Meddelelser* 47(7):1–71.

Aziz, B.

1976a "Ani Chodon, Portrait of a Buddhist Nun." *Loka* 2:43–46.

1976b "Reincarnation Reconsidered: The Reincarnate Lama as Shaman." In J. Hitchcock and R. Jones, eds., *Spirit Possession in the Nepal Himalayas*. New Delhi: Vikas Publishing House.

1978 *Tibetan Frontier Families*. Chapel Hill: University of North Carolina Press.

Berger, P., and T. Luckmann

1967 *The Social Construction of Reality*. New York: Anchor Books.

Bishop, J. M. with N. H. Bishop

1978 *An Ever-Changing Place: A Year among Snow Monkeys and Sherpas in the Himalayas*. New York: Simon and Schuster.

Bloch, M.

1986 *From Blessing to Violence: History and Ideology in the Circumcision Ritual of the Merina of Madagascar*. Cambridge: Cambridge University Press.

1987 "Ortner and her Critics." Paper given at the annual meetings of the American Anthropological Association, Chicago.

Bourdieu, P.

1977 *Outline of a Theory of Practice*. Trans. R. Nice. Cambridge and New York: Cambridge University Press.

1987 "Scientific Field and Scientific Thought: Marginal Notes on Sherry B. Ortner's article on 'Theory in Anthropology since the Sixties.' " Paper given at the annual meetings of American Anthropological Association, Chicago.

Braudel, Fernand

1980 "History and the Social Sciences: The *Longue Duree*." In his *On History*. Chicago: University of Chicago Press.

Bruce, C. G.

1923 *The Assault on Mount Everest, 1922*. New York: Longmans, Green, and Co.; London: Edward Arnold and Co.

Burghart, R.
1984 "The Formation of the Concept of Nation-State in Nepal." *Journal of Asian Studies* 44(1):101–25.

Cameron, I. C.
1984 *Mountains of the Gods*. London: Century Publishing.

Caplan, L.
1970 *Land and Social Change in East Nepal*. Berkeley and Los Angeles: University of California Press.

Carrasco, P.
1959 *Land and Polity in Tibet*. Seattle: University of Washington Press.

Clarke, G. E.
1980 "A Helambu History." *Journal of the Nepal Research Centre* 4:1–38.

Collier, J., and S. Yanagisako
1987 "Theory in Anthropology since Feminist Practice." Paper given at the annual meetings of the American Anthropological Association, Chicago.

Comaroff, Jean
1985 *Body of Power, Spirit of Resistance: The Culture and History of a South African People*. Chicago: University of Chicago Press.

Dash, A. J.
1947 *Darjeeling*. Bengal District Gazetteers. Alipore: Bengal Government Press.

Dening, G.
1980 *Islands and Beaches: Discourse on a Silent Land: Marquesas 1774–1880*. Melbourne: Melbourne University Press.

Dirks, N.
1987 *The Hollow Crown: Ethnohistory of an Indian Kingdom*. Cambridge: Cambridge University Press.
n.d. "Ritual and Resistance: Subversion as Social Fact." Manuscript.

Dozey, E. C.
1916 *A Concise History of the Darjeeling District since 1835*. Calcutta: Mukherjee.

Dumont, L.
1970 *Homo Hierarchicus: The Caste System and Its Implications*. Trans. M. Sainsbury. Chicago: University of Chicago Press.

Edwards, D. W.
1977 "Patrimonial and Bureaucratic Administration in Nepal: Historical Change and Weberian Theory." Ph.D. dissertation, Department of Political Science, University of Chicago.

Encyclopaedia Britannica
1974 "Indian Subcontinent, History of the," 9:334–430.

English, R.
1985 "Himalayan State Formation and the Impact of British Rule in the Nineteenth century." *Mountain Research and Development* 5(1):61–78.

Fantin, M.
1971 "I Monasteri nella Regione del Khumbu." *L'universo* 51(1):61–67 plus photo pages.
1974 *Sherpa Himalaya Nepal.* New Delhi: The English Bookstore.

Fernandez, James
1974 "The Mission of Metaphor in Expressive Culture." *Current Anthropology* 15(2):119–33.

Fisher, James F.
1986 *Trans-Himalayan Traders: Economy, Society, and Culture in Northwest Nepal.* Berkeley and Los Angeles: University of California Press.

Foucault, Michel
1980 *History of Sexuality.* Vol. 1. New York: Vintage Books.

Fox, R.
1985 *Lions of the Punjab.* Berkeley and Los Angeles: University of California Press.

Francke, Rev. A. H.
1907 *A History of Western Tibet.* London: S. W. Partridge.

French, L.
n.d.a "Consolidation of the Nepalese State [with special reference to the Sherpas]." Manuscript commissioned by SBO.
n.d.b "Sherpas in the Darjeeling Context." Manuscript commissioned by SBO.

Funke, F. W.
1969 *Religioses Leben der Sherpa.* Innsbruck and Munich: Universitätsverlag Wagner.

Fürer-Haimendorf, C. von
1956 "Ethnographic Notes on the Tamangs of Nepal." *Eastern Anthropologist* 9(3–4):166–77.
1964 *The Sherpas of Nepal.* London: J. Murray.
1975 *Himalayan Traders.* New York: St. Martin's Press.
1984 *The Sherpas Transformed.* New Delhi: Sterling.

Geertz, C.
1973a "Deep Play: Notes on the Balinese Cockfight." In C. Geertz, *The Interpretation of Cultures.* New York: Basic Books.

1973b "Ideology as a Cultural System." In C. Geertz, *The Interpretation of Cultures*. New York: Basic Books.

1980 *Negara*. Princeton: Princeton University Press.

Gibson, T.

1987 "Are Social Wholes Seamless?" Paper given at the annual meetings of the American Anthropological Association, Chicago.

Giddens, A.

1971 *Capitalism and Modern Social Theory*. Cambridge: Cambridge University Press.

1979 *Central Problems in Social Theory: Action, Structure, and Contradiction in Social Analysis*. London: Macmillan.

Goldstein, M. C.

1968 "An Anthropological Study of the Tibetan Political System." Ph.D. dissertation, Department of Anthropology, University of Washington.

1971a "Stratification, Polyandry, and Family Structure in central Tibet." *Southwest Journal of Anthropology* 27:64–74.

1971b "Taxation and the Structure of a Tibetan Village." *Central Asiatic Journal* 15(1):1–27.

1975 *Tibetan-English Dictionary of Modern Tibetan*. Kathmandu: Ratna Pustak Bhandar.

1978 "Adjudication and Partition in the Tibetan Stem Family." In D. C. Buxbaum, ed., *Chinese Family Law and Social Change in Historical and Comparative Perspective*. Seattle: University of Washington Press.

Hall, S., and T. Jefferson, eds.

1975 *Resistance through Rituals: Youth Subcultures in Post-War Britain*. London and Birmingham: Hutchinson of London, in association with the Centre for Contemporary Studies, University of Birmingham.

Hamilton, F.

1819 *An Account of the Kingdom of Nepal*. Edinburgh. Reprinted as *Bibliotheca Himalayica* 10, ser. 1, 1971.

Hannerz, U.

1986 "Theory in Anthropology: Small is Beautiful? The Problem of Complex Cultures." *Comparative Studies in Society and History* 28(2):362–67.

Hardie, N.

1957 *In Highest Nepal, Our Life among the Sherpas*. London: Allen and Unwin.

Hillary, E.

1955 *High Adventure*. New York: E. P. Dutton.

Hitchcock, J.
1966 *The Magars of Banyan Hill*. New York: Holt, Rinehart & Winston.

Hobsbawm, E., and T. Ranger, eds.
1983 *The Invention of Tradition*. Cambridge: Cambridge University Press.

Hodgson, B. H.
1848 "Route from Kathmandu, the Capital of Nepal, to Darjeling in Sikim, interspersed with remarks on the people and the country." *Journal of the Asiatic Society of Bengal* 17 (part 2):634–46.

Höfer, A.
1979 *The Caste Hierarchy and the State in Nepal: A Study of the Muluki Ain of 1854*. Innsbruck: Universitätsverlag Wagner.

Holmberg, D. H.
1980 "Lama, Shaman, and Lambu in Tamang Religious Practice." Ph.D. dissertation, Department of Anthropology, Cornell University.

Hooker, J. D.
[1854?] *Himalayan Journals*. London: J. Murray. Reprinted 1969.

Hunter, Sir W. W.
1896 *Life of Brian Houghton Hodgson, British Resident at the Court of Nepal*. London: John Murray.

Iijima, S.
1963 "Hinduization of a Himalayan Tribe in Nepal." *Journal of the Kroeber Anthropological Society* 29:43–52.

Jäschke, H. A.
[1881] *A Tibetan-English Dictionary*. Delhi: Motilal Banarsidass. Reprint.

Jerstad, L.
1969 *Mani-Rimdu, Sherpa Dance-Drama*. Seattle: University of Washington Press.

Jones, R. L.
1976 "Sanskritization in Eastern Nepal." *Ethnology* 15(1):63–76.

Kelly, Raymond C.
1977 *Etoro Social Structure*. Ann Arbor: University of Michigan Press.
1985 *The Nuer Conquest: The Structure and Development of an Expansionist System*. Ann Arbor: University of Michigan Press.

Kirkpatrick, W.
1811 *An Account of the Kingdom of Nepaul*. Reprinted as *Bibliotheca Himalayica* 3, ser. 1, 1969.

Kotturan, G.
1983 *The Himalayan Gateway: History and Culture of Sikkim*. New Delhi: Sterling Publishing.

Lang, S.D.R., and A. Lang

1971 "The Kunde Hospital and a Demographic Survey of the Upper Khumbu, Nepal." *The New Zealand Medical Journal* 74(470):1–7.

Landon, P.

1928 *Nepal.* Vol. 2. London: Constable & Co.

Lévi-Strauss, C.

1966 *The Savage Mind.* No translator listed. Chicago: University of Chicago Press.

1969 *The Raw and the Cooked.* Trans. J. Weightman and D. Weightman. New York and Evanston, Ill.: Harper & Row.

MacDonald, A. W.

1973 "The Lama and the General." *Kailash* 1(3):225–34.

1980a "The Coming of Buddhism to the Sherpa Area of Nepal." *Acta Orientalia*, Academiae Scientiarum Hungaricae, 34 (1–3): 139–46.

1980b "The Writing of Buddhist History in the Sherpa Area of Nepal." In A. D. Narain, ed., *Studies in the History of Buddhism.* New Delhi: B. R. Publishing.

March, K.

1977a "The Iconography of Chiwong Gompa." *Contributions to Nepalese Studies* 5(1):85–92.

1977b "Of People and Naks: The Meaning of High-Altitude Herding among Contemporary Solu Sherpas." *Contributions to Nepalese Studies* 4(2):83–97.

1979 "The Intermediacy of Women: Female Gender Symbolism and the Social Position of Women among Tamangs and Sherpas of Highland Nepal." Ph.D. dissertation, Department of Anthropology, Cornell University.

Mason, K.

1955 *Abode of Snow: A History of Himalayan Exploration and Mountaineering.* London: Rupert Hart-Davis.

Messerschmidt, D., and N. J. Gurung

1974 "Parallel Trade and Innovation in Central Nepal: The Cases of the Gurung and Thakali Subbas Compared." In C. von Fürer-Haimendorf, ed., *Contributions to the Anthropology of Nepal*, pp. 197–221. Warminster, England: Aris & Phillips.

Michael, F.

1982 *Rule by Incarnation: Tibetan Buddhism and its Role in Society and State.* Boulder, Colo.: Westview Press.

Miller, B.

1958 "Lamas and Laymen: A Historico-Functional Study of the Secular Integration of Monastery and Community." Ph.D. dissertation, Department of Anthropology, University of Washington.

1961 "The Web of Tibetan Monasticism." *Journal of Asian Studies* 20:197–203.

Miller, R.
1965 "High Altitude Mountaineering, Cash Economy and the Sherpa." *Human Organization* 24(3): 244–49.

Mintz, S.
1985 *Sweetness and Power*. New York: Viking Penguin.

Nakane, Chie
1966 "A Plural Society in Sikkim—A Study of the Interrelations of Lepchas, Bhotias, and Nepalis." In C. von Fürer-Haimendorf, ed., *Caste and Kin in Nepal, India, and Ceylon*. New Delhi: Sterling Publishers.

Nepal, Central Bureau of Statistics
1984 *Population Census 1981*. Kathmandu: His Majesty's Government of Nepal.

Obeyesekere, G., F. Reynolds, and B. L. Smith, eds.
1972 *The Two Wheels of Dhamma: Essays on the Theravada Tradition in India and Ceylon*. Chambersburg, Pa.: American Academy of Religion.

O'Laughlin, B.
1974 "Mediation of Contradiction: Why Mbum Women Do Not Eat Chicken." In M. Rosaldo and L. Lamphere, eds., *Woman, Culture, and Society*. Stanford: Stanford University Press.

Oldfield, H. A.
[1855?] *Sketches from Nepal*. Delhi: Cosmo Publications. Reprinted 1974.

Oppitz, M.
1968 *Geschichte und Sozialordnung der Sherpa*. (Student translation, name lost; SBO files.) Innsbruck-München: Universitätsverlag Wagner.
1974 "Myths and Facts: Reconsidering Some Data concerning the Clan History of the Sherpa." In C. von Fürer-Haimendorf, ed., *Contributions to the Anthropology of Nepal*. Warminster, England: Aris & Phillips.

Ortner, S. B.
1966 (Sherry Ortner Paul) "Tibetan Circles: An Essay in Symbolic Analysis." M.A. thesis, Department of Anthropology, University of Chicago.
1970 (Sherry Ortner Paul) "Food for Thought: A Key Symbol in Sherpa Culture." Ph.D. dissertation, Department of Anthropology, University of Chicago.
1973a "On Key Symbols." *American Anthropologist* 75:1338–46.
1973b "Sherpa Purity." *American Anthropologist* 75:49–63.
1975 "Gods' Bodies, Gods' Food: A Symbolic Analysis of a Sherpa Ritual." In R. Willis, ed., *The Analysis of Symbolism*. ASA Studies 3. London: Malaby.

1978a *Sherpas through Their Rituals*. Cambridge and New York: Cambridge University Press.

1978b "The White-Black Ones: The Sherpa View of Human Nature." In J. Fisher, ed., *Himalayan Anthropology: The Indo-Tibetan Interface*, pp. 263–86. World Anthropology Series. The Hague: Mouton.

1981 "Gender and Sexuality in Hierarchical Societies: The Case of Polynesia and Some Comparative Implications." In S. Ortner and H. Whitehead, eds., *Sexual Meanings: The Cultural Construction of Gender and Sexuality*. Cambridge and New York: Cambridge University Press.

1983 "The Founding of the First Sherpa Nunnery, and the Problem of 'Women' as an Analytic Category." In V. Patraka and L. Tilly, eds., *Feminist Re-Visions: What Has Been and Might Be*, pp. 93–134. Ann Arbor: University of Michigan Women's Studies Program.

1984 "Theory in Anthropology since the Sixties." *Comparative Studies in Society and History* 26(1):126–66.

n.d.a "Patterns of History: Cultural Schemas in the Foundings of the Sherpa Monasteries." Forthcoming in E. Ohnuki-Tierney, ed., *Symbolism through Time*. Stanford: Stanford University Press.

n.d.b *The Monks' Campaign: Religious Reform and Social Change among the Sherpas after the Foundings of the Monasteries.*

n.d.c "The Decline of Sherpa Shamanism." Manuscript.

Ortner, S. B., and H. Whitehead, eds.

1981 *Sexual Meanings: The Cultural Construction of Gender and Sexuality*. Cambridge and New York: Cambridge University Press.

Parker, B.

1985 "The Spirit of Wealth: Culture of Entrepreneurship among the Thakali of Nepal." Ph.D. dissertation, Department of Anthropology, University of Michigan.

Parsons, Talcott

1964 *The Social System*. New York: The Free Press.

Paul, R.

1970 "Sherpas and Their Religion." Ph.D. dissertation, Department of Anthropology, University of Chicago.

1976a "The Sherpa Temple as a Model of the Psyche." *American Ethnologist* 3:131–46.

1976b "Some Observations on Sherpa Shamanism." In J. Hitchcock and R. Jones, eds., *Spirit Possession in the Nepal Himalaya*. New Delhi: Vikas Publishing House.

1979 "Dumje: Paradox and Resolution in Sherpa Ritual Symbolism." *American Ethnologist* 6(2):274–304.

1982 *The Tibetan Symbolic World: Psychoanalytic Explorations*. Chicago: University of Chicago Press.

n.d. "Fire and Ice: The Life History of a Sherpa Shaman." Manuscript.

Peissel, Michel

1967 *Mustang, the Forbidden Kingdom.* New York: E. P. Dutton.

Qu Ai-tang

n.d. "The Relationship between the Sherpa language and the Tibetan language" (in Chinese). Forthcoming in the proceedings of the Lhasa Tibetology conference, 1986. Available from the author at the Nationality Institute of the Chinese Academy of Social Sciences, Beijing.

Rappaport, R.

1986 "Desecrating the Holy Woman: Derek Freeman's Attack on Margaret Mead." *American Scholar* 55(3):313–47.

Regmi, M. C.

1963–1968 *Land Tenure and Taxation in Nepal.* 4 vols. Berkeley: Institute of International Studies, University of California.

1978 *Thatched Huts and Stucco Palaces: Peasants and Landlords in Nineteenth Century Nepal.* New Delhi: Vikas Publishing House.

1979 *Readings in Nepali Economic History.* Varanasi (Benares): Kishor Vidya Niketan.

Regmi Research Collections

1891 "Complaints of Sherpa Kipat-Owners of Solu-Khumbu," Aswin Sudi 3, 1949 (Nepali month and year). Vol. 57, pp. 13–21.

Regmi Research Series

1975 "Landholding, Trade, and Revenue Collection in Solu-Khumbu," 7(7):122–26. Contains documents from 1786 and 1828.

1979a "Ban on Cow Slaughter in Solukhumbu," 11(9):129–30. Contains the document from 1805.

1979b "Regulations for Khumbu," 11(3):40. Contains the document from 1810.

Richardson, H.

1962 *A Short History of Tibet.* New York: E. P. Dutton.

Rose, L.

1977 *The Politics of Bhutan.* Ithaca: Cornell University Press.

Rose, L., and J. Scholz

1980 *Nepal: Profile of a Himalayan Kingdom.* Boulder, Colo.: Westview Press.

Rosser, C.

1966 "Social Mobility in the Newar Caste System." In C. von Fürer-Haimendorf, ed., *Caste and Kin in Nepal, India, and Ceylon: Anthropological Studies in Hindu-Buddhist Contact Zones.* London: Asia Publishing House.

Sacherer, J.

1975 "Sherpas of the Rolwaling Valley: Human Adaptation to a Harsh Mountain Environment." *Objets et Mondes* 4:317–24.

1977 "The Sherpas of Rolwaling: A Hundred Years of Economic Change." In *Himalaya: Ecologie, Ethnologie*, pp. 289–93. Paris: CNRS.

1981 "The Recent Social and Economic Impact of Tourism on a Remote Sherpa Community." In C. von Fürer-Haimendorf, ed., *Asian Highland Societies in Anthropological Perspective*. Atlantic Highlands, N.J.: Humanities Press.

Sahlins, M.

1981 *Historical Metaphors and Mythical Realities: Structure in the Early History of the Sandwich Islands Kingdom*. Ann Arbor: University of Michigan Press.

Samuel, G.

1978 "Religion in Tibetan Society: A New Approach. Part II, A Structural Model." *Kailash* 6(2):99–114.

1982 "Tibet as a Stateless Society and Some Islamic Parallels." *Journal of Asian Studies* 41(2):215–29.

Sandberg, G.

1904 *The Exploration of Tibet: Its History and Particulars from 1623 to 1904*. London: W. Thacker and Co.

Sangye Tenzing (sang-rgyas bstan-'dzin)

1971 *Shar-pa'i chos-byung sngon med tshangs-pa'i dbu-gu* (The unprecedented holy scepter: A religious history of the Sherpa people). Junbesi (Nepal) and Paris/Nanterre (France). (Commissioned translation by Patrick Pranke and Clair Huntington, SBO files.)

Schieffelin, Edward

1976 *The Sorrow of the Lonely and the Burning of the Dancers*. New York: St. Martin's Press.

Scott, James

1985 *Weapons of the Weak: Everyday Forms of Peasant Resistance*. New Haven: Yale University Press.

Sestini, V., and E. Somigli

1978 *Sherpa Architecture*. Paris: UNESCO.

Snellgrove, D.

1957 *Buddhist Himalaya: Travels and Studies in Quest of the Origins and Nature of Tibetan Religion*. New York: Philosophical Library.

1966 "For a Sociology of Tibetan Speaking Regions." *Central Asiatic Journal* 11(3):199–219.

1967 *Four Lamas of Dolpo*. Cambridge, Mass.: Harvard University Press.

Snellgrove, D., and H. Richardson
1968 *A Cultural History of Tibet*. New York and Washington, D.C.: Frederick A. Praeger.

Spear, P.
1965 *A History of India 2*. Harmondsworth, England: Penguin.

Stephens, S.
1987 "Anthropology since the 60's, Theory for the 90's?" Paper given at the annual meetings of the American Anthropological Association, Chicago.

Stiller, L. F.
1973 *The Rise of the House of Gorkha: A Study in the Unification of Nepal, 1768–1816*. New Delhi: Manjusri Publishing House.

Survey of India
1915a *Exploration in Tibet and Neighboring Regions, 1865–1879*. Vol. 8, part 1, pp. 116–20.
1915b *Exploration in Tibet and Neighboring Regions, 1879–1892*. Vol. 8, part 2, pp. 383–99.

Tambiah, S. J.
1976 *World Conqueror and World Renouncer: A Study of Buddhism and Polity in Thailand against a Historical Background*. Cambridge: Cambridge University Press.

Tengboche Reincarnate Lama
n.d.a "Information on Khumbu Sherpa Customs, on Sherpa Religion, on Tengboche Monastery, and on Mani Rimdu." Trans. S. Ortner. Kathmandu (1979). Published by the Lama for distribution at the monastery.
n.d.b "The Stories and Customs of the Sherpas." Trans. F. Klatzel and T. Sherpa. Kathmandu.

Therborne, G.
1980 *The Ideology of Power and the Power of Ideology*. London: Verso.

Thompson, M.
1982 "The Problem of the Centre: An Autonomous Cosmology." In M. Douglas, ed., *Essays in the Sociology of Perception*. London: Routledge and Kegan Paul.

Tilman, H. W.
1952 *Nepal Himalaya*. Cambridge: Cambridge University Press.

Tucci, G.
1969 *The Theory and Practice of the Mandala*. New York: Samuel Weiser.

Tucker, R.
1979 "British Forest Policy in the Himalayan Foothills, 1815–1914." Manuscript.

Turner, Victor
1974 *Dramas, Fields, and Metaphors*. Ithaca: Cornell University Press.

Waddell, L. A.
[1894] *The Buddhism of Tibet or Lamaism*. Second ed. Cambridge: W. Heffer and Sons. Reprinted 1959.

Weber, M.
1978 *Economy and Society*. Ed. G. Roth and C. Wittich. Berkeley and Los Angeles: University of California Press.

Weitz, C. A.
1984 "Biocultural Adaptations of the High Altitude Sherpas of Nepal." In J. R. Lukacs, ed., *The People of South Asia*. New York: Plenum.

Weitz, C. A., I. G. Pawson, M. V. Weitz, S.D.R. Lang, and A. Lang
1978 "Cultural Factors Affecting the Demographic Structure of a High Altitude Nepalese Population." *Social Biology* 25:179–95.

Williams, R.
1977 *Marxism and Literature*. Oxford: Oxford University Press.

Wolf, E.
1982 *Europe and the People without History*. Berkeley and Los Angeles: University of California Press.

Yengoyan, A.
1986 "Theory in Anthropology: On the Demise of the Concept of Culture." *Comparative Studies in Society and History* 28(2):368–74.

Index